Getting Justice and Getting Even

Language and Legal Discourse
A series edited by William M. O'Barr and John M. Conley

The Bilingual Courtroom
Court Interpreters in the Judicial Process
by Susan Berk-Seligson

Rules versus Relationships
The Ethnography of Legal Discourse
by John M. Conley and William M. O'Barr

Getting Justice and Getting Even
Legal Consciousness among Working-Class Americans
by Sally Engle Merry

Getting Justice
and
Getting Even

*Legal Consciousness among
Working-Class Americans*

Sally Engle Merry

The University of Chicago Press
Chicago and London

Sally Engle Merry is associate professor of anthropology at Wellesley College.

The University of Chicago Press, Chicago 60637
The University of Chicago Press, Ltd., London

99 98 97 96 95 94 93 92 91   5 4 3 2

Library of Congress Cataloging in Publication Data

Merry, Sally Engle, 1944–
    Getting justice and getting even : Legal consciousness among working-
    class Americans / Sally Engle Merry.
        p.   cm.
    Includes bibliographical references.
    ISBN 0–226–52068–4.—ISBN 0–226–52069–2 (pbk.)
        1. Law—United States.   2. Judicial process—United States.
    3. Dispute resolution (Law)—United States.   4. Sociological
    jurisprudence.   5. Law—New England—Cases.   I. Title.
    KF379.M47   1990
    349.73–dc20
    [347.3]   89–29627
                                                       CIP

∞ The paper used in this publication meets the minimum requirements of the American National Standard for Information Sciences—Permanence of Paper for Printed Library Materials, ANSI Z39.48-1984.

To Paiche, Sarah, and Joshua

Contents

Preface

My interest in writing this book came from a desire to present the perspective of people who use the courts for help with their personal problems. As I saw people turn to the courts for protection from violence, for help in controlling a neighbor or relative, or for aid in managing rebellious teenage children, I became curious about what kind of consciousness of law draws a person to the courts for help. And as I saw them sometimes turned away frustrated and angry and sometimes pleased even when the case never came to trial, I wondered what these court users learned about the courts.

The book talks about the ways people who bring personal problems to the courts think about and understand law and the ways people who work in the courts deal with their problems. There are important differences between the perspective of the plaintiff and that of the court. Plaintiffs come with a sense of entitlement to law, but the court receives them with great ambivalence. As court clerks, prosecutors, judges, probation officers, and mediators handle these cases in court, they try to make sense of the problems and provide some kind of help. In doing so, they typically reject the legal claim underlying the demand for help. The court endeavors to provide justice by delegalizing the problem, considering it in moral or therapeutic terms, while plaintiffs struggle to assert the legal elements of the situation.

Ultimately, this book is a story of domination and resistance. The court imposes nonlegal interpretations on the problems, and the plaintiffs resist these interpretations, demanding help in legal terms. I was drawn to this problem by my concern with the domination inherent in the ability of some to construct authoritative pictures of the way things are, pictures that others accept. These pictures are powerful in that they suggest what must be done about a situation. Pictures are negotiated between the various participants in court processes, participants who differ in their influence on the ultimate portrayal of the situation. Who constructs authoritative pictures and who goes along with them are central questions, as are the sources of authority that render some pictures compelling and others pale and unpersuasive. Some people resist the pictures painted by others, insisting on their own. How do they do so, and how do they attempt to paint their own pictures? I think that much of the subordination of women operates according to processes of cultural domination of this kind, as well as deriving from more tangible forms of economic and political domination. The growing power of the helping professions in late-twentieth-century America seems to operate according to such processes as well.

Many people have helped with this book. Some of the research and writing was generously supported by the Law and Social Sciences Program of the National Science Foundation, grant SES-86-06023. Much of the earlier data collection was also supported by a National Science Foundation grant, SES 80-12034, and by a grant from the National Institute of Justice, both received with coprincipal investigator Susan S. Silbey. She has contributed greatly to my thinking throughout this study and gathered some of the data on which it is based. A further piece of research was supported by the W. T. Grant Foundation. Wellesley College provided a supportive working environment for several years, both allowing me to take leaves and supporting student research assistants for both interviewing and data preparation. A sabbatical leave year from Wellesley College enabled me to finish the manuscript. Many research assistants have worked with me on this book: Suzanne Banta, Sandy Baldwin, Lisanne Crowley, Genia Demetriades, Timothy Haslett, Kinne Hoffman, Carol Mazzarella, Julie Monteleone, Tracy O'Brien, Ann Marie Rocheleau, Dina Sawayel, Julie Tyler, Ann Webster, Kim Worthington, and Linda Zakas. I am very appreciative of all their good work.

The Amherst Seminar on Legal Ideology and Legal Process provided a stimulating and exciting intellectual environment while I worked on this project. The discussions generated in this group have been important to the development of many of the themes in this book. I appreciate the contributions of its members: John Brigham, Patricia Ewick, Christine Harrington, Brinkley Messick, Ron Pipkin, Austin Sarat, Susan Silbey, Adelaide Villamoare, and Barbara Yngvesson. Several people have read parts or all of the manuscript and provided helpful and insightful comments: Donald Brenneis, Jane Collier, Iona Crook, Rhoda Halperin, Christine Harrington, Robert Hayden, Deborah Kolb, William O'Barr, Austin Sarat, and June Starr. Suzanne Orenstein, Roberta Sawyer, and Ginny Magro contributed significantly with their insights and their wisdom. The people I observed and interviewed gave generously of their time, their insights, and their vision. I can only thank them anonymously.

And—last only in the order of presentation—my husband and children, who thought I was permanently attached to my computer, were patient and tolerant of my long hours of work on this book. How, my children said, could I restrict their TV and video game time when I always was watching *my* screen? For providing a supportive and loving environment and for constantly reminding me that there is more to life than writing books, I am very grateful to them. I dedicate this book to them.

June 1989
Wellesley, Massachusetts

1

Introduction

The lower courts in the United States generally dislike handling problems between neighbors, friends, lovers, and spouses. Yet ordinary people persist in bringing such problems there. Sometimes people coping with a persistently noisy neighbor, an unfaithful lover, or a disobedient child interpret their problem as a legal one and turn to the courts for help. People come to the courts because they think the law has something to offer them: protection from a violent lover, obedience from a teenage child, punishment for a rude and inconsiderate neighbor, control over a battering husband. For women who feel vulnerable to violent men, courts offer the possibility of power.[1]

But the court officials who handle these problems consider them out of place in the court. Most are referred to as "garbage cases," as frivolous and troublesome, and as evidence that people "use" the court. Domestic-violence cases are more likely to be considered serious but may still be categorized as garbage. Judges, lawyers, clerk-magistrates, and mediation-program staff attempt to manage and settle these personal problems as moral dilemmas while not taking them seriously as legal cases, offering lectures and social services rather than protection or punishment. Some plaintiffs insist that they have real problems, however, and try to persuade the court to respond in these terms.

This book is about the people who take their personal problems to court and about the legal consciousness that brings them there. The setting is eastern Massachusetts in the early 1980s; the people are mostly white working-class Americans, largely but not entirely women. They have decided that the legal system has something to offer them and have taken the initiative to bring a problem to the court. Most of the cases I describe came to the lower criminal courts, but some came to the juvenile courts and a few to the small-claims courts. Most also went to mediation programs attached to these courts. All these legal services are virtually free to the public. I have used an ethnographic approach to explore the legal consciousness of plaintiffs and to observe and report the way the parties, the mediators, and the court officials talk about law, rights, property, problems, and cases. I tell stories about these plaintiff's problems, many of which involve violence, about their experiences in court, and about the neighborhoods, communities, and towns they come from.

Most of the people are Americans who have lived in the United States for a few generations or more. Some are white working-class women who have been beaten by their husbands and who finally decide that they should call the police and file a complaint in court. Others are residents of dense neighborhoods whose houses have been splattered by eggs hurled by neighborhood teenagers. Some are parents who despair of teaching their adolescent children to respect them and ask the court to back up their authority. They go to court because they see legal institutions as helpful and themselves as entitled to that help. They see the court as an institution which has a responsibility to protect their fundamental rights to property and safety, rights they acquire as members of American society. Moreover, they think that settling differences by legal rules and authorities is more civilized and reasonable than violence.

Their sense of entitlement is not based on particular legal doctrines, however, but on a broad sense of rights. They believe that, as members of a legally ordered society, they are guaranteed protection of property and person and can use the courts to protect these rights. Rights are not conceptualized as being attached to persons as individuals but as being embedded in relationships and constitutive of these relationships. A person has a right to respect and noninterference from a neighbor, for example, instead of a right to privacy as an individual. Most of these plaintiffs do not feel alienated from American society, nor do they think that its dominant institutions are unavailable to them. But they are not naive about the extent of social and economic inequality within American society or about their relatively powerless position. Despite their recognition of their unequal power, they nevertheless think they are entitled to the help of the court.[2]

Working-class Americans' use of the court for help with family and neighborhood problems reveals that the poorer and less educated segments of American society have a consciousness of rights and entitlement to use the legal system. Plaintiffs often make comments such as "You have no right to trespass on my property!" or "She agreed to live with me—how can she complain now?" or "Somebody should be able to stop him from calling me all day and night and harassing me!"—referring to fundamental legal concepts such as property and contract. Furthermore, legalistic procedures such as using a petition to express disapproval toward a noisy neighbor or passing zoning laws to regulate land use and dogs are common ways of handling personal problems before turning to court.

Yet, recourse to the courts for family and neighborhood problems has paradoxical consequences. It empowers plaintiffs with relation to neighbors and relatives, but at the same time it subjects them to the control of the court. People who take personal problems to court become more dependent on the state to manage their private lives. Recourse to court strengthens the hand of the plaintiff against his or her neighbor, relative, or friend, but at the same time it leaves her dependent on the court for support. After submitting their problems to the courts for help, plaintiffs must then struggle to keep control of their problems as

the courts reformulate and reinterpret these problems' meaning and consequences.

Court users usually turn to court reluctantly and only as a last resort. Filing
charges in court symbolizes a sharp escalation of a quarrel and usually heats it
up. People often postpone this drastic act in hopes that their difficulties will go
away or at least remain tolerable. They threaten legal action more often than
they ultimately go to court. Although most of the people who use the courts for
personal problems belong to the working class, relatively few working-class
people actually bring a problem to court.

Plaintiffs' encounters with the courts are typically sobering and discouraging. They find the system complex, the judge hard to find, and the penalties
surprisingly light. It is easy to get into the door of the courthouse but far more
difficult to arrange a hearing in front of a person in a black robe.[3] It is yet more
difficult to have one's enemy or abusive spouse severely punished. These cases
are typically handled in the lower end of the court system: the lower criminal
court, the small-claims court, the juvenile court. Even within these courts, such
cases are generally processed by lower officials rather than by judges: by clerks,
prosecutors, probation officers—officials who serve as gatekeepers to the bottom tier of the court system.[4] Following the development, in the 1970s and
1980s, of alternative dispute-resolution forums for minor disputes, these cases,
including small-claims cases, are increasingly being siphoned off into structured informal forums which operate within or alongside the courts. Community mediation programs have been created to handle precisely this kind of troublesome problem. Managed by paid staff, often located in the courthouse but
handling problems through lay volunteers from the community and according
to informal procedures, these programs operate at the boundary of the social
and the legal.

There is both power and danger in the use of courts. There is power in wield-
ing a potent weapon, one which is symbolically powerful and can have severe
consequences. But there is the danger of losing control of the weapon, of ini-
tiating a process which cannot be stopped. One risks being stigmatized for
appealing to this form of power. And it may not help. In the courts I studied,
women were particularly likely to find their problems reinterpreted as issues of
character and emotion rather than of legal rights, putting them in the position of
enraging their husbands or lovers by going to court but without winning protection or control. As Kristin Bumiller observes in her research on victims of
discrimination, victims often fail to complain because they fear retaliation and
because they think the complaints are futile (1987). Just as the plaintiffs I studied thought that law was on their side but dangerous, so the discrimination
victims felt that invoking law was a risky business which could make things
worse (1987: 431).

This is not a study of the working class, nor does it claim to represent the experience of the entire working class. It is a study of people who use the courts for help in sorting out their family and neighborhood relationships, regardless of their social class. In practice, such people are largely working class.[5] It is by now a commonplace that different social classes, genders, and kinds of people interact with the legal system in different ways. For example, problems with crime tend to involve the poor and minorities, small property claims involve small businesses, real estate and consumer problems involve the middle class, and large commercial transactions involve the affluent elite. Here I examine one kind of interaction with the courts and then ask who is involved and what the interaction is like. Because I examined family and neighborhood problems, the people I am talking about are primarily working class. Had I focused on a different kind of legal problem, I would have described a different class of person (see Mayhew and Reiss 1969).

Moreover, the population of people who bring personal problems to court is largely women. Women are more likely to take their neighbors, husbands, lovers, and children to court than are men because they are relatively powerless in these relationships. In this social world, relative power depends to a large extent on strength, willingness to use violence, and economic resources. Women are usually less well endowed with these qualities than are men. They turn to court because they feel vulnerable and because they hope it will provide a powerful ally, but it is not a first choice. My conversations with court users suggested that women were also more attracted to settling differences without using violence than were men and that they were more often drawn to the idea of mediation. Thus, both class and gender contribute to the sense of powerlessness which draws plaintiffs to court.

It took a long time to decide how to present this material. It slips out of the conventional categories of anthropological research: the community, the institution, the family. My organizing principle is a pattern of court use, which creates a relatively amorphous boundary. I have had to establish several contexts: the court and its operations, the towns the users live in, the neighborhoods in which the problems occur, the social history of the working class, and the culture of the working class.

Moreover, my information comes from very different perspectives and methods. It includes actions (what people do, such as fighting and going to court), talk (the way they discuss the problems and the discourses they and the court use), and consciousness (the way people think about law and legality). Consciousness is obviously the hardest to know. I talked to people informally, listened to them talk in mediation, in court, and outside the court, and watched what they did about their problems. From these observations I inferred something about their consciousness, but I recognize that such inferences are subjective, the product of an interaction between the observer and the observed.

Legal Consciousness

The law consists of a complex repertoire of meanings and categories understood differently by people depending on their experience with and knowledge of the law. The law looks different, for example, to law professors, tax evaders, welfare recipients, blue-collar homeowners, and burglars. The ways people understand and use law I term their *legal consciousness*. Consciousness, as I am using the term, is the way people conceive of the "natural" and normal way of doing things, their habitual patterns of talk and action, and their commonsense understanding of the world. The consciousness I am describing is not only the realm of deliberate, intentional action but also that of habitual action and practice. Jean Comaroff describes consciousness as "embedded in the practical constitution of everyday life, part and parcel of the process whereby the subject is constituted by external sociocultural forms" (1985: 5). Consciousness is expressed in subtle and diverse ways, in the way people act and speak as well as in the content of what they say (Comaroff and Comaroff 1987). It is embodied in the practical knowledge by which people do things (Bourdieu 1977).[6] Legal consciousness is expressed by the act of going to court as well as by talk about rights and entitlements.

Consciousness develops through individual experience. But this experience takes place inside structures which define people's lives. Further, it changes with contradictory experiences. People question what they are doing and shift directions if it appears that their way of acting either is not working or contradicts what happens to them. The legal consciousness I observed changed as plaintiffs went to court and observed contradictions between what happened to them and what they expected. In general, people have the possibility of creativity and resistance, of changing their consciousness as they test it against the experiences of everyday life.[7] Legal consciousness can itself generate contradictions. Promises of equal treatment in court, for example, are contradicted by the experience of the court's unequal attention to interpersonal problems.

Much of the earlier research on understandings of law has taken place in terms of research on attitudes toward law as these have been ascertained through large-scale survey research (for a summary, see Sarat 1977). But this approach flattens the way people understand and use law. It assumes that each individual has, rather than a series of interpretations of different facets of law, an overall stance toward law as a thing. Legal consciousness, as a part of culture, partakes of both the particularity of a situation and the overall context in which the situation is considered. Moreover, as in any facet of culture, understandings of law are not constant but develop through experience. Finally, attitude surveys presume that a person's stance toward law lies in the realm of the recognized and explicit, so that it can be elicited by questioning, rather than in more implicit assumptions about the nature of social relationships revealed in actions.

Studies which survey the use of law avoid the assumption that attitudes toward law are explicit and constant, but they inevitably miss the complexity of particular situations. For example, Mayhew and Reiss, by using a large-scale telephone survey of households in Detroit, asked how citizens come to define their affairs as legal matters and seek the advice of a lawyer. (1969).[8] Despite the value of this pathbreaking study, it could not examine the social context of individual situations in which law was used. Similarly, the Civil Litigation Research Project, relying on a large-scale survey by telephone, investigated the distribution of civil disputes in the general population and the processes by which they became court cases but could not examine the settings of particular disputes (Miller and Sarat 1980/81; Trubek et al. 1983).[9]

Ideology and Disputing

My analysis begins from the perspective of dispute analysis, in that it examines moments of conflict and their development over time and focuses on the perspective of the litigants (see Nader 1984). As in dispute analysis, the emphasis is on the litigant as choice maker, on his or her strategic decisions in pursuit of interests, and on the cultural and institutional contexts within which these decisions are made (see Nader and Todd 1978). On the other hand, my analysis of disputing is joined with a different approach, one which looks at law as an ideology, as a set of symbols which are subject to various kinds of interpretation and manipulation.[10] From this perspective, disputing is a process of meaning making or, more precisely, a contest over meanings in which the law provides one possible set of meanings.[11] The process of disputing is one of quarreling over interpretations of social relationships and events. Parties raise competing pictures of the way things are as each strives to establish his or her own portrayal of the situation as authoritative and binding. Third parties also struggle to control the meaning—and hence the consequences—of events through their distinctive forms of authority. Law represents an important set of symbolic meanings for this contest.[12] Those third parties able to speak with the institutional support of the legal system and those who claim to voice its interpretations with authority exercise particularly strong influence in these discussions (see Yngvesson 1988). This privileged position empowers court officials to dominate the people whose problems they handle.

I think my approach has some broader implications for the way we go about studying sociolegal phenomena. It demonstrates the strength of joining the analysis of dispute processes with the analysis of ideology. Although I use neither of these terms, I combine the analysis of microlevel interactions around moments of conflict developing over time—the approach which we normally describe as the study of the disputing process—with the analysis of interpretation and contest over the way things are understood, an enterprise which we normally associate with the study of ideology. The focus on dispute processes is attentive to social interactions and to the way the social world is revealed in moments of fight. The focus on ideology foregrounds meaning and the power inherent in establishing systems of meaning.

Attention to ideology raises questions not generally asked in studies of disputing. One concerns how constructing and disseminating ideologies contributes to maintaining relations of power. The critical legal studies movement, in particular, has challenged liberal views of the role of law by asking how law, in an ideological as well as a directly coercive sense, serves to buttress the power of the strong rather than to protect the rights of the weak (cf. Kairys 1982; Kennedy 1982; Gordon 1984; Trubek 1984). Critical legal scholars, among others, have suggested that law serves as an ideology with hegemonic characteristics—that it not only enforces compliance but also constructs a world which is accepted because it is legally ordered, even though some groups are privileged over others.

The domination inherent in the imposition on subordinate groups of a persuasive image of a social order as being *just* has been described as hegemony. In Raymond William's discussion of the concept, he describes hegemony as the capacity of social and cultural forces to produce acquiescence to power (1977: 108). Hegemony in this sense depends on legitimacy rather than on force, on the consent of the governed rather than on coercion. It is a product of the capacity to shape meanings and values by which the whole social world is organized and understood. Political authority always relies to a greater or lesser extent on the consent of the governed, and any form of domination requires some level of consent by the dominated group, some willingness to accept its own subordination. Without this consent, the costs of domination become extremely high. It is clear why people accept domination by violence, but why people consent to their own subordination is less clear. Yet a hegemonic ideology can be founded on the belief that a system is inevitable as well as that it is just.[13] In a cogent summary of the complex arguments surrounding hegemony and consciousness, James Scott argues that compliance by subordinate groups is more likely to reflect a consciousness that the system is inevitable and compliance necessary than that it is just (1985: 314–51).[14] Moreover, Scott argues that the existence of everyday resistance reveals that hegemony is not complete, that there is not full and complete acceptance of the necessity or justice of the system. The appearance of hegemony—of widespread compliance—can be, he argues, induced by repression, not by willing compliance or by an acceptance of the justice of the social order.

The dominating ideology itself establishes the terms for acts of resistance. Examining the relations between rich and poor peasants in a rice-farming region of Malaysia, Scott argues that here it is the capitalist elite themselves who are challenging the dominant ideology as they construct new patterns of organizing labor and of land ownership. Poor peasants resist this change with a backward-looking ideology, condemning the new patterns in terms of the ideology now being dismantled by the capitalist farmers. Thus, resistance takes place in the terms established by the dominating ideology itself: the obligations of a good Muslim, the responsibilities of a landlord to his workers, and so forth. Indeed, Scott argues, every dominant ideology must contain elements which appeal to subordinate groups or it would not be accepted. It is these elements which provide grounds for resistance within the dominant ideology itself.

American working-class plaintiffs in court are, like these Malaysian peasants, contesting their subordinate status within the terms of the ideology of law. They accept that law has the capacity to construct a just society and that it is inevitable. When they discover that their problems are not taken seriously as legal problems and when they are encouraged to view them as issues of morality or therapy, they do not question the overall framework of law itself but only how it applies to their own lives. What is lost is not the consciousness of law as just but the consciousness of their entitlement to use law. Some assert this entitlement anyway, returning to court and striving to get results. If law is an ideology which serves to strengthen existing relations of power, then, indeed, those who return to court and continue to struggle in the legal arena are continuing to support these relations of power.

But I believe the situation is far more complex. As an ideology, law contains both elements of domination and the seeds of resistance. It provides a way of legitimating property and privilege as well as a way of challenging property and privilege. David Trubek has argued that the legal system must provide some benefits for subordinate groups or it would not be accepted as legitimate (1977). Jean Comaroff finds the same ambiguity in the Zionist churches in South Africa: they encourage people to go along with the system, renewing the worker to continue his or her participation in urban wage labor, but at the same time they offer moments of resistance (1985). Similarly, in revolutionary situations, symbols of legality can be used by the poor to challenge dominant groups by prosecuting the rich in people's courts (Santos 1982). Law, as an ideological weapon, has two edges: it is a source of domination and, at the same time, contains the possibilities of a challenge to that domination. It is not a part of a hegemonic ideology in the simple sense of a set of beliefs which induce subordinate groups to go along. Instead, it is an ideology which becomes part of a struggle over control—and it is the language in which this struggle takes place and in which relative power is contested. Thus, law constructs power and provides a way to challenge that construction.

Cultural Domination and Law

Law works in the world not just by the imposition of rules and punishments but also by its capacity to construct authoritative images of social relationships and actions, images which are symbolically powerful. Law provides a set of categories and frameworks through which the world is interpreted. Legal words and practices are cultural constructs which carry powerful meanings not just to those trained in the law or to those who routinely use it to manage their business transactions but to the ordinary person as well. Law in this ideological sense can be described as a discourse, a way of talking about actions and relationships. I use the term *discourse* here in the sense that Foucault does (1980).[15] Like other discourses, law is limiting in that it asserts some meanings and silences others. The discourse of law is neither internally consistent nor unambiguous, of course. It is an intricate, historical accretion of rules, punishments, categories of behavior, and practices which reflect changing notions of crime, individual and environmental causes of behavior, the responsibilities of the state for social life, and so forth. Its ambiguities, inconsistencies, and contradictions provide multiple opportunities for interpretation and contest.

Discourses are located in the world, rooted in institutional structures. Consciousness, on the other hand, describes an individual's understanding of his or her world. It is produced by a person's interpretation of the cultural messages provided by discourses, an active process in which the person uses cultural categories to construct an awareness of self (Comaroff and Comaroff 1987: 205).

This book is a study of the processes of cultural domination exercised by the law over people who bring their personal problems to the lower courts. These processes take place as their problems are interpreted by the lower courts. Although domination usually means control exercised by force, it can also take place in a gentler sense as control over the way people think about themselves, their problems, and the world. Although not violent, this form of domination is nevertheless powerful: it encompasses the ability to determine the thinkable and the unthinkable, the natural and the cultural ways of doing things. This is a form of domination growing out of control over cultural forms, over ways of talking and acting.[16]

Mediation sessions, clerk's hearings, and lower-court trials of family and neighborhood problems are instances of talk in which individuals present images of both themselves and events in ways designed to justify and convince. The conversation is a contest over interpretations of ambiguous events. The parties couch their descriptions in language intended to persuade, interpreting their own actions as fair, reasonable, or virtuous and those of the other side as unfair, small-minded, and irrational. Third parties also develop interpretations of both the event and the character of the people which they introduce into the discussion.[17]

Conversations about events and actions take place within frames of meaning.[18] The participants have already understood the incident within some frame of meaning. When they appear before a third party, they bring expectations about the third party's frame of meaning as well. There is obviously a good deal of uncertainty here, of flailing around for the right combination of concepts and explanations which the third party and the other side will accept. Experience is important: going to court hones a person's knowledge of persuasive ways of presenting problems and claims while alerting him or her to futile ones. Third parties frequently offer instruction about what they want to hear, how it should be phrased, and which labels are effective and which are not. They offer particular visions of how the law works and drop words which carry weight in the court.[19] Parties couch their descriptions of events and character in ways designed to persuade these people. As problems move through the courts, parties quarrel over interpretations of situations, in part by arguing over the frames of meaning within which these interpretations are made. I call these frames of meaning *discourses*.

I argue that the lower courts contain three analytically distinguishable discourses, only one of which is that of law. One is based primarily on categories and remedies of the law, one on the categories and remedies of morality, and one on the categories and remedies of the helping professions. The same discourses exist outside the courts as well. As we will see below, when people come to court, they bring their problems already framed in one or more of these discourses. Once they get into court, they find that mediators and court personnel try to reframe their problems in a different discourse.

All of these discourses are rational and unemotional. Thus, they ignore the emotional side of family and neighborhood problems. But feelings usually constitute the heart of the problems and constantly bubble up during discussions in court and mediation.

Yet, law not only provides a language by which people understand themselves and their social relationships; it also fines, imprisons, and even executes people.[20] Law channels and imposes the force of the state. Whether the legal system applies force (and it rarely does so concerning personal problems), the potential is always present. Thus, its power to shape consciousness depends both on its capacity to generate symbols and categories which persuasively constitute the social world and on its capacity to exert force behind these symbols and categories, to coerce obedience to its renditions of events and relationships. Even when the hand of the law is light and yielding, as it is with interpersonal battles which get to court, the potential of a heavy grasp in the form of a wrenching separation from everyday life, intrusive supervision, or a heavy fine is always present. In the legal arena, it is not possible to draw a sharp distinction between the domination provided by cultural meanings and that provided by violence, between forms of control residing in the ability to shape consciousness and those residing in the exercise of force.[21]

Thus, law exerts both direct coercive power and subtle cultural domination.[22] As courts help people to solve their problems, they characterize and interpret the everyday experiences of the people who seek their help. They establish the discourse within which a problem is framed and its solution identified. Usually plaintiffs bring problems articulated in a discourse of rights and evidence, but court officials and mediators reframe them in a discourse of morality or treatment. Refusing to provide the kind of help plaintiffs seek, they offer instead a different, less welcome form of aid. And from time to time the courts impose force, usually by putting a person on probation or by requiring him to pay a fine or court costs.

Although law provides authoritative definitions of problems, its domination is neither complete nor static. People try to resist its cultural domination, to insist on their own formulations. As with other symbolic systems, the concepts, codes, and categories of law have layers of meaning and significance which are subject to various interpretations (Geertz 1973). This interpretive openness enables people to reformulate their legal consciousness as they find out what happens to them in court. Some people continue to accept the court as equally just and authoritative, but others decide that it is corrupt, weak, or indifferent to their problems. For many, experience teaches that the courts need not be regarded with awe and fear but that they can be a place for manipulation and play. Some court users begin to resist the legal system by asserting their own definitions of the problem, by insisting that they have a *real* legal problem or that they *truly* need protection or help. Some use emotional outbursts which challenge the clerk's or judge's efforts to dismiss the case; others return with new charges and claims.

Through an examination of the legal experiences and changing legal consciousness of plaintiffs in interpersonal disputes, I will indicate some of the autonomy of interpretation, the extent of top-down control and bottom-up freedom of action of these plaintiffs. The working-class people I talked to were rarely the passive recipients of an elite-generated notion of law, cogs in a grinding social system over which they had little control. Clearly, they are often caught in situations which they cannot alter; yet they do not simply accept these situations as just, nor are they always convinced by the vision of society presented to them by elites. On the other hand, they rarely doubt the legitimacy of law itself or the value of a legally ordered society. Still, they question, wonder, and reshape their ideas in response to their experiences. The courts appear confusing and labyrinthine to them. Yet, working-class plaintiffs gradually come to make some sense of the courts and even to use them to their own advantage, although often not in the ways that those who run the courts intend. As I describe the dynamic tension between these users of the law and the practitioners who administer it, I will trace out the tension between the control exercised by the court and the resistance of those who try to use it.

Legal Institutions on the Boundary

Law as it blends into life in communities, in families, and in neighborhoods is not the mythic law of Perry Mason, of civics classes, or of the black-robed justices of the Supreme Court, replete with elaborate procedures and rituals, abstruse language, complex rules, formal costumes, and ornate and awe-inspiring chambers. Instead, it is found in the corridors rather than the courtrooms of busy city courthouses, in the offices of assistant clerks, and in lesser courtrooms, where, despite the formality of the room and the black robe, the judge leans over his raised bench and brusquely asks, with an air of irritation, "What is really going on here? What is this case really about?" and observes, after some of the details of the relationship have been revealed, that his only real interest is in preserving the peace. The ornate vision of law exists here only as a myth. But its power and presence provide one way of determining which problems belong and which do not; one way of deciding which procedures are really appropriate and which are not. The mythic vision creates for the judge, the clerks, and the attorneys a guiding vision of what they ought to be doing, although it exists in a world where things are not generally done that way, where the mythic vision is generally recognized as irrelevant—sometimes even as antithetical to justice. The mythic vision evokes notions of the rule of law: the idea that all persons are equal before that law, that the procedures of the law guarantee justice for all, that every citizen can rely on the law as a bulwark against infringements of his or her rights. The mythic vision portrays a society in which all people possess a more or less equal access to justice and an equivalent bundle of rights.

But legal talk at the boundary between court and community is about how people should treat each other, about relationships, about peace, and about staying away. In juvenile court, talk may concern the need to go to school, to avoid taking drugs. The judge sometimes describes herself as the unnamed parent. In small-claims court, the judge talks about being fair, being reasonable, and getting along. In lower criminal court, the judge, district attorney, or clerk, talk about the need for neighbors to learn to live together, the need for a young man to leave a young woman alone when her parents oppose the relationship, and the duty of mothers to stay home with their children instead of going to bars. Talk of laws, of what constitutes a crime, of penalties for particular offenses is here too. But when problems involve families, neighborhoods, friendships, or romances, the talk is more often of help, treatment, and duty than of legal rules and procedures.

As mentioned above, the dominant discourses in the lower courts seem to be those of law, of morality, and of therapy. The first discourse is elaborated and enunciated by the courts, the second by families and communities, the third by the helping professions. The discourse of law is about rights and evidence. The discourse of morality is about how people should treat one another, about relationships, and about respect and reputation. The discourse of therapy is about treatment and cure and about the way behavior is shaped by environmental and social pressures. Sometimes the discourse of therapy excuses offensive behavior as externally caused, and sometimes it condemns this behavior as the product of an irrational mind. These discourses also exist outside the court and are embedded in the consciousness of the litigants themselves.

Problems Out of Place

The problems people brought to court in the New England towns I studied concerned quarrels with people they knew personally: intractable neighbors, disobedient children, abusive spouses, violent lovers, uncooperative merchants, and irresponsible landlords. These quarrels are fundamentally struggles over the definition and shape of social relationships. They concern the duties and obligations of marriage and family life, the shape of relationships between friends and lovers, the meaning of being a neighbor. Although property claims often become involved as a means of talking about the way people have behaved, the central issues are the obligations and expectations of social relationships. These are conflicts within the domestic sphere of family and neighborhood rather than within the public sphere of politics and economics. They are not crimes, although they may be phrased in the language of crime. Their status as legal problems is ambiguous.

These problems are, in a sense, "matter out of place," to use Mary Douglas's vivid metaphor for talking about the significance of context to meaning (1966). She argues that the meaning of dirt depends on where it is; it is viewed as objectionable "dirt" only when it is where it does not belong. Personal problems, from the perspective of the court personnel and even of the plaintiffs themselves, fit into this category: they are emotional, difficult, and complex problems which are serious as social problems but are of trivial importance in court. Despite the creative efforts made by plaintiffs to present their problems in ways the courts will consider, the problems are often difficult to squeeze into the legal categories available to them.

These are private problems in a public domain. But that statement presumes clear definitions of what "private" and "public" mean. These terms are, however, quite problematic.[23] Public and private are culturally constructed categories peculiar to a historical time and place,[24] susceptible to shifts over time.[25] In the New England courts I studied in the 1980s, court officials identified cases which did not belong in court as being those with ongoing relationships, mutual fault and blame, and a chronic character, stretching long into the past and offering little hope of resolution in the future. These were problems between acquaintances which did not involve significant violence or property damage, or they were problems within a family or neighborhood which often did involve violence and property damage. They concerned differences about how neighbors should treat one another or about how husbands and wives should get along. There was a good chance that, even after the case was "settled" by the court, it would return. These cases fall into a grey area between those regions of behavior unambiguously subject to regulation by the courts and those clearly defined as private and beyond the scope of court intervention. This is a fluid and shifting frontier.[26] During the 1980s, court officials began to see these problems as belonging in mediation programs, particularly those clearly affiliated with the courts.

To the people who work in the lower courts—the judges, prosecutors, and clerks—interpersonal cases are unwelcome. Court officials do not feel that they can refuse these requests for intervention, yet they also feel that these cases are not really "crimes," not "real legal problems." They call them "garbage cases," "junk cases," "shit cases," and so forth. The cases are seen as difficult, troublesome, and often frivolous. Many say that people are simply "using" the court to fight with each other. To clerks and prosecutors, the existence of ongoing relations and mutual accusations, revealed by cross-complaints, are markers of garbage cases. Court officials recognize that plaintiffs seek a form of help—better treatment from spouses; protection from angry jilted lovers; more consideration from family, neighbors, and friends; more money to pay bills—which is hard for the court to provide. Ensuring that the husband stops hitting his wife, that the neighbor turns off his music at 10:00 P.M., that the teenager treats his parents with respect seems impossible. "It doesn't belong here" is another way of saying "We can't handle it here."

To make matters worse, plaintiffs often come hoping to uncover the "truth" of the situation. They want to present the situation to a judge in a black robe or take a lie detector test. Yet, determining the "facts" of these cases is difficult if not impossible: the events are complex, the interpretations manifold. Clerk-magistrates, prosecutors, and judges have a sense of futility, a sense that these problems cannot be easily sorted out or settled.

These problems are also difficult because they are so emotional. The people themselves are likely to get out of control, to violate the rules of appropriate behavior in court. The telltale sign is an angry victim who brings up other issues. A prosecutor who regularly handled interpersonal cases said it can be very embarrassing to bring cases like this to trial, and she tries to avoid it, for if people start shouting at each other in the courtroom, the judge will say to her: "Why did you bring this crap in here?" One prosecutor described these cases as "murky" or "muddy" rather than "clean." Another prosecutor said that no one wants to deal with anything but the most superficial aspect of these cases, trying to avoid everything else. "People know it is there, but no one wants to touch it." A probation officer talked about "throwaway" cases in which people seem crazy or irrational, have some ulterior motives in using the courts, and are likely to fly off the handle or say something crazy. Prosecutors and clerks prefer to send cases such as these to mediation rather than to bring them to trial. Nor do judges like getting involved with them. In a trial, the parties may bring up other things and ramble on, getting angry. In contrast, a clean case, such as a breaking-and-entering case or an unprovoked assault and battery in which the incident occurs between strangers, does not raise these hazards. Everyone but the parties seems anxious to keep emotional cases out of the courtroom.

But the courts cannot entirely ignore the demands of these plaintiffs. The cases are initiated by citizens, and the court is a sensitive political entity. Its legitimacy requires responding in some way to these requests for help.[27] And the problems might turn into something else—injuries to innocent bystanders or serious crimes.[28] Loose cannons on a rolling deck, the problems need to be tied down. Furthermore, court officials recognize that these are intense, persistent, and troubling problems for the people who bring them, even though the legal issues may not loom large. Unworthy of the court's attention, they are still serious conflicts in families and neighborhoods. The court attempts to provide some kind of help while detouring the problems off the road to trial.

In the lower criminal court, these problems are low-status cases. A high-status case has an innocent, respectable victim and an offense classified as a felony or serious misdemeanor. When the parties know each other and are blaming one another for something which is not unambiguously a case of property theft or unprovoked violence, court officials tend to regard the case as less worthy. When emotions are high and the "facts" difficult to determine, a case is particularly undesirable. When it seems unlikely that the court can resolve the problem, it is also viewed as tainted. Indeed, the courts which tend to handle such problems—the local criminal courts, the juvenile courts, and the small-claims courts—are themselves ranked in the bottom tier of the legal system in status and pay.

Inside each court, the people who handle these cases have the lowest status in the courthouse. These cases represent a significant proportion of the workload of the clerks and the mediation programs but are a small proportion of the cases handled by prosecutors and are a fraction of the trial caseload. The clerk-magistrate, below a prosecutor in status, snares and disposes of most in his initial hearing. The few which manage to slip past are usually settled in a pretrial conference. Here, only the most junior prosecutors handle them, except for an occasional more senior prosecutor who happens to like this kind of work. Very few reach the attention of the highest-status person, the judge. With the addition of mediation programs to the court in recent years, most are handled by mediation, although some still return to court. Mediation staff are typically very-low-paid workers, below the clerks in the pay level and status hierarchy of the courts. Many of the low-paid mediation staff are women, while judges are almost all men. The mediators themselves are volunteers, also disproportionately women.

Interpersonal cases are the central mission of mediation programs. The staff and mediators in mediation programs view some cases as garbage cases, but their criteria are somewhat different. They do not feel a similar distaste for emotional, chronic, and murky problems. But they dislike those in which the parties lack any desire to compromise or settle. Neighborhood feuds between people who love to quarrel are considered garbage, for example. Some described garbage cases as those involving either such trivial issues as the placement of trash cans or mentally ill people who are unable to negotiate. If people are unwilling to negotiate and compromise, there is little a mediation program can do to help them. Thus, court and mediation staffs define garbage cases differently, but, for both, the category refers to problems both intractable to their mode of handling and unresponsive to their available solutions. But, like the court, mediation programs try to handle most of the cases that come in the door, even when they think the attempt futile and the case unworthy.

For the parties too, these problems are matter out of place. Most sense that they do not really belong in court. They come anyway, because they are desperate and see no place else to turn. Going to court is a last resort when avoidance, tolerance, and negotiation have failed. Many see the court as legitimate for crimes of property or accidents but not for family-control problems, conflicts with lovers, insults and name calling, or harassment—unless there is serious violence or an ongoing and intolerable situation. Only when they see the problem as involving a fundamental legal right do they feel justified in taking legal action. Some plaintiffs justify their action by defining the defendant as a general threat to the neighborhood or as a person who is dangerous and needs help. They endeavor to present their problems in forms to which the court will respond, while the courts react by labeling these problems as unworthy, trivial, and garbage.

The Debate about Litigiousness

For the legal elites of the 1970s and 1980s too, interpersonal problems in court are problems out of place. The presence of interpersonal problems in court has fueled complaints about the litigiousness of American society. Since the mid-1970s, many leading spokesmen for the legal profession, such as judges, the former Chief Justice of the Supreme Court, law school professors and deans, and practitioners in large firms dealing with big cases, have complained about the litigation explosion and the overly litigious nature of the American public. Pointing to soaring caseloads in the higher courts, they charge that the average American is overly litigious, overeager to sue about the slightest problem. Increasing caseloads are attributed to the breakdown in the authority of the family, school, church, and community (Burger 1983; Cannon 1983; for a commentary on this movement, see Galanter 1983, 1986). The decline in these basic institutions has unleashed a self-interested, me-first population, propelled by an overreadiness to sue over every trivial issue, into a mad dash after justice in the courts. This rhetoric implies that it is family and neighborhood cases which are overwhelming the courts. According to former Chief Justice Warren Burger, for example, "one reason our courts have become overburdened is that Americans are increasingly turning to the courts for relief from a range of personal distresses and anxieties. Remedies for personal wrongs that once were considered the responsibility of institutions other than the courts are now boldly asserted as legal 'entitlements.' The courts have been expected to fill the void created by the decline of church, family, and neighborhood unity" (quoted in Galanter 1983: 8).

Yet, there is no clear evidence that the litigation explosion has touched the lower courts; the congestion appears primarily in the federal and appellate courts and involves largely tort cases, particularly product-liability cases (Lieberman 1981; Galanter 1983, 1986; *Justice System Journal* Special Issue 1986). Thus, this particular version of the concern about litigiousness is another expression of the view that family and neighborhood problems are not worthy of the time and attention of the legal community.

I argue that these plaintiffs are neither litigious nor eager to sue at the slightest provocation. Nor is this necessarily a recent phenomenon. Their recourse to court is rooted in such deep-seated cultural traditions of American society as individualism, equality, faith in the law, and the search for freedom from the control of neighbors and local leaders, traditions noted by Tocqueville early in the nineteenth century. The working poor, who most predominantly use the courts for personal problems, share the mainstream view that the rule of law organizes American social life and that legal means are the most appropriate and civilized way of dealing with disagreements. They share the common American understanding that all members of society are entitled to ask the courts for help in protecting their fundamental rights.

The Research

Two research projects form the core of this book. Both are centered on mediation programs designed to handle interpersonal cases affiliated with lower courts. The first research study, carried out in collaboration with Susan S. Silbey between 1980 and 1983, examined the way mediation functions in different kinds of American neighborhoods and focused on the kinds of disputes citizens take to court and to mediation programs. This study examined two mediation programs and compared each with the courts with which they were associated. One program, in Salem, Massachusetts, was attached to the lower criminal court and handled primarily cases which had been brought to this court; the second, in Cambridge, Massachusetts, was independent and handled cases brought to the small-claims court, to the criminal court, and directly to the program. Conflicts were analyzed in terms of the neighborhoods from which they came. This research suggested that plaintiffs turn to the courts as a last resort, when they are seeking justice rather than reconciliation (Merry and Silbey 1984). It also delineated two styles of mediation adopted by mediators in their efforts to help parties settle cases and to avoid imposing a decision (Silbey and Merry 1986). It argued that mediation and adjudication are similar processes both in the ways they construct interpretations of events and in the kinds of outcomes they impose (Silbey and Merry 1987).

This study consisted of five kinds of observation. First, Susan Silbey and I sat in on 118 mediation sessions and took detailed notes on each one during the one to four hours it usually lasted. (I watched about 75 of these mediation sessions myself, and Susan Silbey observed about 40. Research assistants observed most of the rest. The cases described in this book are those I observed.) Second, when cases failed to settle or when the problem flared up again and came back to court, we observed them in court. I observed approximately 30 in court either before or after mediation. Third, using their records, we did a quantitative analysis of the two programs' caseloads, a total of 868 cases. Fourth, we interviewed 124 people who had been through mediation, many of whom had come to court in the first place and had had some experiences in court. We talked to them in person for an hour or more, usually in their homes. Both plaintiffs and defendants were interviewed. (I conducted about 50 interviews, and several research assistants did the rest.)

Fifth, we did an ethnographic study of three small neighborhoods in Salem in which several of the conflicts occurred. This study included a survey of 93 residents of these neighborhoods; the survey asked them how often they had the kinds of problems we saw in mediation and what they did about them. The survey was part of a more intensive ethnographic study which included long conversations with several of the residents of these neighborhoods. I did the general ethnographic interviewing and background work in these neighborhoods, and several neighborhood residents and students did the survey interviewing. In order to compare these working-class and lower-middle-class neighborhoods with an upper-middle-class neighborhood, in the summer of 1985 I did a similar survey and ethnographic study of an affluent suburban neighborhood. A student did the survey, while I again did more general ethnographic work on the neighborhood,. In addition, I spent hundreds of hours observing court proceedings, including hearings in front of clerk-magistrates; talking informally to court personnel, mediators, and mediation program staff; and doing general historical and ethnographic work on Salem and Cambridge. Susan Silbey contributed greatly, particularly in the observations of court proceedings and interviews with court personnel.

The second research project examined a parent/child mediation program in Cambridge. From 1981 to 1984, with the assistance of Ann Marie Rocheleau, I studied a program which handled cases, referred from the juvenile courts, involving teenagers who were charged with truancy, running away from home, and incorrigibility (Merry and Rocheleau 1985). The general structure of this study was similar: it included observations of mediation sessions for 51 young people, observations of court proceedings on the same families, and follow-up interviews with 128 of the participants. The observations of mediation sessions and interviews were carried out by Ann Marie Rocheleau. I observed only two mediation sessions in this program. The study included general observations of court practices, the analysis of a comparable population in court which was not referred to mediation, and of a population which was referred to mediation but did not appear. We also interviewed mediators, staff, and court personnel. Since both this program and the independent mediation program were located in Cambridge, there was some overlap in the ethnography of the town.

My research focused on these three mediation programs. When I began, I was interested in the mediation process itself: who participated, what happened in the sessions, where these people came from, and how the process differed from the court. I wanted to know the extent to which mediation was linked to informal community social order. But as I studied mediation, I became aware not of differences vis-á-vis the court but of similarities to it. Moreover, I began to wonder how it was that the people I saw in mediation had gotten to court in the first place, not just how they had gotten from court to mediation.

The more I observed the ambivalence with which court officials viewed cases brought by private parties—and, indeed, their ambivalence toward mediation programs themselves (for which these cases were the major responsibility)—the more aware I became of the anomalous status of these cases in court. Court officials were reluctant to do much about them, but they were also reluctant to refuse to handle them altogether. Although they felt frustrated about how to deal with them, they were suspicious of mediation programs and hesitant about referring cases. As a result of this ambivalence, court officials tended to send citizen-initiated cases to mediation for help but refused to dismiss the case and relinquish control of it. Thus, cases were mediated under the aegis of the court. Finally, despite the obvious reluctance of the courts to do much about the personal problems citizens brought to them, people continued to bring such problems, leading me to wonder what these people were looking for, why they decided to come to court at all, and what that decision meant about how they thought about law.

Because the focus of my research was mediation, at times the data I gathered do not exactly fit the questions I want to ask of them. One the other hand, in a serendipitous way, the research strategy I pursued did produce detailed documentation of more than 150 family and neighborhood problems brought to court by citizen plaintiffs, as well as information about where they came from, what the people said about them, and how they talked about them both inside and outside legal settings. I explored the neighborhood and family life of many of the plaintiffs and observed and listened to hundreds of hours of talk by parties, by mediators, and by court officials, both inside and outside the courthouse.

The book is divided into two parts. The first part, chapters 2–4, is an analysis of both the nature of the problems and the kinds of people who bring them. The second part, chapters 5–7, is an analysis of the processing of these problems in court and in mediation. The first three chapters describe the neighborhoods from which the conflicts come and the characteristics of the plaintiffs. Chapter 2 portrays the two New England towns and the courts where these problems were handled. Chapter 3 develops a typology of problems and analyzes the forms of legal consciousness which persuade people with different kinds of problems to bring them to court. Chapter 4 describes the kinds of neighborhoods and families from which these people come and the themes in neighborhood and family problems. The next three chapters focus on the way these problems are handled in the court. Chapter 5 analyzes the distinctions, in the community and in court, between the folk categories of problem and case. Chapter 6 describes the three discourses within which these problems are talked about in court. Chapter 7 delineates both the consciousness of the experienced court user and the subtle ways he or she endeavors both to resist the domination of the court and to extract the help he or she is seeking. Chapter 8 concludes with an analysis of the paradox of legal entitlement.

2

The Setting: Two New England Towns and Their Lower Courts

This study of the legal consciousness of people who bring family and neighborhood problems to court takes place in two New England towns, Salem and Cambridge. In this chapter, I describe the social history of these towns and the organization and functioning of their courts: the local criminal court, the small-claims court, and the juvenile court. This chapter situates the plaintiffs in social and historical perspective and describes the kinds of communities from which they come. It also places their efforts to assert the right to legal help in the context of the changing fortunes of the working class in New England in the 1980s. The majority of my ethnographic research focused on Salem, on its court and mediation program and on its social history and present situation. The chapter is mostly about Salem. The social history and composition of Cambridge are in many ways similar to that of Salem. After describing both towns, I will delineate the more general patterns of economic and social change affecting the New England region in the 1980s. The second part of the chapter describes the courts to which plaintiffs bring their personal problems.

Salem and Cambridge are both parts of the Boston metropolitan area. With a population of about thirty-five thousand in 1980, Salem is a medium-sized town, although it is within commuting distance to Boston. An old New England mill town, it grew from a small eighteenth-century settlement of Yankee artisans and merchants engaged in shipping and shipbuilding to a manufacturing center for leather and textiles in the nineteenth and early twentieth centuries. The town is now a financial, retailing, and medical services hub for a larger region on the North Shore of Boston. It is still dominated by a Yankee elite, some of whom live in the elegant houses built by the successful merchants and shipbuilders of its early years, but the town is predominantly working class and lower middle class. A majority of the inhabitants are white ethnics, second- and third-generation descendants of nineteenth-century immigrants. As the economy has diversified, many have moved into lower-middle-class technical and clerical jobs.

In recent years, a new group has arrived: Hispanics from Puerto Rico and the Dominican Republic. They have taken over the poorest housing, formerly inhabited by less successful white ethnics, but their numbers are small and the town remains a fairly homogeneous white, Catholic community. Salem residents feel insulated from the city at their back. Because there is no easy access by highway from Boston, they remain somewhat separate. The 1980 census reported that the median family income was $19,138 and that the population was 97 percent white. Of those more than twenty-five years of age, 67 percent were high school graduates and 14 percent were college graduates. Twelve percent of the employed worked in a professional specialty. In 1977, three years before the study began, the unemployment rate was 9.5 percent.

Cambridge is also an older industrial center, but because it is the site of two major universities as well as numerous secondary schools, colleges, and other universities, it has experienced an even greater transformation than Salem. With a population of ninety thousand people and a location just across the river from Boston, Cambridge is far more urban than Salem and more intimately connected with the city. It has also attracted a more varied group of immigrants. The 1980 census reported that the town was 84 percent white and that 29 percent of the employed worked in a professional specialty. The population is unusually highly educated: 81 percent are high school graduates, 38 percent are college graduates, and 24 percent have some advanced education (1980 census). Almost half (43 percent) of those more than twenty-five years of age have four years of college or more, in sharp contrast to Salem, where the figure is 14 percent. The median family income in 1979, $17,845, was not much below that of Salem, but the composition of Cambridge is far more heterogeneous. There are pockets of poverty and pockets of wealth in the city. It houses a large number of students, elderly people, and recent immigrants from Central and South America and the Caribbean. There is also a stable white ethnic area whose backbone consists of Italian and Portuguese residents, a community more similar to the population of Salem. Thus, the spread of income level, educational achievement, ethnicity, and background is much broader in Cambridge than in Salem. In that sense it is more like a city in which separate and very distinct social worlds coexist but rarely encounter each other.

The Social History of Salem

The people who bring their personal problems to court in Salem are primarily the descendants of the nineteenth-century ethnic immigrants who fueled its industrial growth and expansion. Like many other New England mill towns, the city was a relatively homogeneous community of artisans and traders until the flood of immigration in the nineteenth century (see Handlin 1941; Higham 1955). And, like other Northeastern cities at present, Salem faces economic shifts which are changing the lives of the industrial workers of the region.

Salem's history dates to the early 1600s, when it was one of the first settlements in the New England area. Graced with a good harbor for shallow-draft ships, it soon became one of the major urban areas of New England, rivaling Boston in the seventeenth and eighteenth centuries. Early in its history it was rocked by the famous witch trials, which, Auerbach argues, shows that even at this point it was a divided and contentious town (1983). At the end of the eighteenth century, it was a major port for the overseas trade to China as well as to Europe, Africa, and the West Indies. The harbor area is dotted with elegant homes built by shipowners and ship captains during this period. But, as the eighteenth century wore one, many moved a few blocks away where they filled two or three streets with gracious brick homes of the Federal style. This area, which I will call the "Grove Street" area, continues to house professionals such as lawyers and doctors, many of whom are descendents of these original elite families.

By 1800, Salem was a highly stratified town with both a wealthy elite of shipowning and merchant families who intermarried and a lower group with high death rates, frequent debilitating diseases, a high rate of matrifocal families after husbands died or deserted their families, and frequent death of parents of young children (Farber 1972). Members of this lower group worked as laborers and seamen and were regarded, by the merchant class, as immoral and unrestrained. There was as well a middle rung of artisans. Early in the nineteenth century, many of the prominent New England families from Salem left for Boston as advances in shipbuilding made the shallow Salem harbor obsolete and as commercial shipping moved to Boston.

In the nineteenth century, Salem began a new career as an industrial center, building textile mills, leather factories, and shoe factories. Droves of immigrants—both rural Yankees and European and Canadian migrants—arrived to work in these mills. These groups were absorbed into existing patterns of stratification in which wealthy elites, bearing the traditions of the English aristocracy, looked down on the poor, viewing their way of life as slothful and intemperate. The new groups formed close-knit ethnic neighborhoods clustered around parish churches of their ethnic group. These parishes still define the social geography of the city. In the 1840s the Irish began to arrive, working first in the mills and then moving into city jobs as policemen, firemen, teachers, and city officials. Part of the city was known as "Irishtown," and there are still some working-class Irish neighborhoods, but many descendants of the Irish immigrants have moved into more suburban areas and have acquired middle-class status, particularly since the Second World War.

In the 1860s, immigrants from French-speaking Canada arrived, working primarily in the textile factories and later in the leather industry. Most were farmers, people with little or no formal education. They settled in the tenement districts around the mills, which became known as "Frenchtown." I have given this area the pseudonym "Green Street." The millowners built tenement apartments for their workers here, and most new arrivals moved into these apartments. As their work and incomes improved, they moved to adjacent streets with better apartments, still rented from the mills. One of their first projects was to build a church and a school. The church, erected in 1873, soon became the center of the social life of the French community. The parochial school no longer operates, however, as the descendants of the French immigrants have blended into American society and moved to the suburbs. Many came home from the Second World War rich enough to buy a house or start a business and moved into areas of single-family or duplex housing. Some, however, remain in the area of original settlement near the mills, in poor, run-down housing.

Polish settlers began to arrive in the 1890s, settling in the harbor area in a section of closely packed houses built during the sixteenth and seventeenth centuries. This area, near the harbor, was first Yankee, then Irish. At the turn of the century, it became predominantly Polish. In an effort to help assimilate the immigrants, Yankee elites built a settlement house in the middle of this section in the 1850s. The Poles worked in the mills and leather factories along with the Irish, the French, and the other, smaller immigrant groups. Gradually they were able to build a church and school as the center of social life. Organizations of well-established Polish citizens offered citizenship classes and assistance to more recent arrivals. The two Polish lawyers in the neighborhood, the Polish police officer, and the Polish store owners helped the newcomers to adjust and provided local social services. The neighborhood, called "Polacktown" into the 1950s, was an urban ethnic enclave. As with other ethnic settlements during the period of immigration, it was fairly insulated both from other ethnic communities and from the dominant Yankee elite of the town. I have given this neighborhood the pseudonym "Oldtowne."

The Italian immigration at the end of the nineteenth century, smaller than that of the other groups, produced an Italian neighborhood centered around an Italian Catholic church. Italians worked in construction and food service. Many have now blended with the generic American population, but some still live in the old Italian neighborhood and identify themselves as Italian.

Thus, by the early twentieth century, Salem had consolidated into five major ethnic groups, each with an affiliated Catholic church, which constituted the industrial and service work force of the city. These groups existed under the economic control and social dominance of an old, aristocratic Yankee elite. A small, affluent Jewish community also exercised some economic control in the town. Overall, this is a part of the world in which the language of identity and difference is the language of ethnicity and national origin. People think about and talk about themselves as being Polish, Irish, Italian, or French, even well into the third generation. When asked to describe Salem as a city, residents invariably begin by describing each neighborhood in terms of its dominant ethnic identity and the Catholic church at its center. Many of these churches have or used to have parochial schools associated with them. The names Irishtown and Frenchtown are no longer used, but residents clearly know which neighborhoods are Irish and which are French. Residents now say that in the past the town consisted of the wealthy elite who ran the factories and the lower class who worked in them; there was no significant middle class.

Between 1836, when the city charter was adopted, and 1917, the old Yankee families provided the political leadership of the town. After 1917, mayors were predominantly Irish and the city council included Irish, French, Poles, and Italians (Hunter et al. 1956: 107). The Irish were very influential in running the schools and were prominent in the courts. In the middle of the twentieth century, one Irish judge, the presiding judge in the lower court for many years and known as a "people's judge," was affectionately nicknamed "Let 'em go Joe."

The population remained relatively stable during the 1930s, 1940s, and 1950s as the tide of immigration slackened. Some members of these ethnic groups achieved social mobility and moved out of their ethnic neighborhoods. By the 1950s, the city was about one-third French Canadian, one-third Irish, one-quarter Polish, and the rest Italian, Greek, and Yankee (Hunter et al. 1956: 5). It was, according to its residents, a very Catholic town. In 1953, 80 percent of the population was Catholic, 16 percent was Protestant, and 4 percent was Jewish (Hunter et al. 1956: 5). The elites were the Yankee descendants of the early founders, people with "old" money. They attended the Unitarian and Episcopal Churches and organized groups to promote tradition and history (Hunter et al. 1956: 250–52).

There were some strikes and sporadic union activity at the mills in the 1930s, but by the 1950s the local industrialists, who tended to be Yankees, praised their French and Polish workers for being both wonderful workers and docile, giving them little trouble with labor organizing (Hunter et al. 1956: 120–1). But there may have been more unrest than these industrial leaders recognized. At the same time, a French city councillor said that the French would welcome new industries but that the old industrialists were blocking their efforts to bring in new ones for fear that it would disrupt their labor supply (Hunter et al. 1956: 122).

The city began a gradual decline in the 1950s. Basic industries relocated. In 1953, a major textile company's departure for the South was a heavy blow. The city center began to look seedy and deserted, and, as in other cities in this region, the inner-city neighborhoods began to deteriorate as the more affluent and successful moved into the burgeoning automobile suburbs. In 1970, however, a dynamic mayor, more closely tied to the city's elite, was elected. He began to revamp the schools, taking them out of the hands of the Irish politicians and administrators who had run them for a long time. He worked to renovate the downtown area with the aid of substantial federal funding he captured. The urban renewal which he began reshaped the city, bringing new life and upgrading shabby neighborhoods which had attractive housing and desirable locations. Oldtowne, the Polish neighborhood, contained, nestled around the old harbor, some of the picturesque seventeenth-century houses of sea captains and shipowners. It was chosen for particular attention (Ryan 1975).

During the 1970s, Salem diversified into the production of electrical machinery, chemicals, fabricated metals, incandescent lamps, and electronics, while service industries expanded rapidly. It has developed major medical facilities, a large college, and some tourism. There has been some gentrification of the older parts of the city where old houses are being renovated. Some neighborhoods have been declared National Historic Sites. The struggle over neighborhood change now takes place in terms of historic preservation versus affordable housing, with the old elites and the new gentry, consisting of people from all ethnic groups, standing on the side of historic preservation and against the remnants of the ethnic working classes who still live in these areas and who fight the loss of their low-rent apartments and low property taxes.

During the 1960s and 1970s, the Green Street area of walk-up brick tenements built in the nineteenth century to house the mill workers became the home of a new population: Hispanics. About half are from Puerto Rico, and half are from the Dominican Republic. The Dominicans tend to have a harder time adjusting than do the Puerto Ricans, since they are less likely to know English or to be familiar with urban America. Originally brought in as workers for a shoe company in the early 1960s, the population has grown slowly. By 1980, the census reported 873 Hispanics, 2 percent of the city's population.

Many Salem residents find this group difficult to accept. The hostility expressed against them is reminiscent of the antagonism with which the Yankee elites greeted earlier waves of Catholic newcomers. Descendents of the earlier immigrants say: "These groups should work to make it like we did. They are getting too much help; they have to learn English and learn to fit in like we did." Others complain: "They don't even put diapers on their children, but they can afford TV sets" and "They don't take care of their property" and "They are a volatile people—they fight all the time." Many Yankees compare them unfavorably to the nineteenth-century newcomers. One older Yankee woman said that the earlier immigrants—the Polish, the French, and the Irish—all worked hard and were clean people but that the Hispanics do not fit in the same way. They make a lot of noise, "They just grate on people, the way they act." Referring to the action of Hispanic tenants who took an absentee landlord to court when he raised rents to cover fuel costs, she continued: "They are always in court, demanding their rights." When I pointed out that the buildings they live in look run down, she retorted that they are new, that they were built soon after 1914, and that it does not matter what you do to these buildings anyway, since the people will just destroy them, tear out the pipes, and throw rubbish out the windows. The Hispanic residents, on the other hand, feel that they are taken advantage of by landlords who charge high rents, fail to maintain their buildings, and refuse to pay for heat. Many of the tenements are owned by absentee landlords, a portion of whom are the French who used to live in the area. The buildings are old and deteriorating, hard to heat, and noisy. The people who dwell in them complain about landlords who fail to provide dumpsters or whose trash containers are inadequate, so that the dogs spread the trash.

The people who come to court with personal problems are typically the less successful descendents of the nineteenth-century immigrants and the descendents of earlier immigrants from rural New England. Those who live on Grove

Street, the sanctuary of elegant brick houses, never come. According to the court clerk, this is because "they control everything. Why should they?" Those who do use the court live in the poorest neighborhoods, such as Green Street. But as Green Street changes from French to Hispanic, it is the French, Irish, and other long-established groups who tend to appear, not the Hispanic newcomers. Despite the observation of the Yankee woman quoted above—that is, that these people are constantly in court—very few actually bring their problems to the courts. An outreach worker in the Hispanic community said that these people do not feel entitled to use the court. Nor do older Polish, Italian, or French residents bring their problems to court; it is their American-born children and grandchildren who do so. People who go to court with personal problems are neither the poorest and the most recently arrived nor the educated and affluent; they are working-class individuals living in dilapidated and dangerous housing in neighborhoods experiencing the influx of new residents, people surviving without two wage earners in the family and coping with relatively low incomes. They also tend to be people who have lived for one or more generations in the United States. In the economic climate of New England in the 1980s, this social class faces job loss and neighborhood displacement.

The Economic Transformation of New England

Both of these towns are experiencing, at different rates, the economic transition felt by many Northeastern cities during the 1970s and 1980s. They are changing from being the centers of older industries—such as textiles, leather, shoes, and other forms of manufacturing—to being service centers providing financial, management, health, and education services to large, surrounding regions. These economic changes have transformed the working class throughout New England in the postwar period (see Nash 1989). In the Northeast, the 1950s was a period of significant job loss as many of the basic industries of the region—textiles, apparel, and shoes—migrated to the American South and, in the 1960s, overseas to regions of lower labor costs and more-docile, nonunionized workers (Bluestone and Harrison 1982: 92–98; Sheehan 1984: 29–30). The New England textile industry crashed, with employment dropping from 280,000 in 1947 to 99,000 in 1964, following a similar decline in the leather industries (Sheehan 1984: 29). In this period, the working class lost its privileged status as valued industrial workers, and the power of unions was undermined by job loss and job reclassification (Bluestone and Harrison 1982).

The reindustrialization of New England in the late 1970s and 1980s offered a different set of jobs. Well-paid and steady industrial work has been replaced by two tiers of work: (1) service and managerial work demanding a high educational level and (2) low-skilled, unstable, poorly paid jobs (Doeringer and Piore 1971; Bluestone and Harrison 1982; see also Susser 1982; Sheehan 1984). The high-technology boom does not provide work for the displaced mill workers but instead creates highly skilled technical jobs and unstable, low-paying service-sector jobs (Bluestone and Harrison 1982: 92—8). The most significant employment expansion in the 1950s came in trade, finance, and professional and nonprofit services (Sheehan 1984: 29), a pattern which has continued into the 1980s. As the jobs in the middle disappear, the gap between highly skilled, stable jobs and low-paid, temporary, service jobs increases (see Sheehan 1984; Susser 1986).

Those who once worked in the mills of this region have found it difficult to acquire the education and skills for the more professional jobs. As the demand for industrial workers declines, these people are left with the raft of new, unstable jobs in food service, maintenance work, clerical work, and other low-paying occupations. This group has fallen into a cyclical pattern of unemployment, welfare, and unstable service jobs, a pattern which Susser describes as common among working-class groups in New York City (1982) and which Pappas reports in Ohio (1989). Sheehan describes the situation in Boston.

> In the emergence of a "new Boston" many of the children and grand-children of the immigrants who had fueled Boston's nineteenth-century industrialization became superfluous. The political and social structures they had created became obstacles to the emergence of Boston as a major financial and service center. While statistically it might appear that the growth of the electronics industry would offset the decline in employment in the traditional manufacturing businesses in the Boston area, it is doubtful that many laid off directly or indirectly found ready employment in the new electronics firms. (1984: 36)

The former workers in the textile and leather industries, the unskilled laborers, and the new arrivals to Boston from the rural South and the Caribbean were unable to make the heavy capital investment in education required for participation in the new economic sectors (Sheehan 1984: 36–37).

At the same time, these groups have also been left out of the revitalization of the Northeast cities. As basic industries fled the region, these cities faced periods of crisis, replaced by a new urban florescence as Boston, New York, and other cities turned into financial, management, and service centers (Susser 1982; Sheehan 1984). Urban renewal, redevelopment, and gentrification reshaped downtowns, increasing the demand for first-class office space, hotels, and luxury housing close to the center of the city. This put pressure on low-rent housing in these areas. Over the past two decades, the greater Boston area in particular has experienced an acute shortage of low-cost housing along with a mushrooming growth of luxury housing, often in renovated buildings carved out of old, working-class neighborhoods. Thus, at the same time as changes in the demands of the labor market threaten blue-collar jobs, the pressure to accommodate new enterprises and to house the new, more affluent workers threatens homes and neighborhoods. As the working class is squeezed out of jobs, it is also squeezed out of housing.

The people who bring their personal problems to the lower courts come from this socioeconomic background. They often aspire to unionized blue-collar jobs, but, in the world of diminishing opportunity for blue-collar workers, such jobs are not readily available. Rather than unionized workers with secure jobs and good pay, a group which is typically at the top of the working class, most plaintiffs are service workers, clerical workers, or nonworkers. While some of the descendents of the mill workers of the nineteenth and early twentieth centuries acquired college educations and moved into more suburban neighborhoods, others were less successful. The people who bring their problems to court are typically those who have not been able to move out or up. They remain in poorer, denser neighborhoods threatened with gentrification or with ethnic transition as poorer groups move in. Mediators and court officials, on the other hand, tend to be the more successful descendents of the same immigrants. Court users in Cambridge and Salem are mostly white, but, in other cities where the class position of ethnic whites has been taken by racial minorities, it is blacks and, to a lesser extent, Hispanics who use the courts for personal problems (see the Appendix). For all these court users, recourse to the law grows out of a sense of entitlement to law, a sense rooted in the history of the working class in that region. The difficulties of the working class have not created this legal consciousness, but because a sense of legality is part of the culture of the working class, it provides a cultural resource to cope with the current strains in working-class life.[1]

The Courts

I observed cases concerning personal problems in three lower courts: the lower criminal court, the small-claims court, and the juvenile court. Each court was affiliated with a mediation program. Although the general assumption in mediation research is that it is quite different from court and that it provides a sharply contrasting way of handling problems, in practice mediation functions as a part of the court process, neither clearly separated from court processing (at least to those who use the courts) nor, as Silbey and I have argued elsewhere, sharply divergent in its modes of operation or ways of talking (see Silbey and Merry 1987). It is one of many informal processes for handling problems which have become incorporated into the lower courts in recent years (Silbey 1981). Further, mediation is an instance of the widespread practice of informally negotiating settlements before trial.[2]

The lower courts I studied handled interpersonal cases quickly and without trial most of the time, but they applied a rough sense of justice to the problems. They generally postponed cases, threatened to act while not acting, and instituted a long series of stages through which the case had to pass on its way to trial. I will describe the processes in each court in detail, then point out the strategies which are common to the way interpersonal cases are handled overall. In Salem I studied the lower criminal court. In Cambridge, I studied the juvenile court, the small-claims court, and the lower criminal court. In Salem I also examined a mediation program attached to the court, and in Cambridge I examined two mediation programs, one affiliated with the juvenile court and one based in the community and taking referrals from the small-claims court, the lower criminal court, and private individuals.

The Lower Court

The lower courts in Massachusetts, called district courts, are limited-jurisdiction courts. Their criminal jurisdiction includes all misdemeanors and some felonies.[3] District courts have bail-setting and probable-cause jurisdiction for all felonies. They usually include a juvenile session and small-claims session as well. The bulk of the caseload of district courts is landlord-tenant disputes, traffic offenses, welfare cases, and neighbor and family fights. Less than a fifth of any day's docket consists of arrests. Most cases arrive through complaints filed by the police and other officials (see Silbey 1981). Citizen-initiated personal problems are not a large part of the court's work, particularly at the trial level, but those who bring these problems are a substantial proportion of the people who voluntarily turn to the court for help. They are also a substantial fraction of the people who begin the court process, but most drop out or are eliminated before trial. Citizen complainants tend to be of the same social class as those who constitute the bulk of the clientele of the district courts, and their complaints almost always arise from interpersonal conflicts.

Interpersonal cases come to the district courts in Salem and Cambridge through a police arrest or through a civilian-signed complaint filed by a citizen or public official. There is no charge for this filing or for pursuing the case in court. Once the complaint is issued, the plaintiff is represented by the prosecutor. Police arrests go directly to the prosecutor, either bypassing the clerk's office altogether or passing through a routine show-cause hearing before the complaint is issued. Civilian complaints, on the other hand, are carefully screened by the office of the clerk-magistrate before a complaint is issued.

Anyone can file a civilian complaint by going to the courthouse and filling out an application-for-complaint form in the clerk's office. This form asks for the date and time of the incident, the charge, and a brief (ten lines or so) description of the incident. The secretaries at the counter set a date, usually one or two weeks hence, for a preliminary hearing in front of a clerk-magistrate, and by mail send the defendant a summons to appear. At the preliminary hearing, the clerk-magistrate screens civilian complaints for probable cause, to determine whether a complaint should issue. Some of the clerk-magistrates have legal training, but others do not. This is typically a political appointment, and some clerks become powerful figures within the courthouse.

On the day of the hearing, a clerk-magistrate calls both parties either into his office or into a small unused courtroom and asks each side to tell his or her side of the story. Depending on the orientation of the clerk, these hearings range from informal conversations to rather legalistic interrogation sessions, but they typically offer each side a chance to present a short narrative of the precipitating incident. The hearings I observed typically lasted about twenty to thirty minutes and usually concluded with the clerk's announcement of his decision and a lecture about how the parties should act in the future. I observed hearings held by seven different clerks in the two towns. Clerks rarely issued complaints in interpersonal problems. In her research on Massachusetts court clerks, Barbara Yngvesson found that only one-third are issued.[4] Sometimes a clerk will "continue" the complaint, threatening to issue it if there is any further trouble.[5]

In Salem, interpersonal cases were usually referred to the court mediation program before or during this hearing. Every day the staff of the mediation program checked the list of complaint applications to determine those which looked appropriate for mediation, searching for cases in which there was an ongoing relationship between the parties. Clerks, prosecutors, and judges also referred cases which had ongoing relationships between the parties. Most of the cases handled by the Salem mediation program between 1979 and 1981 were referred by the court; only 4 percent arrived without an initial complaint application. Of 587 cases in the mediation program's records, the clerk's office provided 58 percent of the referrals, the judge 23 percent, the prosecutor 5 percent, the police 5 percent, the probation office 2 percent, and social service agencies and other sources 3 percent. Thus, almost all the cases handled by the mediation program were initially brought to the court, most often by a private citizen. The independent mediation program in Cambridge also received referrals from the clerk-magistrates, prosecutors, and judges of the district court, but the program did not make a regular review of the docket of the criminal court and received far fewer cases. Instead, this mediation program went over the list of cases filed in the small-claims court.

The Salem mediation program is closely connected to the court. Its office is located in the courthouse, it corresponds on court stationery, and it is partially funded by the court. The staff is in daily contact with clerks, probation officers, district attorneys, and judges. It handles primarily interpersonal problems: 71 percent of its cases are neighborhood, martial, family, and lover disputes, and 29 percent are small-claims cases.[6] The interpersonal disputes processed by the mediation program cover a wide range of grievances, ranging from dogs who mess their neighbors' lawns to assaults by husbands on their wives during a drunken rage. Most are conflicts between neighbors, spouses, and family members, while a few involve boyfriends and girlfriends, roommates, landlords and tenants, merchants and consumers, and employers and employees.

In mediation, an impartial third party listens to both sides of the problem and helps the parties arrive at a mutually acceptable solution. The mediators are community volunteers, trained through a forty-hour course in mediation techniques. The goal of the process is to negotiate an agreement which establishes specific guidelines for future behavior. The agreement often stipulates some transfer of property as well. The sessions are held during evenings or on week-ends in nearby churches. With everyone present, each person is invited to present a description of the situation. This initial group session is followed by private sessions between the mediators and each person individually, conclud-ing with a final group session at which an agreement is drafted and signed by the participants and by the mediators as "witnesses." The sessions last between two and four hours (see Silbey and Merry 1986). If the case is not settled in mediation, it returns to the source of referral. The clerk will hold a probable-cause hearing if mediation preceded that hearing.

After a complaint has been issued, the case is sent to the district attorney for prosecution. At the arraignment, a pretrial conference date is scheduled in which the parties are required to appear for an informal settlement discussion. In these discussions the plaintiff is represented by the prosecutor; the defendant is represented either by his or her own lawyer or, more commonly, by a court-appointed attorney. These are lawyers who know one another. They often work out an agreement together which they then attempt to sell to the parties. Often neither the defendant nor the plaintiff has talked to his or her lawyer before the conference date. If the parties can reach an agreement, the settlement is pre-sented to the judge in the trial. Judges rarely impose a disposition that has not been previously negotiated between the parties. Most interpersonal cases are settled before trial, just as most other civil and criminal cases are.

If the parties refuse to settle at the pretrial conference, a trial date is estab-lished. These problems rarely come to trial, but when they do they are likely to receive a disposition such as "continued without a finding" or "sufficient facts" and court costs; in practice these are simply threats to do something in the future if the problem persists, and they do not take any action in the present. The de-fense usually consists of elaborating the past record and history of the individ-ual (see Feeley 1979; Mather 1979; Silbey and Merry 1987).

Small-Claims Court

Small-claims procedure is somewhat similar. Cases which arrive in small-claims court are first filed at a clerk's office. These cases require a small fee; it was about $6.00 at the time of my research. On the day the case is filed, the office workers schedule a hearing. On the day of the hearing, parties find them-selves crammed into a small room where the list of cases is read early in the morning, and then the cases are heard one by one. Individual parties may have to wait all day. The judge in the Cambridge court called the parties up to the bench, where he talked privately to both sides during the hearing, so that, al-though the hearing took place in a public room, the discussions were fairly private. Sometimes the judge sent the parties involved out into the hallway to try and reach a resolution themselves. For most cases, the judge did not make a decision on the spot but told the parties he would take it "under advisement," sending them a postcard with his decision in a few weeks.[7]

The mediation program I studied in Cambridge worked closely with the small-claims court, although it also received occasional referrals from the district court. The staff of the mediation program looked over the list of new cases each day, selecting those which appeared to involve ongoing relationships. It independently contacted the parties and asked them whether they were interested in having the problem mediated. Many refused. This mediation program was separate from the courthouse, located at least fifteen blocks away, but the court did refer cases from both the criminal division and the small-claims court. Of 281 cases referred to this mediation program, 36 percent came from the small-claims court, 15 percent from the clerk's office, 4 percent from the police, 2 percent from the judge, 1 percent from the probation office, 9 percent from a social service agency, 30 percent from individual initiative outside the court, and 3 percent from other sources.

Juvenile Court

School officials or parents can bring rebellious, truant, or runaway young people to the juvenile court and charge them with being "status offenders." The parent or school official filing a petition to make a child a status offender must first talk to a probation officer handling juvenile matters. The probation officer listens to the description of the problem and then advises, refers, or diverts the case to an outside agency. He or she may also recommend a formal complaint. If the probation officer decides further action is necessary, she issues an application for a petition. The probation officer thus serves as the initial contact with the family and can refer the problem elsewhere or address it directly. This role is similar to that of the clerk-magistrate in criminal cases in that the official endeavors to provide an informal resolution before allowing the problem into the court.

In the Cambridge juvenile court, the judge holds a preliminary hearing at the arraignment to determine whether the petition to charge the child as a status offender should be issued. At the preliminary hearing, the judge, aided by the report of the probation officer, probes into the situation. These hearings may last from a half hour to an hour. They are private, held in relatively small, intimate courtrooms which are not open to the public. Only the judge, clerk, probation officer, family members, lawyers, social service personnel, school personnel, and mediation-program involved in the case are permitted to attend. Although the hearings take place in a courtroom, the symbols of judicial power are muted. The judges sit on a raised platform facing a table where the family members and officials sit. The tenor of the hearings is far more informal, personal, and relaxed than in adult court sessions. The judge usually asks about the overall family situation and offers pungent bits of advice such as, "You should do what your parents say" and "You should know that selling drugs is wrong." Judges typically postpone formally adjudicating the teenager as a status offender or "CHINS" (child in need of services), while arranging for educational evaluations, counseling services, and, sometimes, temporary foster-care placement. The Cambridge juvenile court offers mediation as one of the services available at this point. The court hopes to address the problem through these interventions rather than through formal adjudication.

At this preliminary stage, many cases continue for long periods, with an indefinite number of court appearances while the court monitors the child's family and school situation. Instead of adjudicating a child a CHINS, the judge holds hearings every few months, trying to persuade the child to go to school, to stop running away from home, or to treat his or her parents with more respect. The judges typically combine threats of legal action, primarily placement of the child outside the home, with admonitions to do better and with lavish praise for successes. The discourse of the courtroom is informal and makes very little reference to the categories of the law.

The actual trial of the child, to determine whether he or she should be named a CHINS—or, as the court says, "adjudicated a CHINS"—is a further step which a judge can take if he or she is unable to handle the case informally. If the judge decides that the child should be adjudicated a CHINS, she will hold a formal trial, still in private. This commits the teenager to the custody of the state's Department of Social Services. Often the judge will adjudicate the child a CHINS in order to guarantee that the child will receive services, particularly placement in foster homes or group residences. After a trial and adjudication, the court maintains jurisdiction over the case and monitors both the child's progress and the state agency's provision of services. Adjudication is relatively rare. Of 124 cases Rocheleau and I observed in juvenile court over a year and a half or whose records we consulted, only 8 percent were adjudicated. In only half (48 percent) was a petition issued. But these cases were also not quickly dismissed: only 29 percent had been dismissed by the end of our data collection, after one and a half years. The remainder were still at the prepetition stage.[8]

In the strategies used to handle interpersonal cases there are similarities between all three of these courts. First, hearings, particularly at the preliminary end, are typically informal, neither couched in legalistic terms nor conducted in formal, legal settings. Discussion concerns character and relationships, not legal categories and evidence. These proceedings are not hard for the ordinary person to understand; aside from some procedural terms, much of the discussion takes place in everyday language.

Second, each process contains layers of preliminary, informal discussion of the problem. In the criminal court, the act of adjudication has been subdivided into many small steps, each of which provides an opportunity for the parties to negotiate and settle. The juvenile-court process for status offenders is similarly divided into an elaborate series of stages. A case can stop at any point in the process, and the court official can threaten to proceed further. The stages consist of an informal discussion with a probation officer, filing an application for a petition for CHINS status, issuing the petition for a CHINS, and adjudicating the child a CHINS. Most cases do not move to final adjudication but stall in one of the earlier stages. The stage of adjudication is the end of a protracted process rather than the first step. In all the courts, there is a tendency to avoid imposing decisions; legal action is threatened but withheld. Mediation is simply a part of these informal processes, a pull-off from which the case returns to the court process, another layer of preadjudication negotiation.

Third, each process tends to develop a complex, graduated series of penalties. In the lower criminal court, penalties include (a) continued without a finding with court costs, in which there are sufficient facts to find the defendant guilty but in which the decision is withheld, to be dismissed if there is no further trouble, (b) guilty finding with a fine, (c) guilty with a suspended sentence, and (d) guilty with probation. A prosecutor may also decide not to prosecute a case at all.[9] The technique of imposing a penalty and then withholding it if there are no further problems occurs at each stage of the process. The clerk-magistrate, for example, often says he or she will "issue the complaint" but will continue it for thirty, sixty, or ninety days and then allow it to be automatically dismissed if there is no further trouble. As prosecutors work out plea bargains during pretrial conferences, they threaten recalcitrant parties with going to trial. When judges impose settlements, they also rely on suspended penalties: suspended sentences, probation with conditions such as staying away from the other person, payments due in the future. Probation similarly involves ongoing supervision and the threat of punishment if the terms of probation are violated. One judge referred to the continued-without-a-finding disposition as "informal probation." Thus, each court process is divided into a series of stages with both supervision at each stage and the threat of moving to the next stage if some principles are violated.

Fourth, the courts exert slow but sustained pressure on the parties to work out the situation themselves. At every step of the court process, they are urged again and again to settle, to drop the case, or to come to an agreement before a trial.[10] They are pressured to settle in the clerk's hearing, at the pretrial conference, and at the day of the trial before the hearing in the small-claims court. Those referred to mediation are urged to settle in the mediation session. For example, when a small-claims judge heard a case between an Indian landlord and a black tenant, a case which had already been through mediation once, he urged the parties to go into the hall and try again to reach a settlement, saying: "You know each other. Why don't you talk about this, see if you can settle it yourselves?" A young woman who charged her ex-boyfriend with assault was urged by the police prosecutor to make another effort to settle the case. When parents come to juvenile court hoping that the judge will scare their children into going to school, giving up drugs, or treating the parents with respect, the judge will urge the parties to talk to each other. Sometimes he or she will send them to mediation. Mediation programs simply formalize and extend the practices of informal negotiation and discussion which regularly take place in the courts.

Fifth, the onerous obligation of appearing in court is itself used by these courts as a form of pressure to settle. The penalty for not settling is repeated appearances. In juvenile court, in particular, judges use the threat of appearance in court either to encourage good behavior or to punish backsliding. A child who has done well will be allowed several months before the next appearance, while the child who has refused to obey his parents, to attend school, to give up drugs, or whatever will be told to appear within two or three weeks. Appearances generally require long waits of one or more hours before a case is called. As Feeley points out, appearing in court takes time and means expenses in lost wages, transportation money, child care, and so forth, expenses which often exceed the penalty itself (1979). If the process is the punishment, as he claims, it may be because the process is used to punish without really punishing.

The next chapter looks both at the kinds of problems which people bring to these lower courts and at the legal consciousness of people who see themselves as entitled to help from them.

3

Legal Consciousness
and Types of Problems

Before a person can bring a problem to court, he or she must conceptualize it as something that "law," whatever it is thought to be, can help. The plaintiff needs to have a consciousness that law can provide appropriate aid for the difficulty at hand. He or she must interpret the problem as relevant to the categories of the law as he or she understands them. In forming a legal construction of events, people are often assisted by police officers, friends, or town officials who urge them to go to court with their problem. Behind the recourse to court for various kinds of problems lies an image of the law as appropriate and helpful for this sort of difficulty.

What events are construed by plaintiffs as having this legal meaning, this legal significance? Where do the categories of the law intersect with daily life? By examining the kinds of problems people bring to the court, we can see which categories and meanings of the law they use to frame their experiences so that they seem relevant to the law. Looking at the problems which people bring to court provides, therefore, some insight into the situations which people see as fitting within the purview of the law.

The legal categories provided by the courts refer specifically to the nature of the injury or wrong—assault, harassment, trespass, vandalism, or disturbance of the peace, for example. In small claims courts, cases are categorized by demands for money, and in juvenile court they are categorized by the behavior of the child—stubborn, runaway, or truant. But the parties rarely make reference to these categories when they talk about the problems. Court personnel, mediators, and plaintiffs also rarely use these terms to describe the cases. Instead, they talk about the social relationship between the parties. In district court, cases are described as marital, neighborhood, boyfriend/girlfriend, roommate, or stranger cases. In small-claims court, they are merchant/customer, employer/employee, landlord/tenant, and so forth. Juvenile cases are described as family problems and school problems, depending on whether they center on fights within the family or on disagreements between the family and the school. Thus, the language in which these problems are talked about within as well as outside the courts is the language of social relationships, not that of law.

In this chapter, I describe four of the most common kinds of personal problems in court: neighbor, marital, family, and boyfriend/girlfriend problems.[1] I have organized them by social relationship rather than by legal charge, since this is the way they are described by the people who bring them and by the people who handle them. I then examine the class and gender characteristics of the plaintiffs. Finally, I look at how each type of problem intersects with the legal consciousness of the citizens who bring them. These plaintiffs do not think in terms of specific doctrines or rules but instead think in terms of fundamental rights of property, autonomy, and parental authority. These rights are embedded in relationships with spouses, children, and neighbors. The legal consciousness of these plaintiffs corresponds to provisions within the law itself. For these people, threatening legal action and going to court are alternatives to violence. They describe shouting matches, destruction of property, and hitting as common ways of dealing with differences outside of court.

Neighborhood Problems

Neighborhood fights typically begin around simple issues of shared space. Neighbors complain about noise, dogs, children, and parking spaces. Noise is one of the most common complaints, since it drifts across the boundary lines that neighbors strive to delineate. Dogs and children are also mobile entities. Dogs bark and defecate on other people's lawns, and children play in loud or offensive ways, occasionally breaking things. Children are sometimes rude and insulting to adults. In dense neighborhoods, children's balls fly over fences into backyards or thump into houses. Children fight with each other, and their parents jump in to protect them or to fight along with them. Occasionally children seriously injure each other. Families differ about how much children should be supervised and disciplined. Trees also have a way of growing across boundary lines, spreading their branches across the neighbor's yard or poking their roots under fences. And particularly in older neighborhoods, cars spill out of available parking spaces. The struggle over the shoveled-out parking space in the depth of a New England winter is a particularly intense moment.[2]

In addition to serving as the source of annoyances which lead to conflict, children also escalate conflicts. As they fight with each other, parents are sometimes drawn in, either because they feel the need to defend their children or because they have their own grievances against the other families. When they hear about their parents' fights with each other children themselves often intensify conflicts and take them to the street, shouldering their parents' struggle. As they carry on their parents' battles, of course, new injuries and grievances develop, and the fight expands. Escalation proceeds as an intricate dance. Children may begin to fight, their parents jump in to back them up, the parents begin to fight, the children continue the battle in order to back up their parents, and on it goes.

Dogs similarly exacerbate conflicts. Although, unlike children, they do not deliberately take a conflict on as their own, they are also beloved beings which move around and offend. One person's tolerable dog mess is another person's gauntlet thrown as a challenge to a duel; the difference lies in the interpretation. Many people cannot imagine that their dog is offensive. For some, protecting the dog becomes a metaphor for protecting the self. Dogs play a leading role in the neighborhood conflict described later in the chapter. The woman in this situation was far from the only person who pleaded that she had to protect her vulnerable, elderly dog from some frightening mastiff who usually ate small dogs for lunch (for further discussion on dogs and neighborhood conflict, see Perin 1988).

As in the case of noise, children, and parking annoyances, however, it is the larger social and cultural context which infuses these incidents with meaning and leads some to become sources of confrontation and others to be dismissed as the lumps of life. The particular annoyances themselves are often about mundane details of life, but it is in their very mundanity that one can discern their importance. The fact that most of the time most people can deal with these annoyances without battles suggests that, when they cannot do so, the meaning of the struggle stretches beyond the immediate annoyance. When simple issues of shared space escalate into fights, there is usually something else involved. Sometimes it is a pretentious neighbor who feels superior to others on his or her block. Sometimes it is a family which comes from a slightly lower social class background and does things to violate the standards of cleanliness or order of the neighborhood. Sometimes it is simply the presence of a family which represents a new group moving into a neighborhood, thereby foreshadowing change. A new family can symbolize either the decline of the neighborhood or its upgrading and eventual takeover by more affluent people. Under these conditions, neighborhood disputes take on ethnic, racial, and class overtones. Conflicts appear to be about noise, dogs, and trash, but people talk about privacy and respect, subtle and symbolic markers of neighborhood identity and change. Sometimes they involve serious injuries or significant damage to property.

In these fights, neighbors usually know each other distantly rather than intimately. Most of those I observed involved neighbors who knew each other by name and were superficially sociable, but rarely had a deep and personal friendship or a great deal of interest in reconciliation or restoration of a preexisting relationship. Indeed, most of the parties were tied together only by proximity, by the fact that they could not easily avoid one another. The more they felt trapped together, the more intense and prolonged the battle. When avoidance was impossible or very costly—when there was no room to build a fence, for example, or when the victim of abuse could not afford to sell his house and move away—fights became more intense. In more densely populated neighborhoods, it is harder for the parties to insulate themselves from each other. Consequently, more intense and more frequent neighborhood fights came from working-class and poor neighborhoods than came from widely spaced suburbs, and more came from neighborhoods of homeowners then came from rental neighborhoods where moving away is easier.

Going to court provides a way of separating and breaking away from neighbors. Neighborhood problems typically occur within disintegrating relationships. Plaintiffs go to court to distance the relationship further, seeking "to be left alone," "so he/she won't bother me anymore," "so I never have to speak to her again," and so on. The intervention of the court is part of the process of separation. For many of these plaintiffs, the ideal neighbor is the person who says hello and who is available to help in an emergency but who does not seek or expect further intimacy. This is a person who minds his own business and respects the privacy of his or her neighbors. Plaintiffs use the court to separate, to sever relationships, rather than to reconcile and strengthen them.[3]

What kinds of people bring neighborhood problems to court?[3] Observation of the Cambridge and Salem mediation cases provided information on twenty-nine plaintiffs who brought neighborhood problems to the district court and who were referred to mediation. Usually they were white homeowners. Many of the plaintiffs were women, middle-aged, with a high school education and one or two years of college. They had average incomes for the towns in which they lived. Almost half were not working at the time they brought the complaint.

In the twenty-nine cases, seventeen of the plaintiffs were women, nine were men, and three were couples. Three-quarters (twenty-two) of these cases were between people of the same gender. Almost half (thirteen) were between two women, six were between two men, and three were between two couples.[4] About half the cases were between people of about the same age (twelve of twenty-four for whom age information is available), and about half (eleven) were between an older plaintiff and a younger defendant. People who take others of the same age to court were usually in their thirties;[5] those who take younger people are typically twenty to thirty years older than the defendants. People under thirty years of age very rarely take their neighbors to court; nor do younger people often take older people to court. In sum, people who go to court with neighborhood problems are generally in their middle years or older, and they take either their contemporaries or younger people to court. When older people take younger people to court, they are often old-timers reacting to the movement of a new group into the neighborhood. Women go to court more often than men but, in neighborhood cases, often take other women to court.

About half the plaintiffs (twelve of twenty-five for whom information is available) did not work outside the home. Six were retired, five were homemakers, and one was unemployed. Of the retired, two were secretaries, one a police officer, one a lab technician, and one a nurse. Those who were working had the following occupations: machinist, assistant staff manager, temporary office help, high school teacher, factory worker, secretary, nurse, practical nurse, maid, accountant, hospital administrator, school/community liaison, and cashier. The defendants were fairly similar in work experience. Over half were at home. Of the twenty-two for whom I have information, eleven were homemakers, two were students, and the rest had the following occupations: technical supervisor, payroll clerk, day-care teacher, fisherman, salesman, electronic assembler, carpenter, truck driver, and nurse's aide. Thus, people who go to court with neighborhood problems frequently are not working and spend much of their lives at home. Although many are homemakers, women with small children rarely appear. Those who work have a variety of clerical, factory, and service jobs which are not highly paid.

Income figures for eighteen plaintiffs suggest that they are moderate-income people, close to or below the average for their towns. Thirteen of these plaintiffs have incomes under $20,000, the median family income of these towns at the time.[6] The wealthiest two plaintiffs reported family incomes between $25,000 and $35,000. Those with higher incomes typically had two wage earners in the household, however, so that individual incomes are similar. Defendants showed approximately the same income breakdown, with nine reporting incomes less than $20,000 and four reporting incomes more than that. Again, the higher incomes were typically reported by families with two wage earners. Most of the plaintiffs have a high school education, and many have some college. Fewer have a college degree. The educational level of defendants is similar.[7]

Almost all the plaintiffs were white, but so was the population of the towns from which they came. Two plaintiffs were black and three were Hispanic, while twenty-four (83 percent) were white. Almost half of the whites had an ethnic ancestry, but almost all were native born. Twenty of the plaintiffs were homeowners, eight were not, and for one I do not know homeowner status. In other words, going to court over neighborhood problems is most likely to be a strategy pursued by middle-aged homeowners, people with moderate incomes who have an investment in their neighborhood. Plaintiffs in neighborhood cases are typically native-born whites with average incomes and without advanced education. Those who work have a wide variety of service, clerical, and blue-collar jobs, but almost half were not working outside the home at the time they went to court. People at home all day may be more likely to become involved in neighborhood fights. For these people, the home and neighborhood are especially important arenas for the expression of identity and for safeguarding the self. Ownership of a home elevates them above those who must still rent. They are anxious to guard from intrusion the social status embodied in the house and neighborhood.[8]

An Example of a Neighborhood Problem

The following case illustrates the dynamics of neighborhood problems and shows how the parties talk about them.[9] In this case, property is central to the parties' claims for help from the law. As is typical in neighborhood cases, the neighbors have no ongoing relationship to preserve. Both parties are at home much of the time and both own their own homes. Here, going to court is a strategy employed by older people against younger people for driving newcomers out of the neighborhood, and a strategy used by younger people for digging in their heels and staying. The younger people filed the first court charges, but the older people quickly retaliated with new charges. The younger family eventually gave up and moved away. Here, the court was lenient in its penalties, but its intervention provided a level of harassment which persuaded the younger family that staying in the neighborhood was not worth it.

The feud began with a simple quarrel over dogs. Mrs. Brown's elderly poodle urinated against the fence in front of Mrs. Smith's newly purchased house. Mrs. Smith pushed the dog away with a wooden clog shoe, and Mrs. Brown, incensed and eager to protect her dog, hit Mrs. Smith with a baseball bat. It was a small bat, a child's toy. Mrs. Brown was in her sixties, Mrs. Smith in her thirties. The two women had already been fighting over their dogs, Mrs. Smith's larger shepherd/Doberman mix and Mrs. Brown's poodle. Mrs. Smith called the police, who filed a major-incident report charging Mrs. Brown with assault and battery with a dangerous weapon (the baseball bat). Mrs. Brown's heart condition deterred the officer from arresting her, but there was a complaint against her filed in court. Her name, along with the charge, was listed in the newspaper, and she had to appear for an arraignment. The court referred the case to mediation, where it was settled with an agreement which specified when the dogs were to be walked. On the basis of this agreement, the court dismissed the charges against Mrs. Brown.

But only a week later the Browns organized a public hearing on the town's leash laws, a hearing aimed at the Smiths. For three months, while the mediation program was monitoring the mediation agreement, Mrs. Brown regularly called the mediation-program office to complain about the Smiths and their house reconstruction project: blowing trash, unleashed dogs, insulation escaping as it was blown into the walls, and so forth. As soon as the agreement time elapsed, Mrs. Brown went to court and filed charges of threats and harassment against the Smiths. By this time, the Smiths had owned their house for one year and had lived in it about six months. They retaliated by filing countercharges of threats and harassment against the Browns. At the clerk's hearing, the Smiths failed to appear and the Browns arrived with one of the town's prominent attorneys, who pleaded that Mrs. Brown's health was poor and that the situation was stressful for her. The clerk issued the Brown's complaint and denied the Smith's. The case was again referred to mediation, but although the Smiths were willing to try again, the Browns refused. The Smiths decided to sell their house and move to another town, regretting the investment in time and money they had made in the little house.

About ten months after the first incident, the case finally came to trial. In the ten-minute trial, Mrs. Brown's claims of delicate health were not raised, but her hostility to the Smiths was. She was furious. The judge took the case under advisement, reluctant to generate an outcry by dismissing the case immediately. The prosecutor wanted him to dismiss the case and tried to send him a signal to "dump it." Six weeks later, when it came up for disposition, the judge quietly did dismiss the case. Mrs. Brown was again incensed and threatened to file a civil suit for the costs of her medical care that were due to stress; but I found no record that she actually did so.

These neighbors had been fighting for a year. Crammed together on a narrow dirt road facing an inlet of the ocean, their houses were small and unprepossessing, but the location was attractive. For thirty-five years, the Browns had lived more or less isolated in this area of summer cottages. Then the Smiths bought the small house next door and decided to fix it up and make it their permanent home. As they raised the house twelve feet higher on a new foundation, the window of one house suddenly faced the window of the other house only ten feet away.

The Browns had tried many avenues to block the construction: complaining to the town about blowing trash, to the dog officer about the Smith's unleashed dog, to the U.S. Army Corps of engineers about the filling of wetlands when the Smiths dumped a small amount of trash on the narrow strip along the ocean on the other side of the road, and to the town about zoning irregularities because Mr. Smith was running his construction business out of his home. The Smiths responded with growing anger, shouting obscenities at the Browns when they emerged from their house. The "assault" was simply a moment in this struggle, but it provided a way to move the confrontation from the street into the courtroom. Once in court, the clerk tried to settle it, to no avail. Next, the court-affiliated mediation program tried, and it too failed. When the case came to trial, the decision was postponed. When the judge finally issued the decision that the court would do nothing on this case, the Smiths had already given up and decided to move. For the court, this was a troublesome and difficult case, the kind which is labeled "garbage" in private conversations; for the Browns and the Smiths, it was a desperate struggle over the course of their lives, their neighborhood, and their life savings. At the end, the young couple complained bitterly that the older couple had driven them out of their house and that the courts had not stopped them.

The fight between the Browns and the Smiths was a typical neighborhood problem, although more intense and protracted than most. As with many of these quarrels, it was an ongoing, escalating, and multifaceted struggle. The Browns were resisting the transformation of their neighborhood from a summer colony to a regular street. The people themselves were also typical. The Browns had lived in the town all their lives, as had the Smiths. Although they were neither economically nor politically powerful people, they expressed a sense of entitlement about using the court and were willing to appeal to the mayor and other government officials for help as well.

Legal Consciousness among Neighborhood Plaintiffs

One important basis of claims in neighborhood disputes is the privilege of property ownership. Many of the plaintiffs who bring neighborhood problems are people who see themselves as having "made it" by becoming homeowners. They often justify their demands in court on the basis of property ownership, claiming the right to control who steps on their property, who makes noise over it, or who lets their dog use it. They believe that homeownership entitles them to turn to the courts for protection against infringements of their property.

People also justify recourse to court in neighborhood disputes by claiming superiority over those who use violence. Neighbors fighting with each other will sometimes back away from a fight muttering that "I will see you in court" or "I will take legal action," implying that they are above those who continue to hit or throw rocks. One woman said that she was surprised when a neighbor went to court because she did not think the family was "that civilized." As we will see later in this chapter, the use of law instead of violence is an important aspect of the distinction that the more respectable segments of the working class draw between themselves and those they consider more disreputable.

An emphasis on the social power inherent in homeownership is a widespread cultural pattern in American society. In her study of land use and social order in America, Constance Perin describes the powerful cultural meaning of homeownership in this society (1977). There is a sacred quality, she says, to single-family detached homes. The American system of land use is defined in a hierarchy of uses, with single-family detached houses at the apex. Zoning ordinances protect them against apartment houses, businesses, retail stores, or shops (1977: 47). Indeed, owning a house means moving up on the ladder of life, becoming a better kind of person. Sometimes people can afford houses who lack the education and job to be a homeowner. For these people, the definition of themselves as homeowners becomes very important to a sense of self. It is a culturally valued avenue to social honor and prestige even when the dwelling is not much of a house, because, she argues, of the critical social relationship that homeownership establishes with the banker. When the banker approves a mortgage, he investigates a person's job, finances, responsibility, and wider character. Thus, Perin suggests, the banker serves as a gatekeeper to the status of social maturity; the mortgage is its membership card (1977: 67). Along with the image of social honor, homeownership brings other social assets: a long-term increase in assets, tax advantages, and easier credit—all of which are societal markers of the prestige and importance of homeownership (1977: 70). Thus, to be a homeowner is to be socially empowered, to be a special kind of person. It is also to be vulnerable, however, since the status of homeowner depends to some extent on the nature of the neighborhood. Undesirable neighbors can pose a real threat to this status.[10]

Although people in neighborhood fights talk about property rights, they typically understand property in a rather different way than the courts do. As John Brigham points out, property is conventionally associated with individual possession and control and is thought to include rights of exclusion, of accruing benefits, and of enjoyment of property (1988: 405–6). But these rights are not unlimited, as these homeowners often assume that they are. Instead, property rights depend on the state for their definition and enforcement. They are also, in many ways, limited by competing rights, such as the right of governments to take private property for public purposes (Brigham 1987a).

Property is one of the recurring themes in neighborhood fights. Other themes are consideration for neighbors, responsibility for children, and respect for one another's turf. For example, after a fourteen-year-old boy threw rocks at a neighbor's house and the neighbor, enraged, beat him severely, the latter told the mediators:* *"I just want them to leave me and my property alone."* The boy's mother filed charges of assault and battery against the neighbor who, on the advice of a lawyer, filed a cross-complaint of trespassing and malicious damage. The mother complained to the mediators: *"He told my kids if they rode bikes on his property again he would hit them over the head with a sledgehammer."* When the neighbor's wife came over to the mother's house to complain about the latter's son and the rocks, the mother told the wife to get off her property. When asked what he wanted, the man who had beaten the boy said he just wanted to be left alone, that he had worked too long and hard for his house to be bothered. Here, both sides talk about this fight and justify their actions in the language of property ownership.

Another case was referred to mediation by the planning authority after an elderly woman complained about her neighbor's building a boat in his front yard. She was also angry because he had told her that the fence she had purchased could not be erected between their houses because, he claimed, she did not have enough land. Both parties were homeowners, although the man's house was owned by his wife's mother. The street was built 150 years ago and consists of very small houses on equally small lots, about fifty-four feet by fifty-seven feet, along a narrow street. In the mediation session, the boat builder justified his actions in terms of his property rights. When asked to present his view of the situation, he said he was furious when he received a note from the planning department telling him he must cease and desist from building a boat in a residentially zoned area. He then told the elderly woman that the men painting her house could not step on his property to reattach her downspouts. After

---

*Here and throughout the text, quotations are italicized when they have been derived from notes rather than transcribed from tape recordings.

calming down, however, he told her that the workmen could come on his property to replace the downspouts; but he still refused to let the woman erect her fence. He told the mediators:

> *As far as the fence, she can put it up, but not on my land, and I will not give her a foot of my mother-in-law's property. She can never get a fence on my land. And she can have the downspouts put up, but never again put foot on our land. And next time her house is painted, she has to paint from the roof. I have looked at the records* [of land title in the registry of deeds] *and measured, and I know I am right. If she wants to take it to court, that is her business. I won't appear, but I will sue for damages.*

There are many other issues concerning parking, children playing in the streets, balls bouncing against the walls of the house, and failure to show appreciation for favors done in the past—between these families, but property and rights to control who comes on one's property is a recurring theme. For example, one of the neighbors complained that the elderly lady's dog makes messes in front of her house that the neighbor has to clean up. The elderly woman retorted that the land the dog uses is city property. As for the fence issue, she said that she would have the lot lines surveyed (an expensive proposition), and the man replied: *"She can have it surveyed, but if her house is even on my property one inch, I will have her move it."* The mediators worked toward an agreement in which each side promised not to go onto the property of the other family.[11]

In a third case, neighbors in a development of single-family homes began to fight after a group of teenage boys gathered in front of one house, pounding the fence and chanting the name of the people who live in the house. The victims charged the youths with harassment and trespassing. When the mediators asked the plaintiff what kind of a solution he could see, he responded: *"I want them to stop name calling, stay off my land, and leave my family alone."* The mediators told the other families that the plaintiff wants the trespassing to stop, and the other families agreed not to trespass on his property or to chant names. Although this case, like the others, involves a range of insults and animosities, the parties phrased their demands in terms of property and its prerogatives.

In a fourth case, a twenty-year feud between neighbors in a densely packed settlement of single-family homes, each family calls the police whenever it thinks that the other family has injured its property. As one of the women put it, *"I never say anything, never make comments. And I take care of my property and they never do. That bugs them. And if I shovel snow and it touches their fence, they call the police. They always call the police on everything we do. Their son has a record, and they want ours to have one too."* These families expect the police to help whenever they feel that their property is violated.

Since property is a central social category inscribed within and guaranteed by the legal system, plaintiffs who demand help on the basis of property violations are asserting a fundamental right established by the law. Notions of property are essential aspects of the American legal culture, absorbed by children along with table manners and greetings. They are not routinely questioned in later life.[12] When property is infringed, it makes sense to seek help from the legal system which has provided these rights and constructed the inviolable domain of the homeowner in the first place. In prevailing American legal practice, however, the nature of property rights is determined by the court, with government defining the extent of the property owner's autonomy (Brigham 1987a: 253–55).[13]

In mediation and in court people argue about when one can reasonably expect neighbors to be quiet, what it means to be considerate of neighbors, and where dogs can make their messes. But they take for granted that ownership of a house conveys substantial prerogatives to control what people do on that property and entitles the owner to seek help from the court. When courts accept these claims as the basis for complaints, they lend symbolic assent and validation to participants' notions that the law protects those who own property. The details of the incident may be challenged, but the fundamental notion that property ownership is a source of entitlement to legal protection is not.

Thus, law provides cultural categories which define relations between neighbors, categories which belong to the realm of taken-for-granted understandings of the world. Rights of property and homeownership seem natural and inevitable rather than cultural and arbitrary.[14] They are beyond question or doubt. Among these working-class Americans, the link between self and property owner is part of the natural order of the world. Indeed, the hegemonic character of property rights is reinforced by the folding together of the legal consciousness of property and the consciousness of self as owner of property. Similarly, the notions of respectability that are encoded in the use of the law rather than violence for settling differences reinforce thinking of injuries in terms of law.

Marital Problems

Marital problems are those which occur between husbands and wives. They focus on the marriage relationship and the domestic responsibilities of marriage partners. Violence is often the trigger which brings the problem to court, but the violence usually follows a long period of skirmishing and conflict. In many cases, this is not the first violent incident. The complaint about violence is usually part of fights about other issues, such as alcoholism, differences about how to raise and discipline children, the intervention of in-laws who disapprove of the match, and job and money problems. Women complain about their husbands' failure to support their families and to help with the housework, while men complain about their wives' unwillingness to cook, clean, and raise a family. The woman's complaint about violence typically does not stand out as a separate and distinct concern. Instead, many of the women who come to court regard violence as inevitable and consider it an egregious offense only when they think it is excessive or undeserved.[15]

Men view violence against their wives in similar terms. When a wife complains about her husband's violence, he is likely to complain about her constant nagging. Men attribute their violence to their wives' inability to act like good wives. Some men imply that the violence was deserved. One man angrily told the mediators that his wife acts as if he blows up "out of the clear blue sky." But, he contends, she is a constant nagger, telling him that he is ruining her life and the kids' lives: "I just try to get her to stop." Proudly he points out that he succeeded in getting the family out of the projects.

Marital disputes often emerge when a couple feels trapped in the relationship, money is short, the house is small, and the children are disruptive. In order to cope with these pressures, families sometimes turn to wider networks of relatives for support, particularly older parents who have some extra income with which to help families with young children. However, these relations of dependence bring new stresses, particularly as in-laws who are making substantial financial contributions to a young family try to assert control over the family. Many of the women plaintiffs are raising small children and have no independent source of income. They often experience serious money shortages.

Plaintiffs in marital conflicts often go to court seeking separation, desiring to live apart from a spouse who is abusive, violent, alcoholic, or uncooperative. Most of these conflicts are long-lasting; the incident which brought the parties to court was rarely the first moment of violence or trouble. The conflicts typically come out of marriages of five to fifteen years duration, and most have a history of separations, restraining orders, and calls to the police for help. However, separation is not a solution to a problem of too little money or of too much dependence on networks of kin: living alone is likely to be more expensive. The husband evicted from his home for hitting his wife finds living in a hotel more expensive and is reluctant to contribute the bulk of his income to the upkeep of his wife and children in the house the court has barred him from entering. If the wife found money short while her husband was living in the house, she now finds it even shorter. These problems become most intense when marital disintegration is thwarted, when the couple lacks the resources to separate—just as neighborhood problems become most severe when neither party can afford to move away from the other.

The people who come to court with marital problems are often younger, poorer, less educated, and more often women than those who bring neighborhood problems. Many fewer are homeowners. Of eighteen plaintiffs in marital cases I observed, fourteen (78 percent) were women, in comparison to 59 percent in neighborhood cases. In two-thirds of these eighteen cases, women took men to court. The plaintiffs in these cases were younger than the plaintiffs in the neighborhood cases. Of fourteen whose ages were known, seven were in their twenties, four were in their thirties, and three were in their forties. Most (fourteen of sixteen) plaintiffs were about the same age as the defendant. These people were somewhat less educated than the plaintiffs in neighborhood disputes, with five reporting a high school education only, three some college, and one a college degree. Compared with those in neighborhood disputes, a higher proportion, two-thirds, were not in the paid labor force. Seven were unemployed, of whom two were on welfare, four were housewives, and one was a student. The four who were working were employed as monogrammer, nightshift worker, food-preparation worker, and parts assembler. Most defendants are men. They generally work outside the home: of the thirteen for whom information is available, only one is not in the work force. The rest have the following occupations: hotel worker, traveling salesman, machinist, companion for elderly, delivery truck driver, insurance company worker, clerk/typist, self-employed contractor, technician, and warehouse worker.

Plaintiffs' incomes were a little lower than those of plaintiffs in neighborhood cases, with a higher proportion (83 percent vs. 72 percent) earning less than $20,000.[16] They probably earned slightly less because they were typically younger and because many were separated or divorced and could not rely on two wage earners in the family. In all but one case the parties were white. Of sixteen for whom information is available, half (eight) own their own homes. About half the defendants own their homes as well. This is a sharp contrast to the situation for the plaintiffs who brought neighborhood problems, of whom only eight did not own their own homes and twenty did.

Two Examples of Marital Problems

The following two cases illustrate the range of issues involved, the way complaints about violence are embedded in fights over marital duties, and the role which friends and relatives can play in heating up or cooling off a martial conflict. In each case, the plaintiff turned to the law when she was trying to break up her marriage, not restore it. The examples illustrate the ways the courts deal with marital problems.

A twenty-two-year-old woman took her twenty-three-year-old husband to court after four years of marriage, complaining that she was tired of his violence. He had hit her before but was hitting her harder and more often now. But she was also angry that, because he was going to school, he refused to help with the housework. She worked as a parts assembler and liked her job, but since she was supporting the family, she thought it unfair for her to do all the housework. She had always expected husbands to support their wives and wives to raise a family. Now she wanted a divorce. She had already taken out a restraining order against him and they had been separated for one month. This was the latest in a series of fights and separations. She said he refused to go to counseling with her and that he broke into her apartment all the time.

The husband admitted that he does not like doing the housework and thinks that it puts down his manliness. He pointed out that his unemployment insurance contributes to the upkeep of the house as well. He described himself as old-fashioned. He wants her to stay home while he works and thinks she is a women's liberation person, competing with him. He had other grievances: there were always other people, such as her girlfriend or her brothers, living with them. Moreover, one of her old boyfriends was hanging around and it was making him jealous. He had quit school and had just started a good job in refrigeration and wanted to get back together. He claimed that the violence was just his grabbing her to stop her from leaving and that she clawed him. She once threw a wrench at his head. He said it was she who refused to go to counseling. She denied that she was interested in the old boyfriend and said that he is just part of an old group of friends.[17]

Another case involved an older woman, forty-seven years old, who had gone to court for a restraining order against her husband of twenty-seven years, who is an alcoholic. He constantly drinks and then becomes violent. He has lived with her on and off over the past twenty-seven years while she has raised their five children. Many times over the years she had gone to court about his violence; her last restraining order against him was five or six years ago. The recent incident was precipitated by a fight caused by the stress she feels in caring for her twenty-five-year-old daughter, who had had a stroke and was partially paralyzed, and her three-year-old grandson. In addition to a twelve-year-old daughter and an eighteen-year-old son, both were living with them in a small house. The woman was very upset that her husband had deserted her during their daughter's illness, when she needed his support. She said she was thinking about a divorce. He had stopped drinking for the eight days before his appearance in mediation and was living at home because he could not afford to move out. He was fixing up the house to make it larger for the daughter and grandchild but could not finish the job without more money. He felt the house to be very crowded and confusing. He complained that she focused on the children all the time and would not go out drinking with him. He wanted to go out drinking with his friends, not sit at home. He attributed the latest fight to her time of the month and said she always gets upset then.

The woman paid $150 to get a lawyer to help her get a restraining order for five days, then another $150 to have it extended. At the second hearing in court, on the extension, the two lawyers agreed to send the case to mediation. There, the mediators persuaded her to give up the restraining order, a decision which she later regretted. Her husband continued to drink. She is white, Italian, has less than a high school education, and does not work. He is also white, a self-employed contractor who works off and on fixing up houses and yearly earns, according to his wife, between $16,000 and $20,000. They own their own home and rent one or more apartments to others. He is an orphan, raised in foster homes. She said he learned to drink as a teenager, in the Navy. When I asked her whether courts act as if they have seen all these cases before or listen to individual differences, she said that it depends who you are, whether you have money or education. In her opinion, "for professional people, butter melts in their mouths. They are treated a lot better."

Legal Consciousness and Contractual Responsibilities

Plaintiffs are very reluctant to bring marital problems to court and typically do so only when the situation seems desperate. One of the most common justifications is violence. As plaintiffs talk, however, it is protection from excessive and undeserved violence—not protection from all violence—which they seek. There is an underlying assumption that violence can be deserved, that women have an obligation to tolerate some abuse, and that the issue is what the limits are. Marriage is understood to entail obligations on both sides: in these families, men are expected to provide money and women are expected to cook, clean, and care for the children. Violence is linked to this fundamental sense of marriage as a contract in that the wife is expected to be obedient while the husband is expected to avoid inflicting excessive or undeserved violence. Thus, the claim for relief from the court is really a claim that there has been a contractual violation: the beating was too severe, the offense was not sufficient, the wife is not doing her part of the deal, and so forth. The problems are described as lapses from marital duty, with each spouse accusing the other of failing to live up to his or her obligations.

Many of the women plaintiffs have begun to challenge this vision of marriage, however. After taking for granted their obligations to cook and clean for their husbands, to pay the bills, and to tolerate their husband's violence, they have begun to interpret the blows in new ways—as illegal abuse or as an indication that the man needs counseling. From self-help groups such as Al-Anon, from counselors, from co-workers, and from relatives, many have been advised that they do not need to accede to this relationship. The men do not hear these new voices to the same extent. Husbands are sometimes surprised when their wives take them to court over violence. Some say they had no idea there was a problem and cannot understand why their wives had them evicted when they just "slapped her around a little bit." [18]

These problems are more ambiguous in their appropriateness for court than are neighborhood problems, and they are more difficult to frame in legal terms. Parties claim a right to protection from violence, but the violence is embedded in intense and ambivalent feelings and in conflicting interpretations of events. One can ask the court for protection from violence, but one cannot ask for love, for more discipline in childrearing, or for help with the housework during personal crises. The law has long asserted some jurisdiction over the contractual side of marriage, but has asserted less jurisdiction over marriage's emotional content. But, with Massachusetts' recent passage of a law against domestic violence, a law which offers emergency relief by restraining or removing from the home those who batter spouses, the legal system has more clearly offered a form of help.[19] This has encouraged women to bring marital problems to court despite their own feelings of uncertainty.

Boyfriend/Girlfriend Problems

Boyfriend/girlfriend cases involve jealousy, anger, efforts to revive failing relationships, and efforts to keep undesirable boyfriends away from one's daughter. Sometimes these cases involve a request for protection from an angry jilted lover. Alcohol and assaults come up frequently in this kind of conflict, but they are not central concerns the way jealousy is. Plaintiffs often go to court to end a relationship.

In this set of cases there are two subtypes: (1) those between young people, over jealousy and shifting partners, and (2) those brought by parents against the unacceptable lovers of their children. In the first subtype, people who have rejected a lover seek to end harassment by the jilted person or those trying to break off an unwanted romantic relationship try to get the other person to leave them alone. Some, for revenge, take a person who has jilted them to court. In the second subtype, parents try to break off a tie between their daughter and an undesirable boyfriend.

Of the fourteen boyfriend/girlfriend cases I observed, eleven involve jealousy connected with ending and forming new relationships among young people and three involve parents trying to keep young men away from their daughters. Most (ten of eleven) of the first subtype were brought by women. Ten of the cases involve young people in their teens and twenties. All the cases in the second type involve older people against younger men. These plaintiffs were typically younger and more economically unstable than were plaintiffs with either neighborhood problems or marital problems. Almost all are white and native born. Of fourteen plaintiffs, only four owned their homes and ten did not. Of fourteen defendants, only one owned his home. They tended to be economically marginal young men.

These plaintiffs are somewhat less educated than neighborhood plaintiffs. Five had high school educations or less, one had some college, and two had finished college. Annual incomes were also low: seven were described either as low or under $12,000, one was $25,000/$35,000, and one was $35,000–50,000 (this last income was reported by one of the male plaintiffs who was a contractor).Most (nine of thirteen) of these plaintiffs worked outside the home. In the first subtype, of ten for whom I have information, one of the plaintiffs was unemployed, one was on welfare, and one was a high school student. Others had the following occupations: child-care worker, kitchen help, counter help in fast-food restaurant, kitchen worker in hospital, contractor, waitress and teacher, and social worker. Defendants had the following occupations: custodian, post office helper, gas station attendant, unemployed, welfare recipient, student, and housewife.

Of the three plaintiffs in the second subtype—parents trying to keep young men away from their daughters—one worked as a medical technician, one as a drawbridge operator, and one as a housewife. Of the three young men, one worked as a roofer, one was a cab-driver, and one was unemployed. The plaintiffs were typically white, native born, and homeowners.

The following two situations exemplify the two subtypes. A case of the first subtype involved a fight between two couples, both just out of high school. One of the girls filed a complaint against the other for assault and threats; her boyfriend filed a complaint against the same girl for threats and harassment; and his mother filed a complaint against the same girl for assault and battery. This girl herself filed cross-complaints against both members of the other couple for threats and against the boy for assault and battery. The story presented in the mediation session was that the one couple was constantly following the other couple, driving past the house and harassing them. One day, they got into a fight in front of the house of one boy, and the boy's parents joined the melee. This fight generated the string of complaints and cross-complaints. The situation led to two mediation sessions and two clerk's hearings stretching over five months.

As the complex story emerged in mediation, it appeared that in the past there had been a different pairing; the young man from one couple had dated the girl from the other. He left her for a new girl, and the continued assaults that the jilted girl and her new boyfriend carried out represented her continued rage and jealousy at this desertion. However, the other couple retaliated with harassing phone calls (calling late at night and hanging up the phone), attacks on the boy's mother, and visits to the bank where the jilted young women worked as a teller. Probably adding to the stress in this situation were two other conditions: the young man who was the center of the fight had terminal cancer, and his mother was an extremely excitable person who inflamed the feelings on both sides. A few months after the situation appeared in court, the boy's mother was hospitalized for a nervous breakdown. The family of the girl who filed the cross-complaint has a history of court experience: some neighbors took her brothers to court for attacking their son and complained that the whole neighborhood had had trouble with these boys. This girl worked as a bank teller but was fired and got another job as counter help in a short-order restaurant, earning under $4,000 a year. Her new boyfriend came from a family of ten children which, according to the mediators, had a bad reputation, in both the court and the schools, for getting into trouble. At the time of the mediation session he worked for a landscaper, putting in plants, bark, and so forth. The contested boyfriend worked with his father in the construction business. The other girl worked in a convalescent home. All of the young people still lived with their parents.

A case of the second subtype involved the efforts of an older man, Mr. Lucrette, to keep a young man, Joe, away from his daughter. Joe dated the fourteen-year-old girl, Lynette, for three years, although Mr. Lucrette steadfastly opposed the relationship. Lynette became pregnant and bore Joe a daughter, but they did not marry. To discourage Joe, Mr. Lucrette went to court with three different charges against Joe: assault and battery, trespass, and threats to murder Mr. Lucrette's son. Joe was a high school dropout, on drugs, and unable to hold a steady job. Mr. Lucrette was a man in his forties who worked as a medical technician and prided himself on the fact that his children had all finished high school. Mr. Lucrette felt that Joe was not worthy of his daughter, and he sought to block the relationship at all costs. Yet, they lived a quarter of a mile apart and could not avoid running into each other. Joe persisted for a long time in his interest in Lynette, then married another girl; but he still wanted to see the baby he and Lynette had made. This case is described in more detail in Chapter 7.

Legal Consciousness and Protection against Violence

The ambiguity posed by the presence of these cases in court is even greater than that of marital cases. Lacking any appeal to contractual obligations, plaintiffs in these cases usually refer to acts of violence against them which seem undeserved, unreasonable, and unprovoked. They also demand money for repayment of injuries suffered in fights, either for medical bills or for repairs to a car or other damaged object. The legal system has made few if any efforts to define these problems as being within its purview. Besides the protection from undeserved violence, there is no general legal category which supports a plaintiff with boyfriend or girlfriend problems. Moreover, legally irrelevant feelings–feelings of jealousy, of unreciprocated love, of sadness at the loss of a partner—are even more central to these problems than they are to marital problems. The plaintiffs are young, often females, and often angry. Their legal claims are relatively vague, and their sense of uncertainty about going to court is substantial. The court personnel they meet are quite happy to agree with them that these problems do not belong in court.

But many plaintiffs do not know where else to turn for help. So they try to phrase their problems in ways to which the courts will respond and to ask for things which they think the court can provide. Some say they need protection, others say that they want help for the other person, and others say that they are entitled to damages. One young woman said she wanted to get her ex-boyfriend some counseling so that he would not hurt anyone else as he had hurt her. In the case of the two couples described above, one of the young women said that she wanted $20 to pay for her medical expenses, and one of the young men said that he simply needed protection.

Parent/Child Problems

Parent/child conflicts involve parents and their teenage children.[20] The most common problems these families bring to court are school attendance, the child's social life, friends, curfews, resistance to parental supervision, and the arrangements of family life (including chores, use of telephone and television, private space, and money).[21] Important issues rarely discussed either in interviews or in mediation or court sessions are violence and sexual abuse, but there are hints that these are important as well. Parents commonly demand respect and a better attitude; children commonly demand more autonomy, respect, and less yelling.[22] A significant generational and cultural gulf often divides these parents and their teenaged children.

These conflicts take place within intimate and enduring relationships which are hard to terminate, yet termination is often on the participants' minds. Parents go to court to assert greater control over their teenagers, while the teenagers often want separation and autonomy. The teenagers refuse to go to school, they stay out late, and they resist parental authority. Parents usually go to court in the hope of scaring or changing their teenager. A few want to place the teenager outside the home.[23] The parents who bring their children to court as status offenders are a native-born, white, relatively poor group, most of whom have manual, clerical, or technical jobs and relatively low incomes. Few have an education beyond high school.

Three-quarters of the mediation cases referred from the juvenile court were initiated by the parents, and most of the rest were initiated by the school.[24] We did not record whether it was the mother, father, or both who went to court; however, since almost two-thirds (61 percent) of the teenagers lived in single-parent households, mostly with their mothers, and since almost half the young people saw their fathers less than once a month, it is likely that the plaintiffs were mostly mothers.[25] Most (80 percent) of the mothers were in their thirties, 16 percent were in their forties, and 4 percent were in their twenties. The fathers were slightly older: 55 percent were in their thirties, and 45 percent were in their forties. Most families (78 percent) were white, a quarter (22 percent) were black, and none were Hispanic, although the program handled a few Hispanic cases and a Portuguese case which were not part of the research study. The racial composition of the two comparison groups was very similar. Of those studied, 70 percent were Catholic, 26 percent were Protestant, and 4 percent had no religious preference, similar both to the referred-but-not-mediated group and the not-referred group.[26]

The teenagers were fourteen years old, on the average, ranging from ten to eighteen years of age. They were disproportionately (59 percent) girls. The age and gender of children in both the nonmediated samples and the court sample was similar.[27] Most of the teenagers were middle or youngest children, and more than two-thirds (69 percent) had two or more siblings.

The families were typically working class or lower-middle class. Almost half (47 percent) of the mothers worked full-time; one-third did not work outside the home, and the rest worked part time (see Table 3.1). Among the nonmediated and court samples, almost half (48 percent of each) of the mothers were home-makers, and a few were unemployed. In contrast, very few of the fathers (only one in each group) did not work, but a few were unemployed. The most common occupation for the mothers was clerical employment (29 percent), followed by service employment (18 percent) and executive and professional employment (12 percent). More fathers worked in professional, technical, and sales jobs than did mothers (31 percent) and many fewer fathers than mothers were in clerical positions, but about the same proportion of the men had skilled and semiskilled manual jobs as the women had clerical jobs. Clerical jobs appear to be the female equivalent to skilled and semiskilled blue-collar jobs for men. In court cases not referred to mediation, parents rarely had professional or technical jobs and were more likely to be employed in unskilled or service work. These cases were typically simple issues of truancy, not internal family fighting.

The occupational distribution in Table 3.1 shows that families in which the mother had a more professional job were more likely to be referred to mediation by the court than were other cases. It appears that the court recognized problems concerning internal family dynamics as being particularly suited to the extended negotiation process provided by mediation, while those cases in which the child simply failed to attend school—cases in which the parents typically did not attend school long either—seemed to the judges to be less suited to mediation. In this process, the judge clearly recognized not only the legal categorization of these cases as truant, stubborn, or runaway but the social dimensions as well.

Eighty percent of the mothers have a high school education or less, 14 percent have some college, and 6 percent are college graduates. Of the thirty-six fathers for whom information is available, 78 percent have a high school education or less, 11 percent have some college, and 11 percent are college graduates. One fifth of the mothers and fathers did not go beyond the ninth grade. As Table 3.2 indicates, however, the referred families generally had more education than those which were not referred to mediation.

Most of the families had average or below-average incomes. Seventy-eight percent of the mediated families earned less than $20,000, as did 94 percent of

Table 3.1. Parents' Occupations (percent)

	Mother			Father		
	Mediated (N=51)	Nonmediated (N=42)	Court (N=44)	Mediated (N=29)	Nonmediated (N=12)	Court (N=16)
Professional	12	14	5	14	17	0
Technical/Sales	4	2	5	17	8	0
Clerical	29	10	18	4	0	6
Services	18	14	21	17	17	6
Skilled	2	5	0	17	17	31
Semiskilled	2	2	2	7	0	25
Unskilled	0	0	2	10	25	19
Unemployed	2	5	0	10	18	13
Not in labor force	31	48	48	4	8	0

Note: Because of rounding error, column entries may not total to exactly 100 percent.

Table 3.2. Parents' Education (percent)

	Mother			Father		
	Mediated (N=51)	Nonmediated (N=38)	Court (N=39)	Mediated (N=36)	Nonmediated (N=25)	Court (N=33)
Less than high school	35	37	51	36	40	55
High School	45	32	26	42	40	33
Some college or degree	20	32	23	22	20	12

Note: Because of rounding error, column entries may not total to exactly 100 percent.

the families in the thirty-five nonmediated cases (those in court which were referred to mediation but which were not mediated) for which information was available. Although 22 percent of the mediated families earned more than $21,000 and a few more than $50,000, half earned less than $14,000 and a third less than $10,000. The nonmediated families were considerably poorer: 60 percent earned less than $10,000. Information on the court sample was too scanty to be included. The median family income was $15,500 in the mediated cases and $10,000 in the nonmediated cases. In comparison, the median family income for Cambridge and Somerville, as reported in the 1980 census (two years before this study), was $17,845 and $18,220 respectively. Thus, financial pressures are significant for many of these families, but not for all of them.

These are typically not welfare families but are families supported by the work of one or both parents. Two-thirds are supported by employment and/or child-support payments, 18 percent receive public assistance in addition to income from employment, and only 18 percent are supported solely by public assistance. In 10 percent of the families, the teenaged children are also working. Some of the problems these families face are clearly related to crowded houses, long hours of work, and limited incomes. For example, one mother wanted quiet at night and her son wanted to watch TV; in a small house, both could not be satisfied at the same time. In another case, a child was thrown out of his room because his brother and a girlfriend moved into the room. Many of the battles over who does the chores are particularly heated in families in which the mother is a single parent and a full-time worker; when the mother does not work, these conflicts are less intense.

This is a native and local population, not an immigrant one. All of the children were born in the United States, 92 percent in the greater Boston area. Only one mother and four fathers are foreign born. Three of these four fathers speak Portuguese, and the fourth speaks Italian. Most (86 percent) of the mothers were also born in the greater Boston area. Two-thirds are from the immediate area where they now live.

In order to see how these families compared with the communities from which they came, I compared those who came from Cambridge and Somerville with the demographic characteristics of those two towns. The families in mediation were typically poorer, less educated, and more likely to be native born than were the average families in these towns. They were more likely to be single parents and were slightly more likely to be black, although in these predominantly white towns most families were white. Occupationally, the fathers, typically manual laborers, and the mothers, typically clerical workers, were less skilled than the average for the surrounding community. Eighteen percent of the population of these two towns is foreign born, and 46 percent were born out of state, while the families in mediation from these areas are only 7 percent foreign born and 22 percent born out of state. Although 32 percent of the Cambridge/Somerville work force has executive and professional jobs, only about 6 percent of the parents in mediation from this area have jobs of this type. The educational level of parents in mediation also is less than the average for their surrounding communities. Slightly less than half the parents from Cambridge and Somerville have a high school diploma and none has completed college, but in the general population 74 percent have a high school diploma and 29 percent are college graduates.

One case taken to court and referred to mediation involved a sixteen-year-old girl whose mother, hoping that the court would scare the girl into obeying her, had gone to court for a CHINS petition against her daughter for being a runaway. The mother was disturbed about her daughter's friends, whom she considered prostitutes and drug addicts. The newest boyfriend was a particular worry. The daughter and boyfriend had come home very drunk one night. The mother wanted her to stop seeing him. The daughter, on the other hand, wanted her mother to stop prying into her life and investigating her friends. The mother had refused to let her continue to see a previous boyfriend and was unhappy with one of her present girlfriends. The mother was white, Catholic, native born, in her forties, and had a high school education. She lived in a very small but immaculate apartment. The family income was about $15,000. The mother worked full-time as an instructional aide in a local school and had done so for about ten years. The daughter was her youngest child; she had two older sons. Her husband had died three years earlier. Both mother and daughter were seeing psychiatrists at the time of the mediation session.

Legal Consciousness: The State as Parent

When parents take teenage children to court, they generally hope that the court will help them control the child better. Usually the child is disruptive and rebellious, refusing to go to school and sometimes running away from home. Parents who bring their children to juvenile court are generally desperate, having put up with a difficult situation for a long time, and are anxious for the judge to scare the child and to help the parents get the child to obey and to go to school on time. The courts, according to a doctrine in effect since the early twentieth century, have asserted their responsibility over this behavior. According to the doctrine of parens patriae, the government assumed responsibility as father for children who were getting into bad habits, destitute, living on the street, and so forth (Platt 1969). Parents who go to court in the hope that the court will scare their child, reform it, force it to behave better, or take it away acknowledge this announced responsibility of the courts for wayward and dependent children.

Yet, these plaintiffs, too, feel reluctant and uncertain. Their problems are mostly about feelings: feelings of respect, of love, of anger, of commitment. These feelings are hard to bring into the legal system. They are inconvenient but inevitable accompaniments of problems about obedience, staying home, and going to school. But these problems are less ambiguous in court than are boy-friend/girlfriend problems or even marital problems, since the courts have declared that parents are entitled to help both in supporting parental authority and in compelling children to be obedient, stay home, and attend school. The juvenile court, a specialized institution, testifies to this commitment.

The Social Class of Plaintiffs

Overall, the people who bring personal problems to court tend to be in their thirties and forties (except for some boyfriend/girlfriend cases), often but not always women, and either not working or working in low-paying service, cler-ical, or manual jobs. Most are white and native born, have only a high school education, and are relatively poor. They are neither members of the urban un-derclass nor affluent and educated professionals. Many belong to the category of temporary workers and marginally employed described as the secondary la-bor market (Doeringer and Piore 1971). Few are recent immigrants. A com-munity worker in the Hispanic community in Salem observed that among these new arrivals she sees very little sense of entitlement to use of the courts. They rarely come to court. People tend to take to court those who are similar to them-selves in economic, class, and educational backgrounds. Plaintiffs in neighborhood cases are slightly more affluent, better educated, older, and more often homeowners than are plaintiffs in marital, boyfriend/girlfriend, or par-ent/child cases.

In order to see how typical—how representative of people who bring person-al problems to court in other parts of the country—the plaintiffs I studied are, I examined the literature on court users and mediation programs for information on gender, race, ethnicity, income, and class throughout the United States. In-formation is typically very sparse, available almost only on mediation programs attached to courts. The scanty available literature suggests that the patterns I observed are typical of other regions of the country. These data are described in more detail in the Appendix.

The plaintiffs in Salem and Cambridge can be described as working class. This does not mean that they necessarily share a class consciousness, but they do have a common life situation. They look down on those who have less stable lives, poorer housing, and less reliable jobs, and they look up to people who have professional jobs, college and advanced education, and their own homes. Most aspire to a stable family life, secure job, privately owned home, and the material possessions of a middle-class existence but find they are unable to afford this life. People who bring problems concerning neighborhood and parent/child problems in particular aspire to middle-class status. Those who bring marital and boyfriend/girlfriend problems more often live tumultuous lives without either much job security or an owned home. In the terms developed in the study of working-class culture, plaintiffs in neighborhood and parent/child cases tend to be settled-living people, and plaintiffs in marital and boyfriend/girlfriend cases tend to be hard-living people.

The distinction between settled-living and hard-living people emerges from efforts to distinguish segments of the American working class. Generally comprising people who do manual labor for an hourly wage, the working class incorporates a broad range of service workers, clerical workers, and laborers as well as craftsmen and foremen (see Berger 1968; Levison 1974). This group is generally divided into two broad groupings, although the boundary between them is fuzzy and hard to identify in practice. Howell makes a distinction between "settled-living" and "hard-living" families (1973), a distinction Rubin echoes in her study of working-class families (1976). She describes the categories and their permeability as follows:

> Some families struggled desperately and, most of the time, successfully to remain among the "respectable" poor. Others gave up the fight and, more often than not, escaped their pain in drinking, violence, and desertion. Observing these patterns recently, one writer labeled them as the "settled-living" and "hard-living" life styles (Howell 1973) . . . . Like all such typologies, however, this one, too, should be labeled "Approach with Caution," for at best it is only an approximation of reality. Thus, several things should be clear. First, the hard-living-settled-living styles represent two extremes rarely found in their pure states; elements of each often are found in the other. Second, just as many settled-living men and women may experience some aspects of hard-living in their own lives as they try to grasp and hold the American dream, so most hard livers of one period are settled livers in another. Third, in almost every settled-living family, there are hard-living brothers, sisters, or cousins who, while scorned, are omnipresent and painful reminders of the precariousness of the settled-living lifestyle—of that fact that at any moment external life forces might push even the most determinedly settled-living family off its course (1976: 30–31).[28]

This distinction roughly parallels the differences between people who bring neighborhood problems and people who bring marital and boyfriend/girlfriend problems to court. Neighborhood-problems plaintiffs tend to be settled-living people, while those bringing romantic and marital problems are more often hard-living people. Juvenile problems seem to cross-cut this boundary. Parents tend to be settled-living in life-style, but they fear that their children will slide into a hard-living way of life. Many of the parents who bring their children to court worry that their children's friends will tempt them to abandon the settled-living life-style to which they themselves aspire and to turn instead to drink, truancy, and partying. Those who bring neighborhood problems to court are much more likely to be homeowners than are those who bring marital and boy-friend/girlfriend problems to court.

The distinction between homeowners and tenants serves as a central cultural symbol separating settled livers and hard livers, the respectable, established working class from the more transient, shifting, less respectable part of the working class (Berger 1968: 83; Mackenzie 1973). Owning a house means greater privacy, enhanced status, and freedom from the control of a landlord (Mackenzie 1973). Skilled manual workers who are able to buy a home may live side by side in suburbs with lower-middle-class workers, such as teachers, nurses, and store managers, often earning more money. But these families face economic insecurity, since they do not have any substantial savings. A single economic crisis can wipe out the work of a lifetime. Divorce, alcoholism, inju-ry, illness, and layoffs represent persistent threats to security (LeMasters 1975). Under these circumstances, the house may become the single symbol of afflu-ence, the one real gain for a lifetime of work and drudgery (Levison 1974).

The relationships between homeowners and tenants are close: homeowners typically rent to the poorer underclass, so that these groups share buildings and neighborhoods and schools.[29] Adult children often rent apartments in their par-ents' houses. Moreover, in a world of uncertain employment, the homeowners are never far from the renters, since they face the prospect of foreclosure.

The centrality of homeowning as a symbol of respectable status explains its importance in the talk about neighborhood conflicts. As we have seen, home-owners premise their claims on an expansive sense of property ownership, including the right to throw others off their property. Homeowners in working-class neighborhoods are conscious of the difference between themselves and renters and guard that status. In eastern Massachusetts, with its high housing prices and tight housing supply, the owned home may be an inheritance from parents, something that would be unaffordable to the owner him or herself. Consequently, homeowners often find themselves locked into neighborhoods which they cannot afford to leave.

In addition to homeowning, other central symbols of status within the work-ing class are a stable marriage, a steady job, and education. These are all fragile, however. The first two can disintegrate, plunging the individual into the lower reaches of this social group. One's own education is obviously more du-rable, but the education of one's children is a similarly uncertain project. Parents hope that their children will at least finish high school and aspire to a local college, but this can be threatened by the wrong kinds of friends, lack of motivation, lack of money, and so forth. Although the working class in the 1970s was more educated than in the past, Sennett and Cobb reported a deep sense that working-class people saw education as the key to personal autonomy and control over one's life, a control which they often felt they lacked in comparison to more-educated people (1972). Susser finds that the working-class people she studied were very vulnerable to the power of "expert" advice from therapists, legal advisors, and other educated people (1982: 117).

Conclusions: The Dimensions of Legal Consciousness

Each type of problem arrives in court under the umbrella of a broad legal consciousness and situationally specific legal categories. Working-class people draw on a broad repertoire of legal categories, applying the particular categories relevant to each situation. Each type of problem is associated with a different set of legal categories: neighborhood with property ownership, marriage with contract, boyfriend/girlfriend with protection against violence, and parent/child with a sense that the state is responsible for teenage children in trouble.

This consciousness grows out of legal doctrines announced by the courts themselves, reflecting generally established areas of legal intervention. It responds to announced protections offered by the legal system and to the services which the court provides. But it does not refer to specific laws. The legal categories are not deliberately considered and chosen, as specific legal doctrines or statutes might be. Nor do they conform to the refinements and elaborations of law in the law schools. They are features of the taken-for-granted world of these working-class Americans, a consciousness of law acquired through their life experiences. This consciousness frames the opportunities for help and encourages people to bring their personal problems to court.

These people feel entitled to other government services in addition to law. Many of these people use a variety of government services. Some turn to local politicians for help. They see themselves as entitled to schools, welfare, unemployment benefits, and police protection. The demands they place on the courts are part of a more general sense that the government and its elected representatives are responsible for providing them with a range of kinds of help.

One of the striking features of the plaintiffs who have been described in the present chapter is that they are mostly women. In neighborhood cases women typically take other women to court, and in parent/child cases women take both boys and girls to court. In marital and boyfriend/girlfriend cases, the pattern is for women to take men to court. I think the preponderance of women plaintiffs occurs because women feel relatively powerless in relation to the people they bring to court. Since the prevailing alternative to court is violence, women are at a disadvantage in the competing mode of fighting. They turn to the court as a form of power in dealing with others who are more physically powerful than they are. Women are usually at an economic disadvantage in relations with spouses and lovers as well. Although mothers appear to be more powerful than their children, in parent/child fights mothers frequently face a situation in which their teenage child is being extremely disruptive, rebellious, and unwilling to accept his or her mother's authority. The pattern of older people using the court in battles with younger people grows out of a similar power differential.

Moreover, women seem to be more attracted to a nonviolent mode of dealing with conflict than are men. This is a social world in which male violence is common and fairly well accepted. Thus, the disproportionate use of the court by women grows out of their relatively powerless position in family and neighborhood life and their inability or unwillingness to resort to violence. The court is a form of power for the physically and economically weaker person.

On the other hand, as Chapters 5–7 delineate, there are paradoxical consequences for women who bring their problems to court. Although court sanctions are a powerful weapon, once in court the plaintiffs lose control. Court officials may take the problem seriously or they may not. They may frame it as a minor problem requiring ongoing supervision of the woman's family—an unwelcome outcome. They may simply provide a stern lecture and a threat to impose sanctions if there is further trouble. Or they may take it seriously and impose a strict restraining order on the defendant. There is always the chance that the defendant will be sent to jail, as statutes specify for some forms of assault. The person bringing the problem never knows for sure what is going to happen. She cannot control the process once the problem is a case in court.

But plaintiffs struggle to exert some influence. Defendents also endeavor to shape the process to their desires and to derail the legal process. The chapters on court processes describe contests over control of the case among the plaintiff, the defendant, and court officials as the problem moves into the courthouse.

4

The Social Context of Problems

Where do these plaintiffs live and work? What kinds of neighborhoods and families do they come from? This chapter examines the social contexts of plaintiffs' lives and the meaning, within those contexts, of going to court. People who bring marital and boyfriend/girlfriend problems are particularly likely to live in rented apartments that have absentee landlords and that are in the worst sections of working-class neighborhoods. Those who bring neighborhood problems tend to live in more affluent sections of working-class neighborhoods and to own a small house. Those who bring parent/child problems are of both backgrounds. These differences are subtle, not easily measured by demographic statistics. But they are a powerful part of the way class differences are conceptualized and understood by working-class people.

Indeed, court use is an important index of respectability. In general, frequent resort to court can make a person disreputable. For those who aspire to respectable status, to use the court at all is questionable. But the meaning of going to court varies with the type of problem the plaintiff brings and on the particular cultural world in which he or she lives, a cultural world structured by ethnicity, religion, and history as well as by class. Those who bring marital and boyfriend/girlfriend problems to court are looked down on by the older, more settled residents of the working-class neighborhoods in which they live. Among other drawbacks, taking these intimate, domestic problems to court allows everyone to see one's personal affairs and to talk about them. Instead, respectable people should put up with problems. As one older, settled-living woman said of her problems, "we carry them on our backs." On the other hand, people in hard-living social worlds see the use of law as more civilized than the use of violence. To threaten legal action claims a moral ground above the protagonist who is hitting and yelling.

In Salem as a whole, poor people and people living in more densely populated neighborhoods are most likely to go to court. Residents of affluent, highly private suburbs are much less likely to take their problems to court. The latter endeavor to avoid one another as much as possible and turn to private services such as lawyers and psychotherapists. In order to see how the tendency to take problems to court varied among residents of different neighborhoods, I looked at the geographical origins of 239 cases referred to the mediation program in

Salem during eighteen months in 1980 and 1981. These cases included all types of personal problems, not just the four I have been discussing.

The two neighborhoods with the highest rates per resident were the Green Street neighborhood and another densely populated, rundown neighborhood. There were almost 16 cases per thousand residents in the Green Street neighborhood (21 cases from a population of 1,400) and 16.5 per thousand in the second neighborhood (11 cases from 670 people). This was sharply higher than the town average of six cases per thousand residents (239 from a population of 40,000). On the other hand, a suburban neighborhood on the edge of Salem had only two cases per thousand (3 from 1,900 people), the lowest rate.[1] In general, neighborhoods with higher rates of referral to court mediation tended to have lower incomes, higher school drop-out rates, a higher proportion of renters, and less-educated residents than did neighborhoods with lower rates.[2] They tended to be the most densely populated areas with the most deteriorated housing and lowest rates of owner occupancy. They also tended to be neighborhoods undergoing social change.

In order to explore the meaning of these variations among neighborhoods, I did an ethnography of three working-class neighborhoods in Salem, each with about 1,000 adult residents. I talked to residents informally over a period of nine months about their concepts of class and ethnicity, the history and social organization of their neighborhoods, and the meaning of going to court.[3] I also tabulated the frequency with which, for each of them, personal problems came to court. All three were generally working class, but the first two were less affluent than the third. All were predominantly white and Catholic, mixtures of descendants of Irish, Italian, Polish, French-Canadian, and Greek immigrants. Occupationally, the residents of the three neighborhoods were roughly similar (see Table 4.1). Yet, to the people who lived in these three neighborhoods, they were clearly ranked in a hierarchy. The oldest neighborhood, to which I have given the pseudonym Oldtowne, was a congested area which had degenerated

Table 4.1. Occupations by Neighborhood[a] (percent)

Occupation	Oldtowne	Hilltowne	Riverdale
Professional, technical, managerial	21	14	21
Sales, clerical	11	14	14
Craftsmen	12	13	14
Operatives and transport workers	4	7	4
Laborers, service workers	7	9	6
Retired	15	11	3
At home	20	23	23
Student	11	10	16

Note: Because of rounding error, column entries may not total to exactly 100 percent.

[a] Based on street list of persons seventeen years of age and older that was compiled by city of Salem.

from an ethnic village to a slum. The second, Hilltowne (also a pseudonym), was also fairly densely populated but represented a move up from Oldtowne. The third, which I have called Riverdale, was a recent suburban development to which more successful inhabitants of Hilltowne and similar neighborhoods aspired.

In the eighteen months between January 1980 and June 1981, residents of these three neighborhoods brought to court fifty-one personal problems concerning neighbors, spouses, boyfriends/girlfriends, relatives, and friends. Most cases arrived in the office of the court clerk and were subsequently referred to the mediation program, but some were referred to mediation directly from the bench, and some went to the clerk's office but were never referred to mediation. Unlike the cases discussed in Chapter 3, these include some referred to mediation which were never mediated, usually because the parties refused.[4]

Far more problems came to court from Oldtowne and Hilltowne than from Riverdale. Oldtowne residents brought twenty problems, Hilltowne twenty-five, and Riverdale seven. Moreover, people in Oldtowne and Hilltowne brought many more marital and family problems than did people in Riverdale. The few cases brought by Riverdale residents were almost entirely neighborhood problems (see Table 4.2).

In all three neighborhoods, it was rare for anyone to bring a personal problem to court. I carried out a door-to-door survey of personal problems in all three neighborhoods, interviewing ninety-three residents (about thirty in each neighborhood). This survey indicated that people had many more problems than they ever took to court and that the vast majority of problems were simply endured or discussed with the other person.[5] Fewer than one-fifth of the problems reported in this survey elicited even a call to the police. Very few of the people interviewed said they had taken a problem to court. Problems ended up in court only when one or more of the participants was unusually angry, aggressive, aggrieved, desperate, or stubborn (see Merry and Silbey 1984).

Table 4.2. Problems in Court by Type and Neighborhood[a]

	Oldtowne	Hilltowne	Riverdale
Population of adult residents[b]	1,023	969	719
Type of problem:			
Neighborhood	4	7	5
Marital	4	9	1
Boyfriend/girlfriend	4	3	0
Family	1	4	0
Friends	7	2	0
Total	20	25	6

[a]Cases filed in clerk's office and/or referred to mediation, 1980/81.
[b]From city's Street List of Persons.

Three Neighborhoods and Their Problems

Oldtowne is a very old neighborhood. Originally an elite neighborhood during the peak of Salem's economic importance at the close of the eighteenth century, it contains beautiful houses built at that period plus multifamily structures built in later years. As might be expected of a neighborhood designed and substantially constructed during the eighteenth and nineteenth centuries, the buildings are small and packed together, the streets are narrow, and parks are few. The houses sit directly on the sidewalks and are separated from one another by no more than a few feet. They have back yards of only a few square feet and generally do not have off-street parking spaces. Some of the houses are sufficiently set back to carve out a small parking space in the front. Backyards are generally fenced, and fences are common between houses that are a little distance apart.

During the first half of the twentieth century, this was a Polish ethnic village that housed the recently arrived workers in the textile mills and leather factories.[6] Many immigrants arrived at the turn of the century. It boasted an active community life, numerous self-help associations, two Polish lawyers, and small family stores on every street corner. With the postwar era, however, a long-term decline began as the more affluent and upwardly mobile Polish families moved out, leaving a population of elderly, poor, and single mothers who could not afford to leave. A few are still trapped in the neighborhood because they cannot move away. Another group of old-timers has chosen to remain because they are attracted by the prospect of preserving and upgrading the historic neighborhood and have pursued these objectives in tandem with the Grove Street elite.

During the 1970s, absentee landlords purchased many of the multifamily dwellings and turned them into apartments for low-income and welfare tenants. By 1980, low-income white tenants constituted a significant minority in the neighborhood. However, during the 1970s the city government decided to invest in upgrading the neighborhood, an area of considerable historic and tourist interest. A major urban renewal project on the borders of Oldtowne changed its image and encouraged a flood of young, moderately wealthy professional people who bought and renovated the older "period" houses. By the late 1970s the area was being talked about as "historic" rather than "old." The small size of the houses and the lack of open space guaranteed that young professionals would not remain long after their children were born, however, and they typically stayed only a few years.

The area was extremely transient in the 1970s. A local agency used city poll lists to determine turnover and reported that between 1971 and 1976 63 percent of the total housing units in the area changed hands. In the two-year period between 1974 and 1976 alone, 48 percent of the units changed hands. By the early 1980s, Oldtowne was a very heterogeneous neighborhood. People of varying life-styles, class backgrounds, and values found themselves squeezed together around limited parking spaces and tiny yards. According to the 1980 census, the median family income was $20,050 and $14,972 for the two census tracts into which the neighborhood is divided. Of those inhabitants more than eighteen years of age, 65 percent had finished high school and 15 percent had four or more years of college. Only 37 percent of the households were nuclear families, and only 31 percent owned their homes.

History is an important symbol of status in Oldtowne—but in different ways for different groups. In a city, such as Salem, that is steeped in colonial American history, elite status is associated with things old, with Yankee seafaring, with being there first. The shipowners and ship captains of the seventeenth and eighteenth centuries made fortunes sailing to China and erected elegant brick homes with widow's walks from which their wives could search the sea for their return. These homes still stand as testimony to their taste and power. Historical preservation emphasizes old buildings which connect with this elite past. Not every history confers status; only the history of the Yankee elites, that of the eighteenth century. The young professionals moving into Oldtowne buy up and renovate the desirable "period" houses of the seventeenth and eighteenth centuries because these buildings speak of this past. They are quick to affix to the tiny dwellings date plaques which testify to their connections to this elegant seafaring history, a period which lasted, at the latest, until the mid-nineteenth century. Oldtowne was recently made into an Historic District in order to preserve this particular vision of its past, a move supported by the Yankee elites in the town as well as by some of the more upwardly mobile Polish residents.

The Polish residents of Oldtowne also value history—but a different kind of history. For them, status depends on the history of their family's immigration and adjustment to American, histories which begin, at the earliest, in the late nineteenth century. What is important is how early the families arrived from Poland and what they achieved in job and property ownership once they got to America. Important events include the purchase of a family house, preserved and passed down through the generations. The house is the patrimony, the symbol of what the family is and has achieved. To have a house and a family which has been in Oldtowne for eighty years is to be a person of stature in the Polish community. If one can claim to have forebears who were leaders in this community, one has yet more standing. Thus, history in the Polish community is a history of ancestors and property, not a history of ship captains and the Revolutionary War.

The newcomers who have moved into the neighborhood since 1970 seem to the other residents of Oldtowne to be people with no history. The move in and out, neither buying property nor connecting to elite history. Everyone expects that no matter how intolerable they are at the moment, they will move out sooner or later. There is no historical context within which the other residents can think about these families: no famous ancestors, no family property, no continuity with the past. These people have their own histories of immigration and settlement, but they are unknown to the Polish and Irish residents or to the young professionals with their Yankee ancestry. They have moved too often and have become disconnected from their ethnic communities and their local histories, carrying with them instead the history of their own lives and families. But these private histories are not recognized by those around them, and the newcomers are accorded the lowest status. Many are the less successful members of either the Yankee settler group or other established ethnic groups of Salem. It is these people who turn to the courts for help. A few of those who go to court have Polish names, but more have French, Irish, Italian, or generic American names.

Twenty problems from Oldtowne came to mediation and court: four neighborhood problems, four marital problems, four boyfriend/girlfriend problems, one brother/sister problem, and seven friend problems (see Table 4.2). I estimated that at that time the population of adults (those more than seventeen years of age), in this neighborhood was 1,023 people. Many of these Oldtowne cases involved serious acts of violence. The following accounts of particular cases come from stories given to mediation-program staff during the intake process, when they ask each side privately to tell them what the problem is. Some accounts (as indicated) are taken from the complaint-application forms filed in the clerk's office and composed by the plaintiff him- or herself.

In one neighborhood case, a man went to court against a neighbor, charging her with assault, threat, and trespassing because her uncle had run into the man's yard while yelling that the man's son had stolen something and yelling at his wife. In the complaint application, he described the incident: "He hit my son in the abdomen, harassed my wife, accused us of stealing something, threatened my family with bodily harm." Several of the marital cases involve either 209A applications for restraining orders against violent spouses or struggles over property separations after divorce. One of the marital cases concerned a man's effort to get custody of his son from his divorced wife because he did not think she was taking proper care of the son: she was living with a new boyfriend in a small, unsanitary house with eight children. Boyfriend/girlfriend cases concern either charges of harassment when a jilted lover makes incessant phone calls to the new boyfriend or girlfriend or charges of assault and requests for money damages for injuries. The female plaintiff in the brother/sister case charged her brother with assault and described the situation to the mediation-program staff as follows: *"My brother said a guy was trying to pick me up, but that was wrong. He left and took the guy's brother's car without asking. He was gone for hours. The guy's brother and his girlfriend blamed me. So I called the cops. They arrived. My brother came back and punched me in the ear. Then he ripped my shirt off my back in front of witnesses"* [emphasis is speaker's]. This woman refused mediation.

Many of the cases between friends involved roommates who had moved out and failed to pay bills or who had stolen things. Some cases involved more violence; for example, one woman told the mediation staff the following story: *"A friend of my husband's got into a fight with my husband, broke a table, chairs, and windows. He wanted a ride somewhere and my husband would not give him one. I don't want him to have a record or go to court, I just want things taken care of."* She called the police, who suggested that she file a formal complaint, which she did, charging the friend with vandalism. She did not want to press charges; she just wanted the things paid for. Another case involved a male plaintiff charging three defendants with assault and battery and with assault with a weapon at a party. The plaintiff described the situation to the mediation staff as follows: *"Bit me on the nose, broke a bone in my face—I was beat up really bad. I want something done,—bills paid for. I lost a week of work. Some of the kids I'll feel right in making an agreement with. But one or two I would like to go to court with. They bit me on the face. I do not go for that. They are going around now saying they're going to kill me."* According to the respondent, *"We all want this cleared up. We were at a party. There was a little fight and then Bill* [the plaintiff] *and three other boys came in and a fight started."* One of the respondents lives in Oldtowne, and one lives in the Green Street neighborhood.

The old-timers and the new gentry in Oldtowne look somewhat askance at these people and their parties. They blame them for increases in crime and vandalism in the neighborhood. Some of the new people are single mothers with teenage children. The old-timers complain about these mothers' inability to supervise or control their children. On the other hand, one of these mothers said that after a child reaches the age of twelve, a mother has no more control over him or her. Particularly the older Polish and Irish residents of the neighborhood regret the loss of a close ethnic community and complain about all the "new people" moving in who live in the three-story houses owned by absentee landlords who bought them as tax shelters and investment properties in the 1970s and have not kept them up. These buildings are interspersed throughout the neighborhood and generally serve as the domicile of the younger, poorer residents. The old-timers complain that people with mattresses on their car roofs are constantly moving in and out of these buildings, having loud parties, screaming obscenities on the street, and occasionally shooting off guns. Although they are often called "college kids," this term describes their age more than their academic activities; most are temporary workers in various forms of manual labor.

For the old-timers, particularly the older women, one simply does not go to court with one's personal problems. As one woman said, "it is not in my nature," suggesting, of course, that it was not in her culture. Another said: "I was not brought up that way. Now everybody goes to court about everything, all the time. It didn't used to be that way when I was young." The mediation program staff agreed that older Polish women almost never appeared in court or mediation.

As the older people of Polish and Irish ancestry reconstruct the past of their community, however, they talk about frequent recourse to the cop on the beat, who was first Irish and then Polish, for help in dealing with boys who were troublemakers. The cop would talk to both sides and try to come up with a compromise of some kind. Retired policemen themselves say that "in the old days" they would just talk to the boys themselves and discipline them but that you cannot do this now. Beyond that, older people claim that in the past people just put up with these problems or "took care of them themselves." There were also local ward councilors who were helpful, as well as several local lawyers. Several Polish lawyers lived in Oldtowne in the early twentieth century, at least one of whom was born at the turn of the century and was very powerful in this ward. An older Polish woman said that in Oldtowne anyone could find a lawyer, that there was always a relative or someone you went to school with who was a lawyer. At the time, the local government was largely dominated by the Irish, but the Polish residents gradually moved into politics as they became more numerous.

One retired policeman with many years of service in Salem said that although people glorify the past, some police took advantage of the situation: some were corrupt, some would allow people to sell "booze," some would take free meals, and so on. In the past, he said, the policeman's word was law. Now, he continued, a cop could not act that way and get away with it because there are likely to be people there (in the neighborhood) from Pennsylvania (his example), students from college, educated people, even educated bums, and they all know the law and their rights. A cop could not go in there, he continued, and act the way he used to because people would not put up with it.

Thus, as the population of Oldtowne in the 1940s and 1950s shifted from a predominantly immigrant group of Irish, Polish, and French residents to a second, American-born generation, a generation with more education and a greater sense of rights, there came resistance to the control of local police, store owners, the ward councilor, the local ethnic lawyer. Even when they still live in the old ethnic neighborhoods, young people are not active in local politics or inclined to turn to ward councilors for help. As the postwar generation made more money, it began to move out of Oldtowne to more affluent parts of the city, aspiring to larger houses and wider streets. As this process accelerated with low-cost loans to returning war veterans and with the general process of suburbanization in the 1950s and 1960s, Oldtowne began to deteriorate into a poor area, ripe for purchases of tenement buildings by outsiders in the late 1960s and early 1970s. For most of the older residents, moving up meant moving out and moving away from the old, congested neighborhood, from the tight control of local political authorities and the ever-present gossip of neighbors who were also co-workers, co-religionists, schoolmates, and, often, relatives.

One of the places they moved was Hilltowne, a white, working-class neighborhood of small duplexes and an occasional single-family house. Built early in the twentieth century for the more prosperous and upwardly mobile residents of

Salem, predominantly Irish and French, it still has a mixed ethnic identity. This neighborhood represented a social move up from Oldtowne, a place where the descendents of the first wave of ethnic immigrants to Salem moved when they were "making it" early in the twentieth century. Many of the houses were built then. During that period the neighborhood was a stable Irish and Italian community, with members of each ethnic group attending a nearby Catholic parish church for that group. The neighborhood was closely connected to the city's political life, dominated until recent years by the Irish. Small numbers of French-Canadian and Polish people have also moved in, many from Oldtowne and the Green Street neighborhood. It is still a predominantly Catholic neighborhood. After the Second World War, Veteran's Administration loans enabled more people to move into the neighborhood, making the area even more "mixed," as one resident put it.

People who move here are looking for security in their property, fighting to hold on to what they have but feeling a little precarious about their ability to do so. Their jobs are typically blue collar: security guard, policeman, railroad engineer, janitor, practical nurse, sales clerk, construction worker, night watchman, and so forth. One resident said that there are two lawyers who live in the neighborhood, "but they are not very professional lawyers." These people do not choose the neighborhood because of house values or attractiveness but because family and friends are already there.

This is a very stable neighborhood; many of the people have lived here for ten or twenty years. Frequently young people acquire their houses by buying them or inheriting them from family members. Families often rent an apartment to children as the latter marry and establish independent households. For many Hilltowne residents, buying a home is beyond their means, and inheriting the family house is the only way they will be able to own a home. Mobility is relatively low, and many residents have other family members living on the same street. According to 1980 census figures, the median family income was $20,625. Of those over more than eighteen years of age, 69 percent had completed high school and 9 percent had four or more years of college and advanced education. Sixty-three percent of the households were nuclear families, and 52 percent owned their own homes.

The upper part of Hilltowne is a more settled-living working-class area with small single homes and duplexes which are largely owner occupied. At the bottom of the hill, the houses are far more rundown and are largely absentee-owned apartments and rooming houses. Residents who live in the upper part of Hilltowne view the lower area as a bad area and consider its tenants loud and untrustworthy. One woman said that it is all young people who live there: she does not know any of them, they live in very different ways, and she cannot really understand them. Most of the people from Hilltowne who bring marital and boyfriend/girlfriend problems to court live in this lower part of the neighborhood. For those who live in the upper part, respectability means not going to court over problems unless these problems concern property or victimization by strangers. They too, along with the older Polish and Irish inhabitants of Oldtowne, say that they should put up with problems rather than take them to court. There is a lot of gossip among neighbors in this part of Hilltowne—and, among some, persisting feuds which linger for years. Children are often pulled into these fights, and told whom they may play with and whom they may not.

The residents of Hilltowne brought twenty-five personal problems to court during the same period that the Oldtowne residents brought twenty. The populations of the two neighborhoods are about the same (969 adults in Hilltowne, 1,023 in Oldtowne), so that the frequency with which people bring personal problems to court is roughly the same (see Table 4.2). Since Hilltowne is a more family-oriented, less transient neighborhood, fewer of the problems are between friends. Seven of these problems were concerned with neighbors, nine with spouses, three with boyfriends/girlfriends, four with family members, and two with friends. Most of the marital and boyfriend/girlfriend problems came from the lower part of Hilltowne, while the neighborhood cases came from all over the neighborhood.

Five of the neighborhood cases involved fights between children in school or in the neighborhood, one involved cars turning in the driveway, and one involved a boundary dispute. Some were filed as assault charges, and some as trespassing. In one of the cases about children fighting, a boy on his way home from school was jumped by four other boys. His nose was broken in the fight. His parents charged the other children with assault and battery. In another case, referred to mediation from the bench, the plaintiff, an older woman living with her daughter and grandson, charged her next-door neighbors with harassment. She told the mediation-program staff that her neighbors goaded their son Bill to beat up on her ten-year-old grandson Joe. When she had had trouble with them before, she had her lawyer send the family a letter. She has had trouble with Bill for six years. But recently her husband and Bill's father had an argument about the boy's fighting, and the next day their house was covered with eggs. Bill's father told the mediation program that he intends to pursue this in court if his lawyer agrees and that he will do nothing before talking to his lawyer. Bill's father complained further that the other man was on his porch once—which the other man had no right to do—so he was thinking of getting a restraining order to keep the other man away from his house. He said that would consult his lawyer about this as well. He asserted that things were fine until Joe and his mother moved into the house next door but that Joe is a problem. The plaintiff, Joe's grandmother, agreed to try mediation, but the defendant, Bill's father, never responded to the offer.

Eight of the plaintiffs in the nine marital cases were women, complaining about husbands who drink and hit them (five cases), who steal from them (one case), or who fail to support their children after divorce (two cases). One man charged his ex-wife with threats because she would not let him see their children, aged three and six years. Six of the cases involved temporary restraining orders (209A orders). In one typical case, a woman married four and one-half years filed for a 209A order and charged her husband with assault and battery after he hit her. She told the mediation intake worker that her husband has problems with depression and has been seeing psychiatrists for at least a year but that this is the first incident of violence. She said she just wants time alone and half of the checking account. The husband told the intake worker that the problem is with his wife, who wants him out of her life and has been saying so for the past two years. He says his bills are backed up to about $3,000. He says he slapped her because she would not make his supper. She is white and unemployed; he is Portuguese and works as a machinist. Two weeks after the incident he was again out of work.

The three boyfriend/girlfriend cases involved violence and parents' attempts to break up a relationship. In one case, a young man charged his girlfriend's uncle with threats and with assault and battery because the uncle had started beating him when he was over at his girlfriend's grandmother's house. He complained that the uncle had been giving him a hard time for a long time and had beaten him up four years earlier as well. The uncle lives at the bottom of the hill. Of the four family cases, two were part of a protracted struggle between a young woman who married into a Hilltowne family and her husband and his sister, a situation described in detail in Chapter 7. The third family case is a larceny charge filed by an uncle against a nephew, and the fourth family case is a larceny charge filed by a man who tried to pick up his brother's things from an uncle and was received with yelling, swearing, and a refusal. The two friend cases both involve money or property which one thinks the other owes him or her.

To give a flavor of conflicts in this neighborhood, I will describe two cases which were taken to court. These accounts come from conversations with the participants. They are neighborhood cases, and, in each, the language of property is pervasive. To own property is important in this neighborhood: it establishes the boundary between oneself and those at the bottom of the hill and delineates a space, albeit small, where one is in charge.

One situation in this neighborhood produced several court cases. I received a few accounts of this situation from some of the neighbors, but none from the major participants. It took place in the upper part of the hill. All of the people involved are homeowners, and most have lived in the neighborhood for fifteen or twenty years. A young woman and her mother engaged in a continuing battle, over a period of at least five years, with four neighbor families. They fought with one neighbor over the location of a porch, which the woman's family claimed was on their property. In a dispute over the property line they took the family to court. But there has not yet been a decision, and the other family finally took down the porch. The same woman threw another neighbor's cats over the fence when they came onto her property, then called the health department about the cats. Once she tripped over one of these cats and injured herself so that she was unable to work, and sued the neighbor's insurance company for a large sum. One summer day when a neighbor was mowing his lawn, she claimed a piece of the lawn was her property. She stood on the disputed piece and refused to move while the neighbor mowed across her feet (with a hand mower), turned at the corner, and mowed across her feet again. She charged him in court with assault and battery with a dangerous weapon (the lawn mower). The clerk refused to issue the complaint. A judge described this situation to me as both a funny and an incredible incident to have in court. He asked me: What can you do in such a situation?

Other incidents involved soaking a neighbor with a hose while the woman was on her back porch, an incident which caused the victim to file an assault-and-battery charge,[7] and a neighbor's attack, with hedge clippers, on the young woman and her mother. The mother and daughter had hidden a tape recorder in the hedge, however, and recorded the attack. Both sides filed harassment charges after this incident, and the young woman and her mother brought the tape recording into court. The clerk dropped all charges and told both parties to stay away from each other and learn to get along with each other.

One of the neighbors said that she thinks the young woman thrives on conflict and loves to run into the district court. The young woman is a very attractive woman and draws attention when she goes to court. The court has been heavily involved in this conflict, and the more these people use it, the more sophisticated they become about gathering evidence and building cases. One of the neighbors who described the situation to me says that she keeps detailed notes of all these incidents in case they are needed as evidence in court.

Another problem, located near the bottom of the hill, involved a boundary marker. One family wished to survey its land. The surveyors placed stakes along the boundary about three inches into land which the other family claimed as its own. In a rage, the wife tore up the stakes and shouted at the other family. The family which had commissioned the survey took the other family to court on charges of trespassing and removing boundary markers. The man who wanted the survey worked as a lobsterman. The defendants were relatively new to the neighborhood and at a disadvantage, since the parents spoke only Portuguese. They communicated through their teenaged daughter. Upset about the boundary line and the charges, they turned to a neighbor for advice. The neighbor suggested that they contact a lawyer. The lawyer did not want to handle the case, but his secretary worked as a mediator in the local court, so she suggested that the family try mediation. At mediation, the defendants agreed to have the land surveyed again. Other residents of this neighborhood commented that the "Portuguese are moving into this area," so fears of new ethnic groups moving into the neighborhood probably lay behind this problem.

After the mediation session, the woman in the family which had commissioned the survey complained to me that a neighbor had given the father in the

Portuguese family wrong information about his legal rights by telling him that he did not have to allow anyone else on his land. The person who gave the "wrong" advice was a hotheaded man described by his neighbors as irrational because he and his next-door neighbor were constantly screaming at each other, yelling about restraining orders and so on. Another neighbor, however, said of him: "My husband and I just laugh and think it is funny."

Indeed, in several cases, other, uninvolved residents said that they found the neighborhood fights to be entertaining and engrossing. This is a neighborhood with intimate relations, with considerable talk between neighbors, and with overt conflict and confrontation. To go to court is looked down on, but, when people feel that their rights have been seriously infringed, they go to court anyway, confident that the severity of the injury justifies turning to court. As is clear from the cases described above, there are differences in how people interpret recourse to court; what for one seems to be a legitimate grievance seems to another to be excessive and frivolous. In the third neighborhood, however, people agree more unambiguously that the use of court is, under most circumstances, a humiliating and degrading thing to do.

The third neighborhood, Riverdale (also a pseudonym) is a recent development of single-family homes built in the mid-1960s. This is a neighborhood for working-class families who have moved up to a more middle-class neighborhood. Sometimes they hold two jobs or rely on two wage earners in the family to afford the house. Some are more middle-class families with relatively low-income jobs, such as schoolteachers. One resident described the neighborhood as a place for people "on their way up." Most people who move here do so because they are attracted by the houses' reasonable prices and location, not because of proximity to family. A survey I conducted on thirty-six residents indicated that most (97 percent of those interviewed) moved there because of the location or the houses, not for proximity to relatives or friends. The house is a commodity, not part of one's family or community history or a place identified with one's personhood, in contrast to Hilltowne and Oldtowne, where houses are often part of a family patrimony.

The single-family homes in this development are clustered closely together on relatively small lots, usually about one-eighth of an acre. Overall the houses are quite similar. Each has an individual backyard. The houses are separated from each other by about thirty to forty feet, but this does not provide enough space for plantings to create barriers between the fronts of houses. Sidewalks line the curving streets, which are labeled with quaint names such as Teapot Way. Houses have garages and off-street parking spaces. Many people have fenced in their small backyards, but few have built fences between the houses. With its curving streets and single-family homes of similar design, Riverdale looks like a suburb. Although the neighborhood is attractive, it is densely populated for a suburban development, and the city's planners worry that it will not hold its value in the future.

The population is predominantly white and economically homogeneous, although the neighborhood contains a wide range of ethnic backgrounds. This is a neighborhood of nuclear families.[8] Most residents have a high school education, but relatively few have finished college.[9] The median family income in the 1980 census was $23,951. Many of the residents are skilled blue-collar workers such as truck drivers, carpenters, machinists, or auto mechanics or are low-paid white-collar workers such as night store managers, guidance counselors, clerical workers, and postal workers. Some are service workers such as chambermaids. They could be called settled-living working-class people. There are only a few hard-living people living in Riverdale.

An attractive suburb in a predominantly working-class town, this is a place for people who have moved out of poorer, more congested areas and ethnic neighborhoods. Many come from more close-knit ethnic communities such as Hilltowne and Oldtowne and appreciate the relative privacy of the suburb, the absence of gossip. For many of the residents I talked to, this is their first house, chosen because it was "a lot of house for the money," an economical buy in a suburban-appearing neighborhood. However, it is a very densely populated suburb. Residents complain that they can see into each other's kitchens. The proximity of houses and lack of fences and shrubs enhances the feeling that they have little privacy from their neighbors' prying eyes. As one woman put it, "whenever I sneeze, the next house knows."

This is a neighborhood with considerable concern about relative status and about the financial situation of neighbors. People who live here often talk about how much money their neighbors have and are jealous of those who have purchased a swimming pool (above ground) or new furniture. A question about a neighbor's electric bill is interpreted as nosy behavior. Some residents complain that when the women get together, they compare their husband's jobs, their minks, and their antiques. One woman pointed out that families in this neighborhood buy their children anything they want. At the same time, most people's economic prosperity is somewhat tenuous. Riverdale residents are anxious about stories they hear of people who have defaulted on mortgages and lost their houses. Resources are often stretched to the limit to afford the house; any instabilities in jobs or marriages threaten disaster. There is often talk of unemployment and foreclosure. Overall, people's social status is fragile.

This is not a neighborhood of intimate relationships. There is little close social life between neighbors, although there is considerable speculation about neighbors's purchases and financial troubles. Residents say that there is not much gossip and that that which occurs focuses on lawns, paint, and shrubbery. As one resident put it, "here we only talk about the outside of houses—yards, the paint, the appearance—not the insides of houses." This statement is true at a deeper level as well: the details of family life are, by and large, not known or shared by neighbors. For example, one resident reported that she did not know that her neighbor had been deserted by her husband until the neighbor moved out of her house several months later. Other residents reported that they felt uncomfortable when they heard a family yelling and fighting with each other, that they were afraid to intervene or even to discuss the situation with each other. Privacy is very important here. There is a strong feeling that people should keep to themselves, should not talk to their neighbors about their problems but should mind their own business. Many residents stress that they do not get involved with their neighbors and that that is the way they like it. They only want to say hello and goodby, anticipating that if they need help the neighbor will provide it just as they expect to provide help to their neighbors when asked. Since both adults in a family usually work, there is little time for neighborhood socializing.

In Hilltowne, people talk all the time and often fight; in Riverdale, people do not talk to each other and fight less openly. One woman said that this is a neighborhood where people do not confront each other: when they do not like things, they do not say anything. Most people I talked to in this neighborhood said that they would not think of going to court with any problem besides a traffic accident or a crime. There was a strong feeling that personal affairs do not belong in a public arena. Those who go to court are labeled "court happy" and are avoided. One woman who took a neighbor to court, charging her with attempting to steal her husband, was described as having come to Riverdale from a "lower-class area" and as speaking in a rough manner. Another woman who called the police all the time was labeled "police happy." People stayed away from her.

The difference between Riverdale's and Hilltowne's attitudes toward going to court was epitomized by the subtle distinctions drawn by two women, one from Hilltowne and the other from Riverdale, as they talked about what they thought of people who brought personal problems to court. Both were mediators and handled these problems in the mediation program. The Hilltowne resident had finished high school and some college and worked as a secretary; the Riverdale resident had finished college and some graduate school and worked as a teacher. The woman from Hilltowne said that when you take a personal problem to court, you make it society's problem. Once it becomes society's problem, you lose control over it. People in these situations, she thinks, feel angry and powerless, which is why they turn to the court. They call on the police, but the police only come and help if they know you or if you need a service such as a ride to the hospital.

The woman from Riverdale agreed that people who go to court make their problems society's problems, but she was more critical of them. She said they go to court because it is free. If she herself had a problem like this, she would go to a psychiatrist and pay for it, even if she had to borrow the money. She would not make her problem society's problem, just as intelligent, educated people in general do not. Those who go to court get used to putting the responsibility for their lives onto other people's shoulders. They lean on society for their problems to be solved, and as their children watch them behave this way, they learn to do the same thing. Thus, children follow their parents into welfare and into the courts. They feel entitled to the free services of the court because they expect society to help them cope with their problems. Thus, the first woman sympathized with the use of court but pointed to its drawback—that is, that one loses control—while the second woman condemned people who go to court for their lack of self-reliance. Their different interpretations parallel the two neighborhoods' generally different stances toward court use.

Most of the Riverdale people who appeared in court brought neighborhood problems. In each situation, the person who filed the complaint was severely criticized by the defendants for taking such extreme action. Of the six cases in court and mediation, five concerned neighborhood problems (see Table 4.2). One was a simple case of a barking dog, one an assault-and-battery charge about girls fighting in school, one a charge of vandalism and children throwing rocks, one a charge of harassment and trespassing by neighborhood children, and one a charge of harassment by a woman who feared that her neighbor was stealing her husband. In one of these cases, a man with a hot temper was enraged when neighborhood children threw rocks at his car, and he charged them with vandalism. The mother's complaint application in the case of the girls fighting in school read as follows: "While my daughter was at Salem High, she was harassed and physically assaulted by X and her friend Y. My daughter was punched and had her clothes pulled off her body in the corridor. She in turn did swing at one of the girls in self-defense. There are adult witnesses to this matter that will come forward and make statements." At the mediation intake, the mother said she wanted a restraining order to keep the other girls away from her daughter. The parents of the defendants said that there had been fights between the girls for a long time and that the problem is the plaintiff's daughter, who is very dependent on the other two girls and gets drunk. The mediation program scheduled a session, but the plaintiff failed to appear and dropped the charges. One of the defendants lived at the bottom of Hilltowne.

The single marital case was an application for a 209A restraining order by a woman who said that although her husband had always had a drinking problem throughout their seventeen years of marriage, recently his temper had gotten so bad she was afraid. He had told her the only way he would leave the house was by law, so she went to court for a restraining order. He told the mediation intake worker that the problem was that he was trying to buy a house and was working twelve to thirteen hours a day. When his wife came home from work, she would lock herself in the bedroom. He wanted everything to be OK again. They went to mediation and agreed to separate. This was the separation about which the neighbor living two houses away knew nothing until the woman moved out of the neighborhood; nor did the neighbor know about the court case.

The following example is a detailed study of one Riverdale neighborhood problem which came to court and mediation. Here again the language of property runs through the problem. This fight seems to be partly about social class and its subtle lines of difference. As in some of the earlier cases, it involved a boy who fights and a family which feels superior to its neighbors. This account comes from the mediation session and from detailed interviews with most of the participants on both sides.

This problem began between Jim (a pseudonym), a fifteen-year-old boy labeled a bully and a troublemaker by several neighbors, and the Marks (also a pseudonym), a family regarded as superior and standoffish by their neighbors. Neighbors complained that Jim wandered around with a bow and arrow, played with younger children, blared rock music from his radio at night, and was overly aggressive with the other children. One neighbor said: "That family has been a problem for the whole neighborhood, and there are a lot of people who have had trouble with them." When confronted with Jim's misbehavior, his mother denied it and protected him. The Marks found Jim particularly annoying but put up with him for several years. Seven years earlier they had accused him of ripping a hole in their pool, an incident which began a period of conflict between these adults and the boy.

The Marks lived across the street from Jim. They gave their neighbors the impression that they thought they were superior to the rest of the neighborhood. Both parents worked as schoolteachers and sent their two daughters to private school. Unlike the rest of the neighbors, they did not socialize with those around them. Their neighbors complained that they were strange and nosy, pried into other people's lives and wandered into their gardens, and talked about money all the time. As one neighbor put it, "their kids never play with our kids: they are just too smart for our kids, that is all." The Marks felt that they were more intellectual than their neighbors and took great pride in their children's schooling. They had moved out of a poor tenement district to this suburban neighborhood, as had many of their neighbors. They found money short, and although they would have liked to move out, interest rates and house prices locked them into this house. Both had finished college and reported a family income of $20,000 to $25,000 a year. They were in their thirties.

Involved in this conflict as defendants were several other families, families whose children played with Jim and joined together with him to harass the Marks. One was a couple in their forties with a family income between $25,000 and $35,000. The woman had a high school education. Another consisted of a divorced man who worked as a high school gym teacher and lived with his son and earned between $20,000 and $25,000. He was in his thirties, with a college education. All owned their own homes. All the families involved in the conflict, including the Marks, had lived in the same small neighborhood for eleven years. All said they would like to move out of the development but could not afford to: the houses had been relatively inexpensive but had not held their value. The interest rate was too high to buy elsewhere. There had been a long history of conflict and bad feeling between the families, but no one could escape.

One night in early summer, Jim and a group of friends, most of them age ten or eleven, gathered on the sidewalk in front of the Marks' house, their favorite hangout on their way home from baseball practice. From what all the neighbors said, it appeared that none of these children like the Marks much and took some pleasure in harassing them. This evening they started chanting the Marks's name and with their baseball bats pounded on the chain-link fence and mailbox in front of the house. The Marks were very upset but did nothing. The next night the chanting occurred again, and this time Mr. Marks accused one of the boys, a sixteen-year-old, of chasing Mrs. Marks with a baseball bat. Mr. Marks went to the house of this sixteen-year-old (not Jim), and the boy's father helped him search for the boy. The father punished his son for the assault.

Fearful that these events would continue, the Marks went to court and filed an application for a complaint against five boys: Jim, the sixteen-year-old who had been punished, and three ten-year-olds. They charged each boy with "harassment and trespassing," on the application form describing the incident as follows: "Hitting our chain link fence with sticks and a baseball bat. Shaking the fence to try and dislocate it. Name calling and harassment." They listed two neighbors as witnesses. Before it reached the level of a clerk's hearing, the case was referred to mediation.

When the five families whose sons were charged received the mediation-program notice offering them the opportunity to try mediation to avoid further court involvement, they were furious. The letter was written on court stationary and contains, as one of these parents said, "a lot of legal language." One parent was angry that the Marks had not talked to him first before filing the complaint application. Another was angry that he had punished his son for the assault on Mrs. Marks, because Mr. Marks had subsequently admitted that it had not really happened. All the defendants felt that going to court over this incident was taking things much too far and that these problems should be handled by talking to parents first. It was clear that they all regarded the complaints as a drastic escalation of the conflict. One of the accused neighbors said mediation was a bad idea for this kind of a problem because *"You have to keep the government and the courts out of it. Once you file a court complaint against someone, you can't be friendly. The only thing that you can do is to go to court."*

At the mediation session, the mediators asked each side to present its position. Issues of class differences surfaced in the discussion. Jim's mother, for example, asked the Marks: *"Do you ever wonder why you, such educated people, schoolteachers, get all the children angry at you? You are supposed to be good at working with children, but you must be doing something that they all hate you."* Another neighbor complained: *"For five or six years, Mr. Marks has not talked to us, and he said that my son and Jim ripped his pool apart. I don't want him spreading rumors around."* In a private discussion with the boys, one of them complained of Mr. Marks: *"He thinks he owns the sidewalk. The mailbox we hit is on the sidewalk."* The Marks told the other families that they simply wanted the trespassing to stop, to have the boys stop coming into their yard. Here, the boundaries of self and of privacy are drawn with the language of property, of land, of trespassing. Mr. Marks also said privately to the mediators that he found the chanting particularly offensive because he was Jewish and it reminded him of Nazi Germany. He did not raise this in front of the other families, but the mediators did.

After three hours of discussion, the parties agreed to stay away from each other and the Marks agreed to drop the charges. The defendants' families refused to sign anything. After the session, the boys' parents stopped talking to the Marks, and the Marks said they would have nothing to do with any neighbors any more.

The neighbors whose boys were in court were angry that Mr. Marks had taken them to court without talking to them first. They complained about his uncooperative and unneighborly behavior. But for the Marks this was a situation in which they needed protection from trespassing and harassment. They also felt that they were helping others of their neighbors deal with Jim, who was a difficult boy. Many were afraid to complain about him.

Many neighborhood problems are, like this one, about small differences in social class and life-style, microcultural variations which are expressed in different standards for control of dogs, supervision of children, upkeep of house and yard, and discipline of children. They typically escalate into conflicts around a person who is behaving in a provocative way, as Jim was. Even in neighborhoods broadly similar in social class, as these three are, some people feel slightly above or below their neighbors. Sometimes a family feels superior to its neighbors, as the Marks did, which makes the others angry. Sometimes a family seems undesirable, unwanted, or slovenly by its neighbors who aspire to a slightly higher social class. Car repair in the driveway, for example, signals lower class status in an upwardly mobile suburb such as Riverdale. In some cases, an older person sees a newcomer as foretelling a broader change in the neighborhood and attempts to drive the newcomer out, as the Browns did (see Chapter 3). Sometimes the newcomers use the courts to fight the old-timers, to insist on their rights to stay, as the Smiths did (see Chapter 3).[10]

But the most common result of turning to the court is not victory for either side but separation. The court helps the plaintiff confront the other person but does not usually rule for either side. Instead, the court simply becomes part of the arsenal the two parties use to renegotiate their relationship into a more distant one.

As the present discussion has indicated, court use constitutes a complex marker of social class. Settled-living people aspiring to middle-class status condemn going to court for family and marital problems; they consider it to be embarrassing, humiliating, and typical of lower groups. Taking neighbors to court is more acceptable than taking family members to court. But when settled-living people feel that their lives and property are under severe threat and that their rights are being seriously infringed, they believe that asserting these rights in court is necessary to protect themselves and their family. Of course, one person's excessive use of courts can seem to another to be a legitimate defense of rights; it is a matter of interpretation. For hard-living people, however, going to court is a more refined alternative to violence, a better way of doing things. The threat "I will see you in court" is a way of saying "I am more civilized than you are." Here, law is the symbol of the way educated, professional people deal with differences.

Community Organization and Court Use

The patterns of community organization and court use I have been describing suggest the emergence of a new kind of neighborhood order, one based on the escape from community. People go to court in these three neighborhoods out of a search for an impersonal moral authority with the power to enforce its rules and out of a desire for freedom from the control of local political authorities and from local gossip. The desire for freedom was expressed by the people I talked to as a preference for a more private world in which people were not always talking about each other and were not subject to the control of local leaders. People in Riverdale particularly prized their privacy; the lack of intimacy between neighbors was just fine with them. In the past, life in Oldtowne and Hilltowne was dominated by residents with more education and wealth: the store owner, the landlord, the politician. These were stratified communities with powerful local leaders. Despite our images of harmonious, integrated communities of the past, urban ethnic villages such as Oldtowne and Hilltowne used to be run by those with power, money, and connections. Now people are trying to escape these local leaders. To move out to a community like Riverdale is to be free of these forms of control, to join a community in which the lines of stratification are blurred and in which control is diffused. Riverdale residents prefer this social world yet are left feeling ambiguous and uncertain about relative rank and about how they deal with conflicts.

A new form of order is emerging here in which homogeneity and privacy produce coexistence without contact—living peacefully together by living apart. When conflict erupts in neighborhoods such as Riverdale, people turn to the nearest moral authority connected with the state—the courts—but they do so very reluctantly. Riverdale residents endure problems and stay away as long as possible, hoping to avoid the stigma of using the courts; but if a situation becomes intolerable or an affront to their rights, they use the law. They have escaped from the control of local authorities—from the clubs, the parish, the local merchants, the ward boss—through Americanization and upward mobility, but in their search for authority, they are newly dependent on the courts.

When problems arise, there is no place else to go. The availability of the court makes their private lives possible. Yet it is an institution with its own agenda for managing and controlling people's personal problems.

Family Conflicts

Family conflicts often center on women's challenges to the traditional authority of their husbands. Their use of the court is a challenge to male authority, part of their struggle to redefine family roles. As they move into the work force on a permanent or temporary basis and as they gain from the women's movement new ideas about themselves and the nature of marriage, working-class women begin to want more intimacy from their husbands, more recognition of their importance as wage earners, more help at home, and more respect. They also want less domination, less abuse, and less violence. Inspired by the new visions of women that are portrayed in the media or by their contacts with helping professionals, women who go to court are sometimes seeking a different kind of marriage. They begin to want more from marriage than only domestic duties and children. In her interviews with working-class California families in the mid-1970s, Lillian Rubin also found women seeking communication and intimacy—rather than subservience and distance—from their husbands (1976).

Many of the women complaining in court about their husbands' violence had endured years of beatings but had recently taken a new view of this violence, deriving this new view either from colleagues at a new job, from a therapist, or from new friends. Protest now seemed possible. What in the past seemed acceptable or at least inevitable now appeared something to question and challenge. Many of these women have encountered professionals in the form of therapists, child-welfare workers, school psychologists, and welfare department workers, some of whom advocate new definitions of women's roles. The husbands have had fewer contacts of this sort.

The husbands seemed unaware of their wives' desires for intimacy and respect, for communication, and for shared responsibility for children and housework. They said they were surprised when their wives complained, that they had no idea there was a problem until they suddenly found themselves evicted from the house by a court order. A few conceptualized their inability to prevent their own violence in terms of pressure: they just "had a short fuse" or "things just built up inside." Men often drank and then became violent, but they were unwilling to discuss or question their drinking. For many, alcohol was a necessary escape from strenuous and demanding work lives. Some worked two jobs in order to make ends meet and felt that drink was necessary to help them live with the strain. As Rubin points out, working-class men often experience considerable supervision and control in their work lives and therefore value freedom from restraint and the opportunity for dominance at home (1976).

Both men and women in these cases view one another in terms of fairly traditional roles. However, the women seem more discontent with these roles than do the men. The men typically want wives who keep the house, prepare the food, and take care of the children. Men evicted from their homes seemed more dismayed by the loss of both the house and these domestic services than by the loss of the woman herself. Women, on the other hand, see men primarily as breadwinners. Yet, men often had difficulty fulfilling this role and were frequently unable to support the family on their income alone. Their jobs are low-paying and unstable. Families sometimes turn to their parents for help, leading to financial dependence and conflicts with in-laws. Wives often work to support the family, even though both the wife and her husband regard her job as temporary and part time (see Rubin 1976). Even when women make important economic contributions to the family, their wages are still viewed as supplemental and their primary work is considered to be homemaking. Consequently, women do not strive for high-paying jobs or demand more; they hope instead to be able to stop working as soon as the family can afford it. The women I saw in court with their personal problems typically held low-paying, part-time, or temporary work. None of the women in the marital cases I observed in mediation had a career. Although some enjoyed their work, they viewed it as a necessity which they hoped to give up in the future.

Even with two adults working, these couples often had difficulty paying their bills. Some men felt this was a personal failure rather than a systemic problem, while others blamed their wives for financial mismanagement. One man attributed his debts to his wife's practice of stashing unpaid bills in a shoe box and leaving them, rather than to his own meager income. Some families aspired to a middle-class standard of living which was beyond their means and on small and unreliable incomes, struggled to pay for campers, swimming pools, and houses. As husbands found they could neither perform well as breadwinners nor manage the new expectations their wives had for partners, some became frustrated and violent.

Part of women's desire to challenge their husbands comes from the new economic power of working-class women generally. The economic reality for the working class is that more and more wives now work in order to support the family. During the postwar period, the proportion of married women in the labor force soared from 22 percent in 1950 to 50 percent in 1980, according to the 1980 census. In 1940, only 15 percent of wives worked, but by 1976 45 percent of wives worked, accounting for a major proportion of the rising female component of the work force (Kolko 1978). The growth of the female labor force accelerates during periods of unemployment (Kolko 1978). In other words, women enter the labor force to help their families through hard times. Moreover, poor wives with children are more likely to work than are more affluent wives. In 1976, women with children less than six years of age and whose husbands earned $7,000 or less in the preceding year were twice as likely to work as were similar women whose husbands earned more than $20,000 (Kolko 1978: 266). Kolko argues that the rising household incomes of the working class in the postwar period have not resulted from the shifting position of the blue-collar worker but from the working wife, leading to more middle-class income levels and expenditures. Women's work insulates the family from economic fluctuation and job instability. However, once the wife enters the job market, the family has no further resources to call on. Studies of working-class families point to the fact that these families live close to the edge and that an illness, an accident, or unemployment can push them over the brink to foreclosure, repossession, and the loss of a respectable way of life (see Newman 1988). The changes in the New England job and housing markets simply exacerbate these difficulties.

Parent/child conflicts often revolve around children's challenges to parental authority. In these cases, it is the parents who turn to the court for added support for their traditional authority. Conflicts frequently concern obedience and autonomy, the responsibilities children have to their parents, and the age at which teenagers become independent. Many of the parents in these cases came from traditional ethnic communities with immigrant origins, such as Italian or Portuguese, in which children owe their parents obedience and respect. The children, growing up in a society which emphasizes teenage autonomy and self-expression, were caught between their parents' expectations and the pressures exerted by their own peer group. Philip Slater describes America as embodying the idea of the democratic family, in which children negotiate rules with their parents and make decisions jointly, in contrast to more authoritarian family systems in which children are expected to show obedience to their parents (1968). These young people are, in a sense, asserting the democratic family model in their demands for freedom and autonomy, while their parents, particularly the father, hold on to more authoritarian images.

Power Relationships and Court Use

Many of these fights are weaker parties' challenges to the hierarchies of authority controlling their lives, while others are efforts by embattled superior parties to maintain control. Some arise out of challenges to established relationships of control. Plaintiffs are sometimes weaker parties seeking to assert control over stronger parties: women over men, relatively poor people over neighbors who do not want them, young women over their boyfriends. But plaintiffs can also be from those previously dominant groups whose control is challenged: parents with rebellious teenage children or older people whose neighborhoods are changing.

The use of law is an important part of the demand for change and resistance to change. Conflict here both challenges the status-quo distribution of power and leads to the creation of a new order.[11] It is simultaneously destructive and constructive (see Yngvesson 1985b). An absence of conflict does not necessarily mean harmony or an absence of hierarchy. Indeed, a powerful hierarchy with well-entrenched patterns of domination can secure considerable peace. When the structure of domination is challenged, peace is disrupted. A plaintiff who takes his or her neighbors to court, a women who litigates against a violent husband, a young woman who sues her boyfriend for hitting her—all challenge patterns of authority in these relationships and disrupt the peace provided by established authority.

In sum, going to court provides plaintiffs with a symbolically powerful resource either to challenge hierarchies which are vulnerable or to defend those which seem precarious. At the same time, appealing to the law engages the authority of the legal system and its capacity to define and name problems in struggles over power and authority within families and neighborhoods. Of course, the law is not the only resource people use to struggle over the structure of unequal relationships, but it is one of them. People also resort to physical violence, to attacks on property, to gossip, to complaints to other government officials such as zoning boards or children's protective services, and to ostracizing the person from their social world. I expected that people would turn for help to other types of third parties, such as neighborhood leaders, church leaders, or local politicians, but they did so very rarely. A few took their problems to psychological counselors.

As courts become involved in these problems, their intervention typically strengthens the plaintiff: the wife, the newcomer, the parent, the established neighborhood resident. But the strength comes less from any particular action of the court than from the symbolic power afforded the plaintiff who succeeds in producing some gesture from the court, even if it is only a mailed summons to appear for a clerk's hearing or mediation session. Paradoxically, the plaintiff gains a powerful ally but at the same time loses control. This ally is indifferent and unpredictable and has its own ways of talking about family and neighbor relationships. The next three chapters explore how these problems are discussed in court and shows how and why plaintiffs lose control over them.

5

Problems and Cases

Chapter 3 showed that people who bring personal problems to court conceptualize them as both relevant to the law and subject to its regulation. They interpret these problems in terms of legal rights embedded in relationships and their entitlement to help from the courts. The nature of social phenomena is, of course, always a matter of interpretation, a matter of imposing meanings on a flow of events. People bring neighborhood and family conflicts to court because they have developed legal interpretations of them. But these are complex and ambiguous social interactions which trail long and convoluted histories. They are susceptible to competing interpretations, even of the same events and histories.

In neighborhoods and families, conflict situations are generally interpreted and talked about as problems, growing out of social relationships. In court, they are interpreted and talked about as cases, originating with a charge and channeled by a process for handling and disposing of the charge. It is the court which defines the case and the processes by which cases are managed.

These are both folk categories: terms used by people themselves and the institutions they work in to talk about conflict situations. In communities, people talk about having problems, troubles, difficulties, and fights. Once the problem gets into court, court officials talk about cases. Each term connotes a certain structure to the situation. Cases have beginnings, middles, and ends, while problems often do not. Closure or "resolution" of problems does not make much sense, since problems are simply aspects of social relationships. Problems do not have the definiteness of substance, the smooth development, or the certainty which a retrospective view of a completed or ended case suggests. Instead, they are irregular in progress, ambiguous in meaning, and uncertain in development. They lack a clear beginning and end, persisting in shifting phases which lead not to settlement but to a restructuring of the relationship.[1]

Conflict situations are understood both as problems and as cases. In neighborhoods and families, a problem taken to court is interpreted for some purposes as a case—an interpretation which emphasizes its seriousness—and for other purposes as a problem, part of the flow of everyday social life. In court, judges, attorneys, clerks, and mediators interpret the situations both as cases with particular charges and futures and as problems rooted in neighborhoods and families. As cases, there is an anticipation of settlement, of closure; as problems, there is an expectation that they will go on until the situation changes or the relationship ends. As cases, these situations are trivial; as problems, they are of great emotional importance to the parties and to a wider community of some kind.[2]

Inside the court, the salience of the problem and the case interpretation varies depending on who is doing the interpreting, the institutional interests of the interpreter, and the objectives of the interpreter. In one of the courts I studied, one prosecutor was interested in these conflicts and took them seriously while another viewed them as trivial and tried to avoid them in favor of "serious" cases such as murder or armed robbery. The first prosecutor thought about them as problems and so took them more seriously as cases; the second ignored them as problems and so considered them frivolous as cases. Mediation programs tend to give greater salience to the problem interpretation than the court does, but the case interpretation is also present. If the parties prove intractable, mediators may remind the parties that there are dire consequences in court for failing to settle, thus drawing the case interpretation into the discussion as a threat (see Silbey and Merry 1986). Clerk-magistrates, prosecutors, probation officers, and judges who handle these situations often try to provide some form of justice for the problem while disposing of the case.

Plaintiffs and defendants frequently fight over these interpretations. A plaintiff usually claims that the situation is a case, and the defendant insists it is only a problem. People who are angry about being taken to court deny that the situation is a case, claiming that it is a problem and does not belong in court. For example, the parents whose sons were charged in the Marks case described in Chapter 4 blamed the Marks for going to court rather than talking to them directly. They thought the situation was a problem and should have been handled informally. This chapter describes the way people interpret and talk about problems and cases both outside and inside the courts.

Problems and Dispute Analysis

Conflict situations are usually analyzed as disputes. But this concept inhibits seeing them as matters of interpretation. It focuses on what people do and tends to neglect the way conflict is understood. It tends to downplay the importance of the way people conceptualize the substance of the law. I first began to question the value of the concept of dispute for understanding consciousness and meaning in conflict processes when I realized that the people I was talking to did not talk about their conflicts as disputes. Instead, they talked about them as problems. When they got to court, they discussed them as cases.[3] *Dispute*, in other words, was not a term in common use among the people who brought their problems to the courts, nor did it describe something which made much sense to them. Dispute is an analytic category, not a folk category.[4] This does not mean it is not a valuable concept for analysis, of course, but it is less useful in examining either the consciousness of people with family and neighborhood problems or the way this consciousness changes and the problems themselves are reconceptualized as the conflict proceeds. Despite its value for the analysis of time and process, it is less valuable in its focus on behavior rather than meaning.

Indeed, the concept of dispute was developed to make possible comparative research on the behavioral aspects of law and order by foregrounding the universal processes of disputing (see Nader 1965; Nader and Todd 1978). As far as possible, disputes were presented as social events embedded within a structure of social relationships (see, e.g., Starr 1978). The study of disputes offered anthropologists a way to bypass the difficult and unresolvable question of the universality of law and provided a new way to compare lawlike activities cross-culturally. Incidentally, of course the concept was also compatible with the underlying structure of analysis within Anglo-American common law (see Griffiths 1986; Ietswaart 1986). The conference on law in culture and society reported by Nader (1969) marks the end of the debate about whether all societies had law and the beginning of a new focus on disputes, although the ancestors of the dispute concept included Malinowski's cases (1926), Llewellyn and Hoebels' trouble cases (1941), Gluckman's extended cases (1955), Turner's social dramas (1957), and Gulliver's disputes (1963), to name a few. The concept of law was considered too culture bound, too rooted in Western jurisprudence to grasp the range of ways people in different societies handled conflicts and troubles. The concept of dispute promised to escape this ethnocentric bias by shifting the focus away from rules and institutions to behavior, to the social context of disputes and to dispute-resolution processes. No longer was the question, Do all societies have law? Now it was, What kinds of processes occur under what kinds of social conditions for handling situations of trouble or hitch? Every society has troubles; the important questions concern how they arise, how they are phrased, and how they are resolved. The dispute was both universal—in that all societies had them—and comparable across cultures. It highlighted behavior rather than rules. As the studies of Laura Nader and her students demonstrate, the study of processes of disputing has provided a rich body of information on legal behavior which can be compared across societies.[5]

Disputes are generally analyzed in terms of a series of stages: an initial grievance by one party, a confrontation in which this grievance is delivered to the other party, and a processing of some sort either in a public arena, in front of a third party, or perhaps in a dyadic confrontation (Nader and Todd 1978). There is sometimes, but not always, a resolution; other times there is a prolonged simmering which never moves into the public arena. A dispute is generally defined as a confrontation over a claim which has escalated to a public arena (Gulliver 1969; 14; Nader and Todd 1978: 14–15). In Gulliver's definition, "no dispute exists unless and until the right claimant, or someone on his behalf, actively raises the initial disagreement from the level of dyadic argument into the public arena, with the express intention of doing something about the desired claim" (1969: 14). Others define a dispute simply as a claim which has been rejected, regardless of whether it moves into a public arena. Miller and Sarat, for example, argue that "a dispute exists when a claim based on a grievance is rejected either in whole or in part" (1980/81: 527). Both Miller and Sarat and Lempert emphasize the sense of entitlement inherent in the emergence of a grievance, a sense of entitlement that comes from an "individual's belief that he/she is entitled to a resource which someone else may grant or deny" (Miller and Sarat 1980/81: 527). Lempert refers to this sense as a "normative claim of entitlement" within disputes (1980/81: 708).[6]

Many have argued that the concept of dispute has tended to produce a preoccupation with process to the exclusion of substance—with the delineation of stages rather than with studies of systems of meaning. Many claim that dispute analysis neglects the ways class relations, economics, politics, kinship, and so forth produce conflict.[7] The term *dispute* brings with it the presumption of a conflict of interests between two parties proceeding through rational, strategic moves to maximize their interests (see Merry and Silbey 1984; Silbey and Sarat 1988). Although the initial impetus in the study of disputes was a desire to examine them within particular social contexts (Nader 1965), in practice the approach of dispute analysis has turned scholars toward the examination of behavior and away from an analysis of either the substance of rules or the meanings of law. Moreover, as the concept has been transferred from the anthropological study of village peoples to complex urban societies, it has lost its emphasis on social context.

Thus, despite its undeniable advantages for comparative research on conflict processes, the concept of dispute is inadequate for understanding the complex processes of interpretation which constitute conflict interactions. The concept of dispute presumes that issues are relatively straightforward and that a dispute can be understood in terms of the claims of the parties and the decisions they make about pressing these claims. Instead, conflict processes, like other social processes, consist of exchanges of messages in which the interpretation provided by any one participant may differ from that of any other participant and in which the understanding that each has of the other is never complete or unambiguous. Furthermore, like all social processes, conflict events have contested meanings and uneven and uncertain paths of development. And here, as in other arenas of social life, participants struggle to assert their interpretations of the meaning of events. The meaning of "reality" is bargained through such processes (Comaroff and Roberts 1981; Rosen 1984).[8] Those more powerful assert their interpretations more effectively than those who are weaker, of course, as do those who are more educated, more highly placed socially, more respectable, or more endowed with whatever other features confer authority in their society.

The shift in focus from the analysis of disputes to dispute transformation provided a valuable step toward this way of examining conflicts. Lynn Mather and Barbara Yngvesson showed how the definition of a dispute shifts with the audience to which it is presented (1980/81). That audience may actively redefine it, principally by broadening or narrowing it. William Felstiner, Richard Abel, and Austin Sarat argue that disputes have a malleable and unstable character and that the consciousness and culture of the person with an injury are of central importance in understanding the event (Felstiner et al. 1980/81). They suggest developing a framework for studying "the processes by which unperceived injurious experiences are—or are not—perceived (naming), do or do not become grievances (blaming) and ultimately disputes (claiming), as well as for subsequent transformations. . . . [They] view each of these stages as subjective, unstable, reactive, complicated and incomplete" (1980/81: 630).

However, the notion of dispute transformation presumes that disputes change along a unidirectional path—not that they are reinterpreted by different participants or that multiple interpretations can coexist. Nor does it emphasize how these interpretations are contested. It is not that the dispute itself changes or is transformed but that different participants interpret the meaning of the event in different ways in different contexts. Each of these interpretations has consequences for the way the conflict is handled.

My approach draws on John Comaroff and Simon Roberts's analysis of the ways litigants interpret situations in order to persuade (1981). They describe the process of constructing an interpretation in dispute situations as the development of a "paradigm of argument": "a coherent picture of relevant events and actions *in terms of one or more implicit or explicit normative referents*" [emphasis in original] (1981: 84). A paradigm of argument is a particular construction of the situation of dispute, a construction which orders facts according to normative claims which are seen as persuasive. Arguments may take place within the paradigm, when normative referents remain unquestioned, or a disputant may introduce a competing paradigm based on different normative referents. In the latter case, the facts may not be contested, only their interpretations. If the case is heard by a third party, such as a chief, he or she may order a decision within the agreed paradigm, choose between rival paradigms, or impose a fresh paradigm on the dispute (1981: 85). "Facts," of course, do not exist separately from the interpretations placed on them, but the distinction Comaroff and Roberts draw is intended to highlight the difference between arguments about circumstances and arguments about norms.[9] They argue that veracity consists of the extent to which situations can be persuasively interpreted and presented (1981: 238). Thus, they argue that disputing can be seen in terms of competing ways of construing events and selves within particular normative frameworks.[10]

What does it mean to look at conflict situations in terms of potential contending interpretations rather than as disputes? Attention to the processes of interpretation and reinterpretation provides a way to understand both the apparent malleability and the underlying constancy of disputes. Disputes can be interpreted in different ways at the same time. Even before a problem arrives in court, the plaintiff has thought about it as a case: in terms of rights, claims, and evidence. As the plaintiff arrives at the door of the courthouse, there is some negotiation with the clerk or mediation-program staff about how the problem is to be labeled and understood in court. In this process, it is reinterpreted as a case by the court. As a case it has a label, two sides, and one or two issues supported by evidence about a particular event. But its interpretation as a problem does not vanish. Neither inside nor outside the courts is there a settled understanding of the conflict.

Viewing conflicts as contests over how they are to be interpreted also provides a way of analyzing the relative power of the parties involved. Power depends in part on various actors' ability to sell their version of the problem, to assert and maintain their interpretation. Since all parties, including third parties, are struggling to dominate discussions of the event by promoting their interpretation of the problem, those whose interpretations ultimately prevail have the most power in the situation. Authoring the prevailing interpretation is particularly important because the meaning of the event implies its solution. Struggles over the prevailing understanding of a problem are really struggles over consequences. The person able to determine the prevailing interpretation is the person able to establish what will be done about it.

Problems as Extended Conversations

These situations can be analyzed as an exchange of messages, as interactions within which meaning is created. The conflict is a form of communication, a kind of extended conversation. The participants exchange messages which express their interests, feelings, and their interpretation of the situation. But these are not simple or straightforward messages. They are instead encoded communications, subject to interpretation by their recipients in terms of their own cultural frameworks and their assessment of the social relationship of communication. Messages include both words and actions; the meaning depends on the ways words and actions are coupled. The interpretation of the message, as is generally true with language, requires not only knowledge of the code itself but also the use of extralinguistic factors of context and situation, so that the receiver selects or reads a message compatible with the circumstances as he perceives them (Bourdieu 1977). The reception thus depends on the objective structure of the relations between the interacting agents' position in the social structure, their power and authority, their emotional intensity, and their identities as derived from gender, age, and class (Bourdieu 1977: 25; see also Arno 1985). It is talk in context, and the context defines part of the meaning of the talk. But the nature of the context is complex: it includes other people, shared understandings, principles of fairness and justice, perceptions of the legal system, definitions of community, and so forth. Moreover, the timing of messages is a significant part of the way communication is carried out. Each side uses delay, speed, and the timing of response as part of its repertoire of communication. There is as well always uncertainty about how this timing will be interpreted.

Messages are inevitably ambiguous in meaning. There is always the possibility of misreading a message. When the common code is undeveloped or when the contextual features of a communication situation are not understood in the same way by sender and recipient, interpreting messages becomes more problematic. Messages may be read in ways which are rather different from the intention of the sender, particularly when they are strangers to one another or when they lack a common cultural code or framework for understanding messages. Even when these shared frameworks are well established, the process of disputing is one of multiple encodings and decodings: the message is encoded by a sender and is read and interpreted by a recipient, who codes and sends a return message. In situations of conflict, in which messages tend to be oblique and fragmentary, the possibilities of misreading are substantial. Thus, the experience of conflict is one of uncertainty. The participants know neither how the other participants are going to react to their messages or exactly how the messages they receive were intended.

In several neighborhood problems, feelings between people who lived next door but did not know one another intensified as they placed hostile interpretations on one another's actions. In one such case a new neighbor moved in and left a note asking the other neighbor to move her car. The recipient felt the impersonal note was extremely rude and refused to move the car. She was miffed that the new neighbor had not even stopped in to introduce herself. In another case, a woman complained bitterly that she had gone out of her way to help a neighbor who had to take her child hit by a car to the hospital. This woman said she had taken care of the neighbor's one-year-old, buying diapers, feeding the child all day, getting out an old playpen for it, but had received no thanks from its parents or even money for the diapers. After this incident, the two women became enemies. In a third case, a man described how angry he had become when the neighbor in a house behind his cut down, without telling the man that he was planning to do so, a large hedge on his own property but on the line dividing their properties. The man was angry because he had relied on the hedge for a sense of privacy but also because he had not been told first, which he felt showed a lack of respect. Although many of these situations blow up because of underlying conflicts based on subtle class and life-style differences between neighbors, misreadings of messages intensify them.

The retrospective analysis of disputes as completed exchanges or as resolved problems restructures their meaning. They appear as balanced exchanges between two sides. But, as Bourdieu points out with the example of feuds, the view of an reciprocal exchange in the past, once it is already finished, is very different from the perspective of a person in the middle of an exchange who does not know what is going to happen and who must weigh the meaning of his actions to the other party, his assessment of the other's position and will, the kinds of risks he wishes to undertake, and the length of time he wants to wait before making a reply (1977). The tension and uncertainty of the participant is lost when one looks back over the event and sees a sequenced and completed set of exchanges.

Catastrophic Shifts in Meaning

Nor do these conflict situations follow an even course of development. Disputes have been described as following a trajectory, a metaphor suggesting a smooth, gradual evolution over time; but the problems I observed had more the character of prolonged periods of stasis followed by moments of rapid, catastrophic change.[11] Problems often remained quiescent for long periods of time while the groups involved struggled to live with the situation. The filing of a charge in court or an act of violence typically produced a rapid shift in meaning, a substantial escalation of the conflict. The prevailing mode of dealing with neighborhood and family problems seemed to be avoidance and inaction, putting up with a difficult situation as long as possible, until some small event tripped off a reaction, an intense response which was often out of proportion to the incident itself. The intensity of emotion at the point of confrontation was related to the long period of building tensions. Social networks between people and norms of tolerance serve as binding forces which postpone confrontations and hold social relationships together, providing the groundwork for more intense explosions. Where such relationships and normative systems do not exist, confrontation occurs more readily and easily. Without such binding relationships, the pursuit of a grievance is more a matter of convenience or indifference than one of risk and danger.

These catastrophic shifts involve reassessments of the seriousness of the problem and provide new contexts within which messages are interpreted. In the Marks case described in the previous chapter, for example, the fact that Mr. Marks had taken the chanting boys to court incensed their parents, who felt that he had shifted the meaning of the event in drastic and unnecessary ways. The parents spent most of the mediation session attacking the Marks for going to court without talking to them first.

Particular events trigger catastrophic shifts in meaning. Some small incident often constitutes the last straw in an intolerable situation, leading to a move which appears drastic to the other side and seems like a radical escalation of the conflict. What constitutes such a triggering mechanism is obviously highly variable and culturally specific, yet it seems, in the cases I looked at, to be related to a future vision of the problem rather than to a gaze over the past. It is when they fear that the situation will remain intolerable long into the future that people seem to take actions which sharply change the course of a conflict. The actual incident which triggers this response, however, is often trivial. It acquires significance only when viewed in the course of the whole history of the relationship. The triggering mechanism is neither the "cause" nor the heart of the conflict; it is simply the last straw in one level, escalating the conflict to another level.[12]

In court, however, the triggering incident is often presented as the charge, confirming the clerk-magistrates' and prosecutors' suspicions that these problems are trivial. Why, indeed, should a person come to court because her sister-in-law has borrowed her ring? Or because a neighbor's child hurled an insult? These incidents make more sense when they are viewed as triggering mechanisms in the long course of a problem, as last straws which finally persuaded a plaintiff to make a cataclysmic shift in the meaning of the conflict and define it as a legal case. To the participant, this is risky business, since he or she is not sure what will happen in court or how his or her legalization of the problem will be received by the other side. Although the courts see many cases, for each plaintiff this is an unusual and unprecedented experience.

The Folk Concept of Problem

What do people mean by *problems?* Problems are parts of social relationships which contain many features besides those of the conflict. They are moments in an ongoing process of exchange of offense and counteroffense which stretches back in time. Problems are multifaceted and emotionally intense. They may begin with a simple incident, such as a bit of gossip, added onto another, such as a rude word, onto another, such as a feeling of threat that a new group is moving into the neighborhood, added onto an act of retaliation, such as turning music up loud—until this slow dance of hostility intensifies to a situation in which someone calls the police. Summoning the police often creates a catastrophic shift of meaning for the parties, leading to a new context for interpreting the subsequent messages between the parties.

The "Bad Character"

When people talk about problems in their neighborhoods, they often see them as involving a person or family whom everyone recognizes as a bully or a troublemaker. People talk about a person or a family who is difficult for the whole neighborhood, friendship circle, or family. They describe the other person as generally annoying because his music is too loud, her children are wild and unsupervised, her dogs bark all night, or he feels superior toward the neighbors. Problems are caused by the neighborhood bully, the snobby neighbor, the chronic drunk, the teenager who likes to fight and throw rocks. In the problems described in the last chapter, there are frequent references to "bad characters": the neighbors who have a bad kid or the woman and her daughter who are always eager for a fight. Plaintiffs often complain that "all the neighbors" have trouble with the people they have brought to court or that "the whole family" knows the boy is a "bad match" for their daughter. As parties talk about these situations, they say: "the whole neighborhood has trouble with them," "everybody knows he is a bad kid," and so forth. They talk about the fact that all the neighbors will support them, even though supporting neighbors rarely appeared in court or mediation and often failed to come even when expected. By the time these situations get to court, most people say that the problem is almost entirely the other person's fault.[13]

Court officials and mediators also assume that the problems they see generally involve "bad characters". But identifying *who* is the bad character is hard. Plaintiffs are eager to prove that the other side is a bad actor; but as long as third parties have no independent source of information, they can only choose between conflicting interpretations. Third parties usually have only the statements of the parties—who are clearly interested in presenting favorable views of the situation—to go on. However, knowledge provided by outside sources, even if fragmentary, usually carries great weight. A probation officer may mention in passing that so and so comes from a family with a bad reputation, or a police officer in court on another case may say that "the Jones family is in court all the time." An outside party such as a community organizer or a police liaison officer may drop a scrap of information, but usually only informally and often by chance. Mediators and court officials also hear about families' previous cases in court. Since such murky situations provide them with little information to go on, court officials are desperate for "objective" interpretations on which they can base a reasonable course of action which will provide some kind of justice. If an interpretation that a person or a family is generally troublesome is presented in a way which the clerk, judge, prosecutor, or mediator considers reliable, it often changes the way he or she handles the case. In a world of uncertain and partial knowledge, these fragments provide something to go on, as the case at the end of this chapter shows.

Emotional Intensity

Problems are almost always emotionally intense struggles rather than rational differences of interest. Mediation sessions frequently involve angry shouting matches between the parties or tearful accusations of neglect and hostility. Many of the people whom I interviewed after their problems were in court and mediation said that it was painful to talk about the problem again, and most reported being upset in the mediation session and in court.[14] A court clerk in Cambridge complained about the stress his job placed on his heart because people who bring their problems to court are typically very angry.

A case, however, is seen as a cool difference of interest. The courts work to assert this cool interpretation of the situation by keeping the problems out of the courtroom and sending them to clerks and mediators. The parties are still upset and angry, but the plaintiff and the people handling the problem assert its meaning as a set of issues and interests outside its emotional meaning. While recognizing the event as a "hot" problem, those who handle it in court present it for court proceedings as a "cool" legal case. In those few cases which come to trial, the attorneys—the prosecutor and the defense attorney, almost always court-appointed—play an active role in screening out the emotional intensity of interpersonal problems and in protecting the court from a witness who explodes on the stand or who goes out of control by bringing in "irrelevant" materials. They serve as a mechanism for containing and controlling explosive feelings and their potentially anarchic effects.[15] The emotional intensity of interpersonal problems is one reason why they seem troublesome and out of place in the court.

Protecting The Self

These problems often have implications for the participants' vision of themselves as respectable, reasonable, and fair people. That a sense of self is at stake explains some of the emotional intensity of these problems. These conflicts are rarely matters of simple interest and rational argument but instead tend to be passionate encounters in which the whole person is on the line. Some conflicts have meaning for how the person thinks about himself or herself and his or her social world, her ability to cope and to defend herself, and her ability to create an acceptable image of herself and her life. This is characteristic of all types of problems, although particularly so for neighborhood problems. When feelings come out in these conflicts, as they usually do, they do so not as a matter of strategy or plan but as an expression of the connectedness of feeling and interests, as a measure of both the extent to which important issues of self are at stake and the uncertainty of the encounter: what is going to happen? how will one's actions will be interpreted? how can one convey one's message clearly, and how can one live with a situation which exists or which one is in the process of creating? When one observes, as I did, a $30 small-claims case between a professional woman with a good salary and a repairman whom she claims damaged her floor and used her kitchen utensils, one cannot help but suspect that there is more riding on the conflict than the money. The repairman is concerned about his reputation and his vision of himself as a good worker; the employer feels that her house has been violated and that she has not been treated with respect. The $30 is simply a symbol of contested visions of self.

The Folk Concept of the Case

When a problem gets to court, it is reinterpreted as a case. In order for it to get to court, of course, the plaintiff must already have interpreted the problem as a legal one. When it arrives in court, a case acquires a label such as assault, harassment, breach of contract, or, in juvenile cases, truancy or "stubborn child." These labels derive from the legal arena, not from the world of social relationships. Each label points toward a kind of resolution, since, by naming the problem, one also names the way of solving it.[16] For example, an assault requires punishment, harassment implies that it must be stopped, theft requires the return of property, and truancy requires a return to regular school attendance.[17] But the particular label which the problem acquires in court does not grow directly out of the problem itself; it is imposed during a fleeting and not well understood moment in which a plaintiff faces an office clerk and fills out an application form. In other jurisdictions, the police or the prosecutors play a more central role in the decision of how to label a problem, but in the Massachusetts lower courts citizen complaints are filed at the office of the clerk-magistrate of the court, by individuals who do not have legal advice.[18] Thus, the label the case assumes depends on negotiations between plaintiffs and people who give advice inside and outside the court, people such as police, lawyers, office clerks, and friends who have been in court before. Obviously the plaintiffs's previous experience in court—and any instructions he or she received at the time—are also very influential.

The filtering of the problem into one court or another is itself somewhat haphazard. It depends on how well informed a plaintiff is, where he or she has been before, what the police or her friends have advised her to do, what she has seen in the media about courts, and what room she walks into in the courthouse. Many of these problems can be interpreted either as civil or criminal matters or as different kinds of criminal matters. The choice of criminal court rather than small-claims court depends on the plaintiff's knowledge and experience as well as on the nature of the problem. Some cases begin with a problem which could be described as civil, rooted in a property argument, but which, as it progresses and as feelings rise, leads to an insult or a blow, which entitles the aggrieved person to take it to the criminal court. Landlord/tenant cases often follow this progression and end up in criminal court even when they begin over overdue rent or poor housing conditions. A rebellious teenager who steals from his mother, hits her, and runs away could be taken to the judge for a restraining order, to the clerk-magistrate in the criminal court for a larceny or assault charge, or to juvenile court as a runaway. David Engel and Eric Steele describe the arbitrary nature of the division between civil and criminal jurisdiction (1979); this arbitrariness appears in interpersonal cases as well. Some cases are even reassigned to different courts during their time in court, as lawyers, magistrates, and judges put various interpretations on the problems they see in the courthouse. The second case in this chapter illustrates the reassigning process.

In sum, when a problem arrives in court, a new interpretation of the problem as a case, labeled with a charge, is superimposed through a negotiation between the plaintiff and entry-level court officials. Even in court, however, as Chapter 3 pointed out, interpersonal cases are generally talked about in terms of the underlying relationship between the parties rather than in terms of the legal charge. The problem interpretation and the case interpretation coexist in the court.

But the case interpretation can lose its salience. What appeared at first as a serious case—such as threats of violence against innocent people or theft of a roommate's property—may be reinterpreted as a problem between two feuding families or as a way of getting back at a roommate for an unpaid telephone bill. As court officials strive to provide justice, they assess whether the situation is better handled as a problem or as a case. Court officials may propose new case interpretations or refuse to acknowledge that the problem has any status as a case at all. Defendants often join in, arguing that the situation is only a problem. Thus, the problem and the case coexist in a state of tension; court processing consists in part of struggles over which interpretation will prevail. The interpretation, of course, dictates what is to be done about it.

The following two examples describe this struggle. In the first example, the plaintiff initially succeeds in convincing the clerk-magistrate of her interpretation of the situation. She presents it in terms of harassment and fear of assault, justifying her appeal to the court in terms of her need for protection from violence. But she has trouble making this interpretation stick, as the other side and a community worker try to undermine it. They press the clerk-magistrate to reinterpret the case as a problem by emphasizing that the plaintiff is a troublemaker and welfare cheat, that there has been a long series of exchanges concerning many issues from jealousy to noise, that there has been mutual provocation and fault, and that there are strong feelings at stake. The clerk gradually decides that the case warrants an informal discussion of the sort that mediation provides, not a legal remedy such as a special police watch or criminal proceedings. The case interpretation falls apart, and he refers the problem to the mediation program.

The second example concerns a problem with jealousy and landlord/tenant relationships. This problem followed a longer course through the courts than did the first. Initially interpreted as a criminal case, then as a problem for mediation, it was ultimately seen as an eviction case. Here also, the plaintiff struggled to assert that the situation was a case and the defendant insisted that it was a problem not worthy of any legal intervention such as throwing her out of the apartment she lives in. The first problem comes from Salem, the second from Cambridge.

In the first example, the quarrel arrived in court as a threat of serious violence against a Hispanic woman, Sandra, from her neighbor who lives in the apartment below, a Hispanic woman named Carlita (pseudonyms). Both are young women, mothers of several children, and originally from Puerto Rico, although Sandra speaks fluent English and has been in Salem for a long time. The women both live in the Green Street neighborhood.

Sandra came to court on a Friday and persuaded the clerk-magistrate that she was in fear for her life from her downstairs neighbor and that she was worried about the safety of her children. The clerk was sufficiently concerned that he asked the police to keep a special watch on the house over the weekend, pending a formal clerk's hearing on Monday. A police officer regularly stationed at the court identified the neighborhood as one with a serious gang problem and a bad reputation. He agreed to alert the police. He commented to me, in an aside, that the Hispanics are excitable people. The clerk responded: *"You know, this family should move, but they can't afford to. What can you do? They all live in the same building. They are not really trespassing, they are not breaking any laws. They have the right to be there."* Thus, both the clerk and the police officer interpreted the situation as serious based on their knowledge of the community. Both concluded that this situation warranted some help from the law.

I spoke to Sandra on Monday morning before the hearing, and she told me she was very scared to be in court and that it was her first time. She described the problem as one of fear because there were all these men in the hallway downstairs, and last Friday night she had been so scared that she finally got a big kitchen knife, sort of like a machete, and opened the door and called down to them that they might just as well come get her and do whatever they wanted to her. She complained about the obscene words on her stairwell and about the comments and obscene remarks of these men, who are Carlita's friends. Emotions were clearly central to the way she thought about the problem. When I asked her what she thought the court would do for her, she answered, with an air of surprise, "I don't know, I have no idea."

During the 20-minute hearing, new visions of the problem emerged. The clerk began with the assumption that the situation was one of threats on the life of a woman and her children. But as it unfolded, it seemed to have many more sides. Sandra brought her sixty-seven-year-old father to the hearing, and Carlita, who spoke no English, brought a local antipoverty worker and volunteer in the mediation program as translator. Sandra was fluent in English, but her father spoke only Spanish. The clerk-magistrate began by saying that he had from Sandra an application for a complaint regarding threats and harassment, an application which contained the following list of statements: "Carlita said 'I will cut your face and hit your father.' She has sent friends to the front of my house to make noise and once a friend came into my house and exposed his private parts in front of my father and children."

The clerk continued:

> *Sandra came in here on Friday in fear for her life. The situation sounded so bad that I contacted Officer Jones of the police department to keep a special watch on the situation. The court wants people to live in peace and quiet, and it is against the law to harass and frighten people. I am not saying Carlita is guilty, and I want to hear from her, but if this is going on, it* must *stop. I will talk to Sandra first, then Carlita will have a chance to talk* [emphasis is speaker's].
>
> SANDRA: *On Friday, people came up and knocked on my door. People are writing obscenities on my walls.*
> CLERK: *You are in fear of your safety and that of your children?*
> SANDRA: *Yes, my children are afraid to go to school.*
> CLERK: *I worry about the children in particular. I have four of my*

> *own, and I think that anything that affects the safety of children is*
> *very important. Is there anything else?*
> SANDRA: *They said they would tie up my father and hit him.*
> FATHER: *I am sixty-seven, I have never been to court before, and these*
> *people come and knock on my door.*
> CLERK: *I am afraid something very serious is going to happen.*
> ANTIPOVERTY WORKER: *I am an advocate here and don't want to be in*
> *the middle. I think this case should be transferred to mediation. I*
> *think you should hear the other side, because there are serious*
> *problems on both sides. The father is unhappy because they are*
> *knocking on the ceiling while he is sleeping, but he should not be*
> *sleeping there at all, because he lives elsewhere and this is subsi-*
> *dized housing, where he is not supposed to be.*

Here the outsider introduces new information providing a different perspective on Sandra, a vision of Sandra and her father as troublemakers and welfare cheats. This perspective seems to make a difference to the clerk.

> CARLITA: *I have three children. I get up early with my children, and*
> *her children are already jumping upstairs, and they keep on jump-*
> *ing upstairs until late. I knock on the ceiling with my broom handle*
> *to get them to keep quiet. They don't have any carpets on the floor to*
> *keep quiet.*

Pounding on the ceiling is a mode of exchanging messages which is likely to escalate a conflict, as it seems to have done here. This case involves other messages which have also escalated the conflict: writing on the walls, knocking on the door, allowing children to jump on the floor.

> CLERK: *The situation sounds much more serious than children jump-*
> *ing. What about the writing on the walls?*
> ANTIPOVERTY WORKER: *Carlita is illiterate, she couldn't have done*
> *it.*
> CLERK: *But her friends could write on walls. And Sandra fears for her*
> *children.*
> CARLITA: *Sandra's children play with knives. And they spill garbage*
> *all over. I have two witnesses that Sandra's children are throwing*
> *burning paper out the window.*
> ANTIPOVERTY WORKER: *This is what I mean. Both sides are doing it.*
> CLERK: *Is Carlita aware that making threats to Sandra is against the*
> *law?*
> CARLITA: *I never threatened Sandra. I have never been to court before*
> *like this.*
> CLERK: *I think this sounds like a case for mediation.*

The clerk then calls in an intake worker from the mediation program.

> CLERK: *We have a typical neighborhood problem here. Sandra lives*
> *on the third floor, Carlita on the second, and the complaint is*
> *against Carlita. There is a problem of obscenities in the hallway*
> *and Sandra is fearful for her safety. This seems like a volatile situa-*
> *tion, and I don't want anything to happen. [To the parties] I want to*

*work with you and with the mediation program to find a way to keep
the peace, since you must find a way to live together and to do so
peacefully. I want to see this resolved and I don't want to see anyone get hurt. If you don't like what others do, you should not get
involved but should ignore it. Sandra, would you try to keep your
children quiet at night? I want you to work on making an agreement
to live peacefully together. You don't want this to come into criminal court,—it is embarrassing and not the place for mothers and
their children. I hope I won't hear about this case again, but if so, I
will continue to work with the mediation program on it.*

By this time, the clerk seems to have changed his mind about the situation.
He no longer sees it as a worthy legal case, entitled to special police protection.
Instead, it has the characteristics of mutual fault, history, emotional intensity,
and ongoing relationships which signal to him a problem appropriate for mediation. The salience of the problem is greater than that of the case. The clerk does
not want to intervene legally except through the informal court-supervised negotiation process provided by mediation. He has abandoned his idea that this is
a situation of an innocent victim terrified by her "bad" neighbors. He now sees
it as a situation in which there are many issues and some history of provocation
on both sides. He has been influenced by the community worker's suggestion
that the plaintiff is really a "bad character." He refers it to mediation and gives a
lecture on neighborly consideration and the need to get along because he thinks
this will provide the best way to get a just resolution of the problem. The clerk
takes the situation seriously, but he has interpreted it as a serious problem rather
than as a serious case.

At the private intake interview with Sandra and her father in the mediation
office, both describe the basic problem as the noise of Sandra's children. Sandra
says that Carlita now sends her friends to attack her. Carlita's boyfriend is also a
big part of the problem because he stares out the window at Sandra and laughs at
her. The problem began a few months earlier when Carlita said that Sandra had
men up to her apartment. As the mediation intake worker assures Sandra that
mediation would be a good way to handle this problem because it would help
them to talk and live together, Sandra insists that the problem has to go to court
because she doesn't think it could be settled otherwise: *"They drink down
there, all the time, and then they get violent and take out knives."*

At the private intake interview with Carlita, Carlita identifies the problem as
Sandra's children's habit of jumping on the floor above her until 1:00 A.M. or
2:00 A.M. She knocks on the ceiling to keep them quiet. She has a daughter with
a heart condition who is frightened by the noise, and she has to change the light
bulb all the time. She is afraid that they will burn down the house because Sandra's children light paper in the halls and outside and throw it out the window.
Sometimes Sandra leaves the children alone with a baby sitter, and sometimes
she is gone all weekend, down to New York. Carlita cleans all the stairs, and
Sandra's children strew them with garbage. Finally, Sandra's father walks with

something hidden under his jacket—"I don't know what it is." The real problem, she says is Sandra's father.

> *He came down to tell me to stop knocking on the ceiling and used bad words. The trouble started three weeks ago when he went to where my boyfriend works and told him to stop knocking on the ceiling. Then, my boyfriend said, "but I don't live there." I thought Sandra should talk to me directly, not send her father to my boyfriend. I can't read or write, and someone put bad words on my door, but I don't complain about it.*

Here the complaint is not only about the message but about the way it was delivered.

After the mediation process is explained to her, Carlita says that she had not been to court before and that the prospect is frightening. Both parties agree to try mediation. After a fairly brief mediation session, they reach an agreement to deal with each other with mutual respect and agree that there will be no threats or harassment from any of them or from Carlita's boyfriend. Sandra agrees to drop her charges against Carlita.[19]

Thus, the conflict contained a complex set of feelings and grudges which emerged in the clerk's hearing and in the mediation intake interviews. There is gossip about sexual affairs, noise from children, messy stairs, glances out the window, a failure to communicate directly, threats of violence, and obscene words written and spoken. There is not one part which is the "real" issue and the rest superficial issues, since each depends for its meaning upon its connection with the others. It appears that during the clerk's hearing the clerk is stumbling across these aspects of the problem, endeavoring to make sense of the situation in terms of his original interpretation—that it is a serious case—but ultimately coming to see it as a problem best served by a referral to mediation. He comes to view the situation as an argument between two women with children rather than as a dangerous situation for Sandra. The problem interpretation has become more salient than the case interpretation.

The voice of a knowledgeable outsider has a powerful impact in this case. The antipoverty worker, introducing her knowledge of the community, insists that it is Sandra alone who causes trouble, that she lies, complains to government agencies all the time, and has illegal residents in her subsidized apartment. Given the ambiguity of the problem, the antipoverty worker's voice carries considerable weight and succeeds in derailing the clerk from his original intent to provide protection for Sandra as an innocent victim of neighborhood toughs. Given his own lack of information about the situation, he turns for help to her information, and her comments move him toward seeing the situation as one of mutual injuries. But these comments do not totally reverse the clerk's opinion; he refuses to see Sandra as the source of the problem rather than as the victim and concludes with a lecture to both. His concern here seems to be to create some kind of peace.

This situation develops as an extended conversation during which messages are exchanged and interpreted, subject to rapid and cataclysmic shifts in meaning. Acts of violence, calling the police, or filing charges in court trigger a sharp escalation of the problem. It is a struggle fraught with uncertainty about what it is and where it is going. This is a risky, emotionally intense, and dangerous event which unfolds in unpredictable ways. The problem here, as is often the case, is on the boundaries of violence. For most people, there is an open-ended and volatile quality to problems which encourages them to avoid confrontations as long as possible. For some, of course, the risk and the danger are a form of excitement and stimulation.

The second example began in the criminal court as a case of malicious damage, based on a door broken in anger. As the complex relationship between the man and woman emerged in the hearing, the clerk-magistrate referred the case to mediation. Whey they failed to reach an agreement in mediation and when it appeared that the fundamental problem was that a landlord wanted his ex-girlfriend to move out of the apartment she occupied in his house, the clerk sent it to a civil court for an eviction.

A soft-spoken, weary-looking young man in his thirties appeared in court with a criminal charge, against his tenant, of wanton destruction of personal property. He charged her with breaking the door to her apartment. His tenant, an attractive, raven-haired young woman in her twenties, had moved into the apartment in his house rent free while the two were dating. After a while, she had broken off the relationship but had continued to live in the apartment. She had invited other men to visit her there, provoking the jealousy of the landlord. He had retaliated by turning down the heat, cutting off the electricity, and playing loud music while he was out of the house. The young woman still paid no rent and refused to move out, alledging that a contract had been made permitting her to live there rent free, albeit a contract made while the landlord and she were dating. She claimed she should still retain the benefit of that promise. Furthermore, it would be a hardship to move her children, aged six and ten years, to another school. Since her mother lived across the street, the woman was quite content to stay in the apartment. The landlord, desperate to change this stressful situation, said he would not attempt to collect the back rent if she would only move out. The situation was complicated by the fact that she had no money to find another apartment, since her divorced husband was unemployed, and also by the fact that one of her children is deaf and a very disruptive, difficult child. The landlord's sister was very opposed to the relationship and had been trying to persuade her brother to get the tenant out. The tenant's mother, who vociferously condemned the landlord for his behavior, had no interest in having her daughter and her children move back in with her.

The case was heard by a clerk-magistrate on the basis of the charge of malicious destruction of property, the damage to the apartment door inflicted by the tenant. At this hearing, which I did not attend, the clerk referred the case to mediation. In the mediation session, which I did attend, the parties were unable to settle. The tenant offered to look for another apartment but was unwilling to promise when she would move out. The landlord, foreseeing long-term stalling, refused to accept this offer. During the four-hour mediation session, the broken door was not mentioned.

When the case came back to the clerk without being settled, he held another hearing on the criminal complaint and asked whether anything had happened since. I attended this hearing. The young woman began to complain about the lack of both heat and hot water and about a defective stove, but the lawyer the landlord had by now retained pointed out that these issues were not germane to the criminal complaint. The lawyer then suggested a month's delay in the issuing of the complaint, which would be dropped if the premises were vacated by then. He was attempting to use the criminal charge as a lever to evict the woman. The clerk decided that the issue was not one for the criminal side, however, and dismissed the charges. He advised the landlord to proceed civilly for an eviction. The clerk was aware of the nature of the relationship between the parties because they had explained it to him in the first hearing. When the clerk asked the man and woman whether they had anything more to say at the hearing, the tenant again stated her intention to move out but said that it would take time. This hearing lasted about fifteen minutes.

As the parties were about to leave the hearing room, the woman's mother asked to speak. She complained that the landlord was being terrible to her daughter, that he had turned off the heat, and that the apartment was in deplorable condition. The clerk cut her off, telling her that he had decided not to issue a complaint. Thus, the mother tried to paint the landlord as a "bad character," but the clerk refused to listen to her string of complaints and did not change his position.

After the hearing, the clerk told me that he thought this was just a lover's quarrel, that they would probably be back together again in a few months, and that he suspected that there were other problems as well, such as a drinking problem on the man's side and emotional instability on the woman's side. Thus, he did not interpret the situation as a case of malicious damage but as a problem of jealousy between emotionally intense and possibly unstable people, a problem he did not wish to handle through issuing a criminal complaint.

The couple returned to civil court for a summary-process hearing on the application for an eviction. This hearing was a private affair in which the two parties stood before the judge at the bench, talking quietly rather than addressing the whole courtroom. I stood alongside the parties, listening to their conversation with the judge. The young woman immediately announced that this was a lover's quarrel, that they used to be together but that now the man wanted her out of the house. She said she was trying to move but that she has a handicapped child and another child and received only $33 a week in child support. She admitted that she had not been paying rent, but she produced the "love note," handwritten on lined yellow paper, with the promise to let her stay rent free. She also complained about the heat, hot water, electricity, and stove and said that she had called the board of health about these matters. Finally, she said that the landlord had hit her deaf son, which was why things had broken down between them. In his turn, the landlord pointed out that she had paid no rent for four months but that he really wanted not the money but for her to move away. He said that the present situation was very hard on him.

Thus, the woman immediately brought the problem to the fore, while the man described the case. He presented himself as a landlord seeking eviction, while she presented herself as an abused and victimized woman. After listening to them, the judge announced: *"This is a social problem, and I would like you to handle it as a social problem. But if you can't settle it that way, then I will have to handle it as a legal problem."* He sent them out to try to reach their own agreement. After they again failed to settle, he called them back to the bench. The tenant repeated the same complaints about the apartment, the difficulties of finding housing with a handicapped child, and her lack of money. She mentioned that the case had already been to criminal court, where she had triumphed. The judge did not seem interested in the criminal complaint but observed that this was a situation in which there were a lot of strong feelings of love and hate mixed together. He then asked the tenant why she did not have a job, since her children were in school, and he told her that she would have to go to work. He advised her to consider her children's welfare, suggesting that the present strife was hard on them.

Finally, he concluded: *"Since I can't settle this as a social problem, I guess I will have to make a legal decision."* He ruled that the "love note" was not legally binding, since it had not been notarized, and he dismissed the complaints about the condition of the apartment, since the woman was not really a tenant. He ordered her to leave in ten days or be evicted. The hearing lasted twenty minutes.

Talking to me after the hearing, the judge said that he suspected right away that this was not a normal landlord/tenant case because the woman seemed so emotional and so hostile. He knew that other things, besides a simple rent dispute, were going on between the landlord and tenant, and he had concluded that she was a very bitter, angry young woman. He talked about the parties in terms of their ethnic identities. He complained that the courts were often asked to deal with social problems although their training is for legal problems, and he felt the need for more appropriate training to handle such problems. Throughout the hearing, he was courteous and affable, eager to have the parties arrive at their own settlement rather than having to impose a legal decision. The tenant did move across the street with her mother within the ten-day period and, a few months later, moved out of state, although she still did not have a job. The landlord sold the house and moved away.

Thus, the judge interpreted the situation as a problem but used the case interpretation to settle it. The landlord persisted in interpreting the situation as a case warranting eviction. The young woman tried to assert that it was a problem, complaining about the landlord's bad treatment of her and about her personal difficulties with money, housing, and a deaf child. Her mother, when she managed to wedge her story into the court process, supported this perspective.

Furthermore, over time the situation was interpreted as three different cases: first, as malicious damage in criminal court; second, as an interpersonal fight in mediation; and, third, as an eviction proceeding in civil court. From the clerk-magistrate's perspective, the broken door was a legally trivial case, not worth further consideration. However, he recognized that the problem was intense and protracted. Consequently, he sent the case first to mediation and then to civil court for an eviction.

Both these examples show court officials trying to provide what they consider to be just settlements for complex situations in which it is hard to be sure what is going on. In their efforts to deal with such cases, they consider the nature of the relationship between the parties, the kind of neighborhood the parties live in, and any other information they acquire, formally or informally, about the parties. Although they generally do not take these situations seriously as cases, the court officials I observed did, by and large, take them seriously as problems and endeavored to provide justice in these terms. This often meant referral to another court or to mediation or delivering a stern lecture to both parties, along with threats to do something if the problem recurred. It rarely meant imposing a penalty on the defendant.

Problems, Cases, and Domination

Before these situations come to court, they are social relationships with strain and conflict. In court, they are interpreted as cases. The case structure is one of the ways the court attempts to manage, contain, and control these problems. As cases, they are framed as a confrontation between two parties over a particular issue or incident, including only the plaintiff and the defendant. Other players are not included. The tenant's mother, for example, although a powerful player in the drama, was permitted only a postscript at the end of the clerk's hearing and was not part of either the deliberation in court or mediation. Her comments were ignored. The case acquires a label—a charge—which, in effect, crystallizes a few issues out of the wider matrix of the problem. The Sandra-Carlita situation became a case of threats, and the jealous-landlord situation, initially a case of malicious destruction of property, became one of unauthorized tenancy. But in both cases the clerks and the judges also interpreted the situation in the framework of problems between neighbors and ex-lovers.

Interpreting a situation as a case implies a different form of handling than interpreting the situation as a problem does. There is a presumption of finality to the process of handling cases: problems may go on and on, but cases are settled. With a case, the court personnel take control over the volatility of the dispute, containing and deflecting anger, managing passions, protecting both parties from each other, and preventing violence, at least in the courthouse. The court stands in as the "community," representing, in a sense, the community opinions that shaped the problem in the first place but lacking the knowledge of the problem that the neighborhood or family members possess.

Yet, the structure of the case sometimes contradicts the plaintiff's experience of the situation. The experience of the conflict is informed by its history, yet history is not included in the structure of the case. For example, when people come to the courts to file complaints, they are asked to fill in the date, time, and location of the incident which serves as the basis for the complaint. Plaintiffs often feel that it is the repeated, continuous nature of the problem which is troublesome. A single incident can be ignored; a repeated one demands action. One woman, for example, filled out this form by writing "all the time" and "everywhere" for her description of the incident. At the clerk's hearing, the clerk informed her that she had to base her complaint on a single incident, not on an ongoing pattern of harassment. Other plaintiffs endure violence, harassment, and aggravation for a long time, until they suddenly feel that it is too much to take and that they cannot go on this way any more. The event is usually a last straw, not a first offense; but, as a case, it appears as the only offense.

Whether the situation is interpreted, at any point in the court proceeding, as a case or as a problem is not settled but remains a struggle. Plaintiffs usually fight to define the situation as worthy of the law's attention, while defendants are usually eager to claim that it is not. Plaintiffs want the court to do something to help them, and as long as this requires presenting a case, they endeavor to do so. Sometimes the court views the case as trivial, however, and pays more attention to the problem. When they see that the case is going nowhere, plaintiffs who are sophisticated can shift to describing the difficulties of the problem they face. Naive plaintiffs unable to phrase their situations as cases may also stick to the problem.

In sum, if one thinks of these events as having different but coexisting interpretations—as problems and as cases—some of the complexities of the way in which they are handled in court begin to make sense. Whether or not the court imposes serious penalties depends on the course of the struggle to define the situation as a problem or as a case. The dual existence of problems and cases emerges because the cases are on the boundaries of social life and law, belonging to both. The tension between these two arenas explains the continuing dissatisfaction with their processing, a dissatisfaction shared both by court officials and by the parties.

6

The Discourses of the Lower Court

The preceding chapter examined differences between the folk concepts of *problem* and *case,* differences reflected in the structure of problems versus the structure of cases. These categories were shown to be constructed by the court and by the community, respectively. The preceding chapter also explored the tensions and ambiguities resulting from the coexistence, in the same arena, of these two different interpretations of conflict situations. The present chapter examines the way meanings are raised and contested during discussions of conflict situations within the court, exploring, in particular, the way parties argue about meanings and about frames of meaning. The present chapter describes the dynamics of the process by which conflict situations are reinterpreted in court and mediation.

Distinct ways of talking and of interpreting events constitute discourses. I am using *discourse* in the sense which Foucault uses the term, rather than in the quite different usage of sociolinguistics, in which discourse refers to conversation in context (Sherzer 1987; Conley and O'Barr 1990).[1] In his view, discourses are means of exercising power in subtle, disguised ways (Foucault 1980: 100–106). Modern discourses or languages, such as psychiatry, penology, criticism, and history, are invisible but are also a language of control.[2]

Discourse here refers to systematic, impersonal modes of talking which govern the production of culture. A discourse is a specialized language, a particular jargon. It is usually signaled through particular phrases or modes of explanation but rarely spelled out. Every discourse, as I am using the term, contains a more or less coherent set of categories and theories of action: a vocabulary for naming events and persons and a theory for explaining actions and relationships. Each discourse consists of an explicit repertoire of justifications and explanations and an implicit, embedded theory about why people act the way they do.

Discourses are aspects of culture, interconnected vocabularies and systems of meaning located in the social world. A discourse is not individual and idiosyncratic but part of a shared cultural world. Discourses are rooted in particular institutions and embody their culture.[3] Actors operate within a structure of available discourses. However, within that structure there is space for creativity as actors define and frame their problems within one or another discourse.

Discourses are sometimes raised explicitly in discussion, but to a large extent they are implicit, assumed, part of the taken-for-granted world. Although a person may learn or elaborate a discourse through explicit instruction, many discourses are part of a culturally constructed world, not deliberately raised or questioned. They are part of the culture through which experiences are formed and by means of which an apparently objective social world is created (Bourdieu 1977). When an individual learns a particular discourse, it becomes part of his or her consciousness. The apparent naturalness of the cultural forms of discourse constitutes one explanation for the power of discourse.

The same event, person, action, and so forth can be named and interpreted in very different ways. The naming of an action or event within a particular discourse, thus interpreting the event's meaning and assessing the motives behind it, is therefore an act of power.[4] Each naming points to a solution.[5] If the family problem is interpreted as caused by a mean and vengeful father, the solution is different than if it is caused by a father afflicted with the disease of alcoholism, under whose influence the man becomes hostile. The ability to name and interpret is therefore a central feature of the power exercised by those who handle problems (see Sudnow 1965; Edelman 1977; Mather and Yngvesson 1980/81; Silbey and Merry 1987). Since names are part of discourses, the contest over naming is largely a contest over which discourse will be applied to the problem at hand. Critical to the power of any participant is his or her ability to determine the reigning discourse.[6]

Actors attempting to assert the discourses within which their problems are framed operate from structurally unequal positions. The supplicant, asking for help, is inevitably constrained to present his or her request in the language of the institution from which help is sought. In her study of marriage and inequality, Jane Collier argues cogently that when women seek to divorce their husbands they must present their demands in the discourse of marriage found in that society (1988). For example, if the discourse specifies that men are entitled to women by virtue of their prowess in war and raiding, women must contest their entitlement in those terms, not in others which might give them greater power. Thus, she argues, the choice of discourse itself is a product of the structure of the society, and the supplicant must adopt the discourse available to her. Although I was unable to do so in this project, it then becomes important to explore the origins and spread of discourses (see Scheingold 1974; Lasch 1977; Bellah et. al. 1985).

Three Discourses

After listening to and reading notes of discussions of about 170 cases in mediation and court, I began to identify three recurring discourses or modes of talking about problems.[7] I think that these three discourses constitute the dominant frames of meaning in court and mediation. They are derived from my own intuitive sifting and organizing of this material—an inductive, ethnographic approach—rather than from the observations of the people themselves. They are not the only possible discourses in which interpersonal problems could be or are discussed. They are simply the ones I heard. Some discourses, such as the discourse of community or the discourse of religion, were notably absent.[8] The dominant discourses I heard were those of rights and law, of fairness and morality, and of therapy and help.

In court, the discourses of law, morality, and therapy weave in and out of the discussions of particular problems. In the course of mediation sessions and court hearings, all three discourses usually appear in the discussion, raised by different parties who try them out to see how they work. As they argue their cases, justify their actions, condemn those of the other side, and strive to elicit the support of the mediator or judge, parties switch discourses, gauging the effects of each one. Mediators, clerks, and judges also struggle to establish and maintain a particular discourse and, when one seems unproductive or leads to trouble, switch to another. A person who is not succeeding in one discourse will often shift to another to see whether it is more effective.

The discourse used most often in both mediation and pretrial court processing is that of everyday morality. Legal discourse is pulled into the discussion from time to time, and most participants refer to therapeutic discourse as well. Some people use one discourse more than another. Men tend to use legal discourse more often than women, and women are more likely to refer to therapeutic discourse. Legal discourse is most common in neighborhood problems (in a sample of thirty cases, six of the seven which used legal discourse extensively were neighborhood problems). Marital and parent/child problems were discussed largely in terms of moral discourse, with legal discourse raised much less often. Marital cases frequently involve discussions of marital role relationships: of six marital cases, four used predominantly moral discourse. Therapeutic discourse appears more often in family problems and in boyfriend/girlfriend problems, probably because it is in the ordering of family relationships that the helping professions have been most heavily engaged, more so than in neighborhood relationships.

Legal Discourse

This is a discourse of property, of rights, of the protection of the self and one's goods, of entitlement, of facts and truth. Legal labels for wrongs, such as "harassment," "assault," "breach of contract," "malicious damage," and "trespass" and concepts such as property and contract constitute its core. It includes reference to evidence, to the presentation of documents, written lists, pictures, and witnesses. Solutions to problems in this discourse require weighing evidence and determining the applicable rules. Some individuals invoke the "rule of law" or rights to privacy, protection, or freedom from harassment. Some demand lie detector tests. Plaintiffs demand protection, insist that "something must be done to stop this situation."

Legal discourse here does not refer to particular laws or legal doctrines but to folk understandings of legal relations and procedures, to notions of contract, of property, and of decision making based on rational discussion and on the presentation of evidence in order to determine "the truth."[9] Concepts of property ownership, privacy, and rights to protection from violence and insults constitute this discourse. These general legal categories fade into political and religious understandings. Parties are rarely aware of particular rules or doctrines which bear on their case but instead have a general sense of fairness which derives from conceptions of property rights, contract obligations, and rights to personal security (Hunt 1985). For example, a landlord whose tenant left without the required thirty-day notice made no effort to rent his apartment for thirty days, instead taking the tenant to small-claims court. He did not realize he had a legal "duty to mitigate" his loss. When the judge heard his case in small-claims court, however, he refused to grant the landlord the full month's rent as damages because the landlord had failed to try to rent the apartment. Similarly, homeowners in neighborhood cases often hold notions of unlimited rights as to the control of activities on their property. They say they are entitled to throw anyone off their property at any time. These people refer to general legal concepts—not to specific laws, which they rarely know in detail. They often go to court asking for "something like a restraining order" but without a clear sense of when they are entitled to such an order or of what it means. Nor are they aware of the details of evidentiary rules, beyond the general recognition that written lists, diaries, and pictures are more persuasive than talk. Some people bring witnesses with them, even though the witnesses have not seen the incident, so that the witness can attest to their character and their credibility.[10]

Moral Discourse

This is a discourse of relationships, of moral obligations between neighbors, parents and children, brothers and sisters, and so forth. The language is of responsibilities and obligations tagged to definitions of social relationships. Interpretations are moral judgments in terms of relationships: should neighbors be quiet at night? is Mary a good mother? should Joe stop drinking? does Susie "mouth off" at her parents too much? Court officials or mediators sometimes tell parties that they should stop drinking, take better care of their children, treat each other like neighbors. Privately, mediators and court officials describe people as "flakes," "crazies," "from a nice family," or "good-hearted." Solutions to problems rest on a reciprocity of fairness, reasonableness, and compromise. Agreements detail rules of housework, of polite social interaction, of the importance of treating one another as "neighbors," "with respect," "as strangers." This is the talk of everyday life, of the normative ordering of family and neighborhood life, a talk people share without specialized training. Since much of the talk in these courts takes place in this discourse, at least here there is not a prevalence of mystifying language.

One aspect of moral discourse is concern about reputation and respect. Some people complain about what others are saying about them. They want their names cleared in court, their actions interpreted as reasonable or responsible. Particularly in close-knit communities, there is talk about preventing slanderous comments, mocking, name-calling, gossip, and insults. One woman complained about her neighbors, for example: "Your daughter says we are trash pickers and calls our kids scum." A man with a speech defect was angry because the neighbor child made fun of his way of talking. In a marital dispute, a husband became furious about the sloppy way his wife kept the house and yard, fearing what the neighbors would think. One young man was very upset because his girlfriend pressed charges against him for violence and therefore his name appeared in the paper as a defendant. He came from a town which he described as a small town and in which his family had had a good reputation, now sullied because people say that he likes to beat up girls. He said he had lost the respect of his father. He wanted to plead not guilty so that he could be exonerated by the court. In sum, moral discourse includes talk about gossip and reputation as well as about fairness and proper performance of family and neighborhood roles.[11]

Therapeutic Discourse

This is a discourse drawn from the helping professions, one which talks of behavior as environmentally caused rather than as based on individual fault. Crowding, stress, or low levels of tolerance for frustration–rather than inborn evil, lack of consideration, or a lack of respect—are blamed for offensive behavior. Offensive behavior is socially caused, not the result of individual will: "He is not well. I don't want him to go to jail; I just want him to get help." The model of illness and disease, which describes difficulties without attaching fault or blame, is the dominant explanation for behavior. Alcoholism, mental illness, "acting out," and emotional immaturity tag this discourse. Offensive behavior does not reveal innate evil but, rather, a need for help. Solutions depend on "treatment," "cure" for the person with the problem. People using the therapeutic discourse sometimes seek help for themselves and sometimes try to force others to accept help. This discourse sometimes links physical ills and emotional problems. For example, some men describe their inability to control explosive violence as the result of high blood pressure, or people talk about the pressure a conflict exerts on their nerves. Some talk about their "issues," rather than about their anger.

This discourse withholds judgment—but at the price of denying the person described full personhood and responsibility for himself (see Foucault 1977). The individual, understood within therapeutic discourse, is less than a full adult, since less is expected of him or her—and therefore he or she cannot be blamed. He has a disease, a problem. Thus, the control inherent in the therapeutic discourse is different from that in the legal discourse, which refers to rights and evidence. Both the legal and the therapeutic discourses are specialized, developed by professionals, although both have spread more widely as a mode of talking in the general population. Some of these court users have experienced counseling, and more have been urged to try; but most have some familiarity with the language (see Edelman 1977; Lasch 1977; Bellah et. al. 1985).

Therapeutic discourse takes the form of excusing offensive behavior, since action is seen as environmentally caused and therefore is understood and accepted. Blame is mitigated. Of her husband's violence, a woman may say: "But he works hard and gets tense and frustrated." Or, when her husband drinks too much, a woman may say: "He had a hard childhood and had to move around a lot." But the same language of therapy can be used to label and condemn. In a neighborhood case, for example, one man said of his neighbors: "They drink too much; that is a lot of the problem." Another man said of his opponent in a neighborhood case: "She will deny she did it. She is cuckoo. She has been in and out of a mental hospital." The language of therapy here is used to condemn and belittle, to diminish the credibility of the other side rather than to understand and help.[12]

The entrance of therapeutic discourse into legal arenas appears to be largely a twentieth-century phenomenon in the United States, one which has accelerated in recent years. With the emergence of the helping profession in the 1920s and 1930s, new ideas of crime as caused by environmental forces rather than inborn evil and of juvenile delinquency as caused by family situations spread into the courts (Platt 1969; Lasch 1977; Rothman 1980). Therapeutic discourse is now pervasive in the management of domestic-relations situations, juvenile problems, and alcohol and drug problems. As Silbey points out, lower courts now dispense services as much as punishments (1981). In a recent article, Martha Fineman shows how the discourse of social work has entered the discussion of child-custody decisions in divorce cases as well (1988: 731). As she traces out the implications of this shift in discourse for decision making about the custody of children after divorce, she demonstrates the power of discourse to frame the issue and to point to one or another solution.[13]

Discourses in Mediation and Court

All four types of problem—neighborhood, marital, boyfriend/girlfriend, and family—are initially presented in legal discourse. During mediation and court processing, parties are steered away from legal discourse to moral and therapeutic ways of talking. Indeed, the objective of mediation is to handle these problems in ways which respond to the relationship between the parties rather than to their legal claims. Clerks and judges also employ moral discourse, although in a different way. After they have dealt with the legal issues, they give moral lectures.

The nature of the discourse shift is distinctive to each type of problem. Neighborhood cases are commonly presented in terms of property rights or rights to legal protection from violence. During court processing they usually shift to a discourse of neighborly cooperation, getting along, and avoidance. As they attempt to shift from legal to moral discourse, mediators often talk about how neighbors should treat one another. In contrast, legal discourse in marital and boyfriend/girlfriend cases emphasizes violent assaults and the need for protection. In court and mediation, plaintiffs are urged to consider this violence in the context of the relationship and to think about what they themselves might do to mitigate it. They are sometimes encouraged to think about therapy for the offender. In family cases, parents arrive demanding greater respect from and control over their children and are urged to negotiate rules for curfews and for sharing chores.

The following three problems, two neighborhood ones and a boyfriend/girlfriend one, illustrate the discourses and their interplay in the course of mediation and court processing.

Neighbors

This problem occurred in Salem, in a dense, working-class neighborhood very much like Hilltowne. This is an old and established area. The problem arises out of subtle differences in social class: a newcomer plaintiff who feels slightly above his neighbors and an old-timer defendant who has a more hard-living life-style. At the center there is a boy, the defendant's son, whom everyone agrees is aggressive. Furthermore, the plaintiff is a man who—by his own account, as well as that of others—is an angry person. The description of the situation comes from interviews with both parties, a visit to the neighborhood, and my observation of the mediation session.

The plaintiff in this situation comes to court with his complaint framed in legal discourse—in terms of rights to privacy, to property, to being left alone. He buttresses these claims with "official evidence." The mediators persuade him to reframe it in moral discourse. They ask about the relationship between the parties, whether they were friends in the past, whether they ever got along, and why the friendship disintegrated. They persuade the defendant to go along with moral discourse as well, although her argument was initially couched primarily in moral discourse. From time to time, she raises the issue of property rights and occasionally adopts therapeutic discourse.

Bobby, the aggressive fourteen-year-old, repeatedly fought with his neighbor, George, a man in his thirties.[14] George and his wife both work, he as a salesman and she as a secretary. His wife has some college education but not a college degree. Together, they earn between $25,000 and $35,000 a year and own their own house. They moved into the neighborhood three years ago. He has been in the military for several years, traveling all over the world, and served in Vietnam. Their only child, a ten-year-old boy, spends the afternoons at home alone. Across the narrow street in a neighborhood of small single-family and duplex houses lives Bobby's family. His mother, Jane, a divorced woman with five children ranging in age from two to fifteen years, struggles to survive on less than $12,000 a year. She has a high school diploma. Her ex-husband is a police officer in town. Her oldest son (not Bobby) has emotional problems. She has lived in town for sixteen years and has lived in her present house for seven years. She owns the house. Jane is an attractive, vivacious woman in her thirties. George is an intense man, and his wife is more gentle and quiet; both are also in their thirties. George's wife grew up with Jane in a nearby neighborhood but they were not close friends.

After a series of incidents between the two families—primarily involving confrontations between Bobby and George in which Bobby threw eggs at George's car, George overturned a picnic table in Jane's yard, and both made obscene phone calls to each other—George went to court and filed a complaint against Bobby, charging him with annoying telephone calls and harassment. The description on the complaint form read as follows:[15] "Repeated obscene telephone calls, damaging personal property, constant harassment from said family. Death threats to my 10-year-old son and flashing knives. Constantly threatening my son on the way to and from school and while playing on and around our own property. Has thrown eggs at my property on numerous occasions." At the clerk's hearing, the clerk refused to issue the complaint and referred the case to mediation, over George's intense and angry objections. Jane was willing to try mediation. I did not attend the clerk's hearing.

Three weeks later, at the mediation session, which I did attend, the two mediators introduced themselves, described the procedure of public and private sessions, emphasized the confidentiality of the private sessions, and noted that they hoped to reach an agreement. If they did, one copy would be left with the mediation program. They emphasized that they had taken an oath of confidentiality from the court and that the only written record of the session would be the agreement. Thus, they defined the event as private, connected to the legal system, and governed by explicit rules of procedure. Only George, his wife, and Jane were present for this session; the children did not come.

George, as complainant, was invited to begin. He began to describe the situation in everyday terms. *"This has been going on for two and a half years. No one is totally innocent in the situation. I've ignored things and so have they, but things are now getting out of hand. They are quieter, then things start up again. Now there is catcalling, abusing people, abusing property."* The mediators press him to be more specific about the nature of the complaint about Bobby, in particular. Jane describes the situation in her initial statement, shifting between addressing the mediators and addressing George, as follows:

> *The complaint was harassing phone calls, but it is much, much more. George's family moved in two years ago. They have a little boy, and my son was friendly with him. The problem was their son's inability to communicate with his peers. They all picked on him, and the kids started to fight, especially Bobby and their son. George would inter-*

*vene and start to fight with my children. This is the problem. There
have been eggs thrown at both houses, and we have tried to get at a
resolution for the bickering. My biggest complaint is that whatever my
children did to his house, George did to mine; then he boyishly admits
it. He has a low frustration tolerance and quite a temper. He is childish—he has knocked over a picnic table, hit Bobby with a baseball—
and I had to call the police. I am at home all the time, and I see this.
My son has been disrespectful to George, but he is disrespectful back.
I intervene to protect their son sometimes. George once kicked in my
door, and my kids were afraid. George also called my son, and I wrote
down what he said. I told him: "When my children do wrong to you, I
knock on the door and tell you and tell them to take the eggs off. I don't
think you would do the same for me." I feel intimidated. I am recently
divorced, and I don't need this aggravation. And the problem is not
the wife or son; it is George. I am not the type of person to call all the
time and say what your son does, but it is George who has chased us
and hit us. He always blames us for things we do and don't do. The
day that the children were playing with wood in our back yard I was
nice about it. I had an idea that other things bothered you, but you had
a camera and were taking pictures. I said in court what was happen-
ing last summer, but he denied it, he was full of lies. I never damaged
your property.*

Both of these statements plunge the listener into the middle of the situation
without providing the contextual background and history with which to situate
the stories. The discourse of both parties is primarily moral, including assertions of one's own virtue and attacks on the moral character of the other side.
Nevertheless, legal discourse is also present, particularly in George's statement
about abuses of property and in his complaint-application form which mentions
harassment and threats of violence. George's use of legal discourse is not surprising, considering that he went first to court and only with great difficulty was
persuaded by the clerk to try mediation. Moreover, in their introduction the mediators emphasized the connection between this process and the court rather
than the difference.

Jane frames the problem in a more therapeutic way, blending assessments of
George's character as "childish" with psychological terms such as "low frustration tolerance" and describing his son as "unable to communicate with his
peers." But she relies primarily on moral discourse, blaming George for not
talking to her directly and for retaliating against a child, behavior not suited to
an adult. In her statement that she is home and that she sees things, there is a
subtle dig against working parents. Jane refers to evidence and to legal claims as
well, although largely in response to George. She has written down the text of
the offensive phone call, she observed his taking pictures, presumably for evidence against her, and denies that she damaged his property. Jane's concern
about George's alleged lies reveals her construction of the event as one in which
truth will be uncovered and a decision made. Yet, as the following discussion
indicates, assessing the "truth" of the myriad incidents in the fight is not possi-

ble; each person has his or her own interpretation of what went on. Yet both are concerned about lies. George responds to Jane's statement as follows:

> *You said in the courtroom that I threatened you, and that is a lie. You say I hit your children. I never hit your child, and the baseball was a softball, not a hard ball. I have never laid a hand on your child. I have never thrown an egg. I am not saying my son didn't. For the last two and a half years, your defense has always been that my son flipped you the finger and said "fuck you." He may have, but we have not raised our child to act that way and no one else has complained. And you always say that at every incident. He was only seven, and it is not normal for a boy that age. Maybe he thought he could because your children are ten and twelve and he sees them doing that and saying things like that to you. And he doesn't say it to us, he never talks like that to me. I know he uses discretion. He doesn't use the kind of language in our house that I hear coming from your house.*

Here the conversation shifts to respectability, encoded in language use. This is an argument about reputation and about the obligations to treat adults with respect. George continues to list his grievances, reading from a long list written on several sheets of lined yellow paper, detailing a series of interactions with the other family. Jane replies: *"This was malicious damage of people. Normal people don't do that. Kids can get together or fight; parents shouldn't fight."* Here she deftly combines legal and moral discourse, referring to the legal charge and then asserting a general moral principle about the way adults should deal with children's conflicts. George seeks again to defend his reputation, pointing out that he does not have problems with his other neighbors and that he has lived all over the world, has got along with people and has worked with those he does not like. He counters her claim that both he and his wife work for lust of money by saying that they cannot afford not to, that they need to make payments on their house, which they bought recently rather than long ago, when Jane bought hers. The argument continues over who did what to whom, intermingled with challenges to one another's reputations. George's wife, Betsy, asks Jane if she is on welfare, and Jane says no, that she is hurt by the question. Betsy says her son has no friends because Jane's sons chase them all away.

Jane says that her kids do use profanity but that she does not think a grown man should become involved. The complaint in court was annoying phone calls, but George called Bobby and said (she reads): "You fucking asshole, I will break your neck." George denies the first part of the sentence but acknowledges the threat to break Bobby's neck. Betsy adds that that day they got fifteen phone calls, including death threats and the threat that Bobby had a knife. Jane retorts that her children do not have knives and that George can get a search warrant and see. After both sides insist that they want only peace, they discuss the fact that both call the police all the time and that it was the police who told George to go to court. When the mediators ask George what he really wants, he replies: "*I don't want to put anyone in reform school, I just want peace, to be left alone.*" The mediators respond that it is up to the families to resolve this problem—no one else will—and urge them to return for another session with the boys.

In a private meeting with the mediators later in this mediation session, George says that he thinks Bobby is disturbed because the boy does not have a father. He admits chasing Bobby down the street but says he did not catch him. But he thinks Bobby wants to pursue the conflict. He says that Bobby says that he wants George to hit him so that he can sue him.

Despite the predominance of moral discourse in this discussion, the legal is not far away. Both sides sometimes raise a legal defense or present more formal kinds of evidence when it appears advantageous to them. Jane offers to have her house legally searched for knives. Bobby threatens to sue George. George has obviously been thinking of reform school for Bobby. The discussion of lies suggests that they interpret this forum as one dedicated to uncovering "truth." There is also some therapeutic talk: George sees the possibility that Bobby is disturbed by the divorce.

The discussion is a contest over the meaning of events and the character of the participants. These are in fact the same debate, since actions are evaluated in the light of the persons who did them. For example, Jane claims that George's retaliation against Bobby is achieving peace inappropriate for an adult. In her effort to make sense of George's actions, she labels him a child and a psychologically disabled person ("low frustration tolerance"), employing diminishing labels from two different discourses. Both sides in this conflict are willing to accept some responsibility for the problems; what appears to be at stake for both is achieving peace and retaining a positive image of themselves in their interpretation of the conflict. Legal discourse and therapeutic discourse are employed as subsidiary tools to support the image of the self created within moral discourse.

At the second mediation session, the mediators have a long discussion with the boys—both alone, without parents, and with the parents. This discussion is couched entirely in moral discourse. The boys agree to talk to each other about their differences. When the mediators bring George and Betsy in for a private discussion, George complains that he cannot accept either the children's agreement to talk to each other or Jane's proposal that she will talk only to his wife—not to him—an arrangement which excludes him from communicating with the other family. "*I couldn't go along with that. It concerns our property—and damage to it.*" The mediators counter that the boys have made this agreement themselves and emphasize that the boys want to be friends. The end of the discussion concerns how parents should act, what they should do if their children have conflicts, and so forth. The final agreement reads:

> 1. The parents, expressing full confidence in the ability of their sons to solve their own problems, agree to allow them to resolve their differences.

2. The three boys [including Bobby's older brother] will feel free to talk with one another over any problem that may arise.

3. All agree that there will be no further harassment.

4. Jane and Betsy will feel free to discuss any future problems on a one-to-one basis should the need arise. All three parents will encourage friendly terms.

The mediators call all the parties back into the room, and each signs the document, with the mediators signing as witnesses. The mediators tell the parties that the mediation office will monitor the agreement by calling each person at two weeks, two months, and three months. At the beginning of the session, one of the mediators had described the agreement as an "official document." Now she reminds them: "*Boys, remember: responsibility lies on your shoulders. It is now up to you to show your parents you stick by your word.*" This session lasted three hours. The one the week before had lasted two hours.

Comparing the initial complaint application and the final agreement reveals a shift in the discourse from the legal to the moral. The mediators favor moral discourse and discourage legal discourse. Despite their initial framing of the mediation session as a legal setting, by reference to both the "oath of confidentiality" from the court and the support of the court, the mediators endeavor to stick to a moral discourse, resisting both the legalistic arguments and the psychological characterizations of the parties. Several times George, in particular, shifted to a legal discourse and presented "legal" evidence. Each time, he was encouraged to think in terms of friendship, neighborly obligation, and the responsibilities of parents; his documents and pictures were ignored. The agreement itself is couched in moral discourse, indicating that, by the end, this discourse dominated the framing of the problem.

All three discourses exist in the repertoires of these people, and they shift rather easily from one to the other. There are some individual differences, however. George is quicker to turn to legal discourse, Jane to therapeutic. George thinks in terms of a fundamental right to the protection of his property, while Jane is more inclined to use psychological labels. It seems likely that, in the course of dealing with her older son's emotional problems, Jane has encountered counselors who have taught her how to use and frame issues in therapeutic discourse. There may be gender differences in preferred discourse; I have the impression that women prefer therapeutic discourse, men legal discourse.

A Boyfriend and Girlfriend

A second conflict concerned a young woman who went to court for protection against a young man who lived next door and who had fallen in love with her. The plaintiff had considerable experience in court, and the defendant was also well known to court officials. Again, there appears to be a subtle class difference between them, with the boy being of slightly lower social class. Yet both these people fall into the category of hard-living people. Neither owns a home. They are more concerned about protecting themselves from violence than about respectability. I interviewed the plaintiff in her home and observed the mediation session and clerk's hearing, and I also talked to the plaintiff informally at some length.

As is characteristic with marital and boyfriend/girlfriend problems, the discussion takes place largely in moral discourse, sometimes moving into therapeutic talk. However, the plaintiff's initial request for help was framed in legal discourse: a request for protection from an angry and violent ex-boyfriend. She allows the mediators to shift the discussion to moral discourse, but when the mediation agreement fails to provide her the protection she seeks, she returns to court, more assertively demanding protection. In her second experience in court, a hearing before the clerk, she is more insistent about maintaining legal discourse, detailing the incidents of violence she has suffered. The clerk persists, however, in framing the problem in moral discourse, concluding with a lecture on how she should behave.

Mediators and clerks generally attempt to delegalize the discourse of people who are trying to invoke the power of the court to protect themselves and their property. As they derail legal discourse and reject cases, clerks and prosecutors sometimes offer advice—as they do here—about how the case could have been framed to generate legal action. Thus, in justifying inaction, clerks and prosecutors provide the tools for future legal action. The court officials teach plaintiffs legal discourse. In this case, the clerk provides fairly explicit instructions to the plaintiff about how to present her problem legally: she needs to provide specifics of date, time, and place, to file soon after a particular incident; and to focus only on a particular event rather than on a general pattern. Thus, paradoxically, at the same time as these forums derail legal discourse, they offer instructions in how to use it to build a more persuasive case.

The plaintiff, Bridget Jones, lived on Green Street, the worst street in Salem, a dim row of four-story brick tenements built in the nineteenth century by mill owners to house their recently immigrated mill workers. At twenty-eight years old, she was a heavy woman with curly brown hair who looked older than her age. My impression was of a strong woman with warmth, vivacity, and a sense of caring. Bridget came to the court about a problem with a young man, Billy, who was in love with her and who called her and harassed her all the time. Billy was seventeen years old, a slight, short boy with a meek expression who sat through the mediation session slumped over and silent. He seemed very sad. He refused to be interviewed afterwards, but I talked to Bridget for about two hours in her apartment and again when her case returned to court. She seemed very self-confident, he apologetic but angry.

Bridget and Billy lived next door to one another on Green Street for about two years. Bridget moved away from Green Street for a few months, but after the mediation session she moved back to Green Street. While they lived next door, Billy began to babysit for Bridget's three children, aged five, seven, and ten years and to spend a lot of time at her house, talking to her and playing with her as well as with the children. She was separated from her husband at the time and confided her problems to Billy. However, then Billy wrote her a love note and she told him that the relationship was off. He began to harass her, attack her, pull her hair, lie in front of her car to prevent her driving away, and call her at work all the time. He threatened to kill himself by jumping off the roof if she did not change her mind. He sometimes sat in her car and waited for her, and once she had to call the police to get him out of her car. This situation lasted about a year. Bridget said that she had threatened many times to go to court if he did not stop harassing her, and she had finally filed a complaint with the clerk, charging him with harassment. Billy was very surprised and hurt that she had.

Billy lived with six or seven brothers and sisters and with a mother who was often absent for weeks at a time. When I talked to her at her house, Bridget told me that Billy was often left to take care of the younger children, including one who is seven years old and one who is ten years old. She said:

> It was really kind of sad. He would spend all day cleaning up the apartment when his mother was coming home, and she would just come in and not notice it at all or say anything. He would do the same thing for me, clean my apartment from top to bottom. Once the little boy, the seven-year-old, and another boy set a mattress on fire, and fortunately Billy came home in time to call the fire department. But they are too young to be left alone without any one to watch them. I guess that Billy or his older brother provides food for them.

When she kept calling the police about her troubles with Billy, the police urged her to take out a restraining order against him (for which she was not eligible, since they did not live in the same apartment). She thought that they were eager for her to take him to court because they thought he was a troublemaker. On the basis of my observations of similar cases, however, I suspect that the police also grew tired of responding to her calls.

At the time of this mediation session, Bridget was working as kitchen help in a local school and Billy was working in a temporary job in the post office. He had dropped out of high school. Bridget also worked off and on in a local bar. Both lived in rented apartments.

The mediation session lasted seventy minutes. The mediation staff member who did the intake told the two mediators that this was a problem of a young boy with an attachment to a married woman and that their role was to tell the boy that he had to end the relationship and stop harassing her. Thus, the problem was initially framed in moral discourse by the mediation program. Bridget's initial statement also presented the problem in moral discourse, adding a reference to his need for help:

> The problem is that he won't leave me alone. He is calling at work, bothering me all the time. This is really aggravating me, and it has just got to stop. He calls me out of work down the hall to the phone

several times a day. It is making me sick and getting me so aggra-
vated. It has been going on for two years now. And furthermore, I was
at a friend's house cooking dinner one day and he sent me a letter
saying that he would kill himself if I didn't leave the house. It was a
male friend. He is very jealous of my male friends and gets very upset
if I ever talk to them. I live in the next town now, but when my husband
and I were separated, I lived near Billy. He would bother me then. His
sister used to babysit for my children, and I got to know him then. He
would come over and play with my children. He needs someone to
care about him and listen to him, and I always did that; I was always
there for him. I helped him in his relationship with his girlfriend. I did
this when I lived near him; but now I have moved to the next town, and
this continues. He calls me when I am at the club [a local bar], *he calls*
my male friends there, and he called one a black bastard. He gets very
upset about all my male friends.

When the mediators ask Billy for his side, he responds only: "I have nothing to say." In the private discussion with the mediators, Billy says only that he has his reasons for harassing her, that she had hurt him very much, but that he will not talk about it. When they asked Billy whether he knows why she does not want to see him any more, he replies: "*I don't know. I guess I am harassing her. She says so, so it must be true. And besides, she took me to court, didn't she?*" Here and later he seems very angry that she has taken him to court. He called her several times at work the morning of the mediation session, to complain to her about it. Invoking the court seems a drastic step to him. When the mediators ask him whether he could treat her like a total stranger, he replies: "*It would be hard, but I could do it. And I have to, because, if I don't, she will take me to court. But I could take her to court too. I could charge her with statutory rape.*" With this comment, Billy shifts from moral to legal discourse, indicating that he has some power within this discourse, although it seems that he does not want to use it. The mediators do not pursue this possibility.

When the mediators ask Billy what he would like to see in the agreement, he replies that he would like her not to come to his neighborhood at all. The mediators demur that this is not fair, she has friends there she wants to visit. He responds that then there is nothing that he wants, refusing to enter into the conversation any more. When the mediators urge him to make another demand, claiming that this is not a one-way street but an agreement for both of them, he replies: "*But she always has a one-way street, and the complaint is against me.*" The mediators attempt to draw him out by asking him about his job, his friends, and his social life. They never return to the charge of statutory rape. Thus, they steer away from legal discourse and encourage Billy to think in terms of relationships. He resists, persisting with legal discourse. He sees the situation as a legal charge against him and threatens another legal charge in retaliation.

In her private discussion with the mediators, Bridget moves into moral and therapeutic discourse rather than into legal discourse. She says she thinks Billy needs counseling. He has refused, saying that he is not crazy. In her description of Billy's mother, she continues to talk in these terms:

> *Billy complains that his mother is never home. She leaves for weeks at a time and leaves him to take care of the children, and there are a lot of children he is responsible for. His older brothers beat him up. He breaks out all of the windows in his bedroom, which are now covered with boards. When I go to my girlfriend's house near his house, he sees me; and then the police always get involved. He knows I go out with my friends on Friday and Saturday nights, and he always waits for me. I want him to stay away from me. He seems to be in shock, ever since I filed these charges against him. I don't think he thought I would really do it.*

The mediators work out an agreement in both moral and legal discourse. Bridget agrees to drop charges of harassment against Billy, providing that he stops trying to see her or talk to her. Both agree to treat one another as total strangers should they accidentally see one another. The third clause reads: "Billy realizes that Mrs. Jones will immediately reactivate her charge of harassment and pursue it in court if there is the slightest breakdown in the agreement." The mediators inform Bridget and Billy, as they sign the official-looking document with a court logo at the top, that one copy will be given to the clerk and that another copy will stay with the program but that there will be no record of criminal charges.

Six months later Billy comes into the mediation office to say that Bridget is still bothering him. The mediation program writes to Bridget, who has moved back to Billy's neighborhood, and she comes into the office to say that he is still harassing her, calling her five times a night in the bar where she now works, and that she has filed a complaint against him in court. The charge is harassment and assault and battery with a knife and rocks. The written complaint-application form reads as follows: "This kid refuses to leave me alone on a constant basis. He constantly harasses me and my children with his threats. If I don't talk to him he gets *very* violent and starts to cause trouble. All I want is this kid to leave me alone. Mediation did not work. Everybody on Green Street knows everything he does to me." In the blank for date, she wrote: "Everyday." In contrast to the mediation session, in which she spoke of Billy as a "super person" who used to be a friend, in this application form the problem is phrased entirely in legal discourse.

The clerk-magistrate holds a forty-minute hearing to determine whether a complaint should be issued. Billy fails to appear, although he has been summoned by the court. The first thirty minutes of this hearing are conducted largely in legal discourse. The clerk emphasizes why this is not a legal case, but he provides substantial instruction about how it could be presented as one. He tells Bridget she needs to provide specific dates, times, and incidents, not a general pattern of harassment. He assures Bridget that if anything else happens she should come right into court with the specifics but tells her that, as it now is, he can do nothing. Harassment is not a crime. Making threats is, however, and when the clerk asks whether Billy has ever threatened her, she brightens up and says: "Yes, all the time." But he threatens not that he will hurt her but that he will call the Children's Protective Services about how she mistreats her children. The clerk says that is not a threat. As she tells him more about her problems and about Billy's violence against her, he seems more sympathetic but still says that he must have a better legal case in order to do anything: "There is not much to go on here." She describes assaults with rocks and a knife, but he asks her if she has medical records: "*Dates are very important. Do you know when these incidents happened? If this goes upstairs* [i.e., to the judge], *and the district attorney asks you for specific dates and you can't provide them, you will lose the case.*" The clerk advises her to call the police, but Bridget points out that the police have stopped coming. She insists: "*This has been going on for three years. Something has got to be done.*" She reminds him that she has already tried mediation. When the clerk refuses to issue the complaint, she keeps repeating: "*Does that mean nothing can be done? That he can just get away with this?*" As she insists on her legal right to protection, the clerk takes a new tack, moving away from legal to moral discourse: "*But this is also your fault, in a way. You have let this go on and on. You should have done something sooner. Now it doesn't look so convincing. And the incident you mention* [which precipitated her complaint application and the mediation session] *was too long ago; it is now seven months ago. The judge will say: 'Why didn't you do something sooner?' If he touches you again, come right down.*" Bridget sighs and looks disgusted. Her friend, who came with her to the hearing, says: "*Bridget, they have to do this legally, you know.*" The clerk concludes, in a final decisive shift to moral discourse: "*I advise you to stay away from that bar. Get some beer and go home and drink it. It is better for your kids, anyway. If there is any more trouble, just come in and I will issue a complaint. You let too much time go by.*" After Bridget leaves the hearing, the clerk confides to me that she is the type who goes to bars and drinks; that, although he has not seen Bridget before this day, he knows the friend who came with her, who is "no prize either"; and he knows the bars they drink in. He also knows the neighborhood they come from, which is a bad one, and knows that the police will not do anything there. He has seen Billy in and out of juvenile court many times and is sure that he will go to jail sooner or later. Billy's older brother is already in trouble with the law. Thus, although the clerk responded to Bridget in legal discourse, he considered the situation in moral terms as well. He adds, in justifying his decision to me: "*This is a serious case; it is assault and battery with a dangerous weapon; but without any dates or evidence, they will throw it out upstairs.*" Although legally serious, the evidence is weak. Six months later, he told me that he never heard from her again.

In the mediation session, Bridget initially phrased her problem in legal discourse but during the discussion, shifted somewhat to moral and therapeutic discourse, guided by the mediators. At the end, she said she was interested in help for Billy rather than in legal sanctions. When she went back to court, however, she insisted on legal discourse, demanding protection rather than help. However, the clerk refused—just as the mediators did—to accept her legal framing of the problem. He turned down the application for a complaint, then shifted to moral discourse, and ended by offering advice. In the process, he provided considerable instruction in legal discourse, telling her how to present the problem if she wants the court to do something about it next time.

Neighbors and Strangers

The third case contrasts with the previous two since it involves neighbors who are strangers. Here the problem is framed more unambiguously in legal discourse. After trying unsuccessfully to settle it in these terms, the mediators move to moral discourse. When they are unable to persuade the parties to abandon their legal framework, they pull in therapeutic discourse, along with appeals to the defendants' sense of themselves as educated people ("You are college students, . . ."). This tactic finally succeeds in moving them into moral discourse, as the final statement by one of the young men indicates. The move to moral discourse is aided by the departure of the two particularly adamant defendants, however. These young men were particularly resistant to the mediator's efforts to shift away from legal discourse. In general, my observations suggest that women are more likely to shift away from legal discourse than are men. Furthermore, when the situation involves a more intense and emotional relationship, it is more amenable to the shift to moral discourse.

In this case, a man named Fred filed a complaint about noise, against three young men living in the apartment above him in a building located on a busy main street in Salem. The three young men, all students at a local college, had moved out of the dorm into this apartment. Fred, an older man who worked as a machinist in a factory, lived in the apartment with his wife and, from time to time, a daughter from a previous marriage. He wanted quiet; the students claimed that they were fairly quiet, particularly in comparison with the dorm. Neither side had ever spoken to the other before; the young men said that, until they read the same name on the mailbox, they did not even recognize the name on the court summons they received. Fred charged them with disturbing the peace. The court clerk referred the case to mediation, describing it as a "student problem."

At the mediation session, all the parties began by describing the problem as one of noise and disturbance, framing it in legal terms. Fred says that he wants to put an end to the noise and disturbance above his apartment, particularly on Sunday and Monday nights. The young men retort that they study at the library those nights. Fred responds: "If you don't want to settle, we can take this downtown [to the court]." He points out that he complains to the landlord all the time about the noise but that it does no good. One of the young men observes that the building is old, that the walls are paper thin, and that they are paying $500/month rent and have the right to make some noise. Another continues: *"We pay a lot of money for this apartment. We don't want to think about you whenever we walk anywhere. And we don't have loud parties; we are restrained, not like in the dorms. There it was loud."* Fred replies: *"You have to live differently in an apartment."* Here the discussion shifts slightly to normative standards of quiet in different places. The young men quickly change the discussion to a complaint about Fred's failure to talk to them directly before going to court with the complaint. They assert that no one else has complained and deny again that they have parties or that they ever have more than ten people in the apartment. Fred counters that their living room is over his bedroom and that it sounds like a basketball is being bounced over his head. One young man responds: *"We can't be conscious of every footstep."* Fred falls back on his own reputation, pointing out that no one has complained about him and that he has lived in the apartment for two and a half years. One young man, tall, heavy, and assertive, says he cannot change his habits of walking. All three students claim that the problem is Fred's, not theirs: they have been doing nothing out of the ordinary.

Here, the discourse is largely in terms of competing rights and evidence concerning infractions of these rights by the plaintiff and the defendants. In order to move the discussion away from this stalemate, the mediators emphasize to both sides that this is a difference in life-style and in ideas about quiet and that they need to understand each other. Privately, the mediators decide that Fred is "very strait-laced," "kind of an oddball," and that the defendants are just boys, some of them big, who cannot really be quiet.

In the private discussion with Fred, the mediators ask for his demands and point out that what one person thinks is quiet may differ from what another person thinks is quiet. The mediator goes on: *"They are big people. They can't really help the noise. They may think they are being quiet."* In the private discussion with the boys, the mediators again point out that the parties have different ideas of quiet and ask what the boys have to say, commenting that it does not sound as if they have been particularly rowdy. The mediators offer several concrete suggestions for masking the sound, such as putting rubber coasters on the TV or changing the room they use as the living room. The students continue to deny that they slam doors or make noise. They ask what will happen if they refuse to sign. The mediators say that the case will go to court, and the boys quickly ask how the mediators evaluate the strength of their case. The mediators refuse to reply, saying that they do not judge. They suggest an agreement that says that the boys will continue to be considerate and will be careful on Sunday and Monday nights. The students resist signing anything that makes changes in their way of life. One continues: *"I don't feel I should sign to do anything that I am already doing. I might be loud sometimes. I don't want my signature on that. I don't care about going to court. I don't mind. There is so much traffic noise there anyway. I am going to settle this by moving out. And what will he give?"* The mediators continue to reframe the problem in moral discourse, suggesting: *"Maybe there is another way. Maybe you could sign that you are a little more aware that there is a problem and that you will continue to be considerate. You could say you are more aware of the problem."* One of the young men objects: *"If we sign that, we are admitting we have done wrong. Now we are aware of his problem, but we don't need to sign it. I will sign only that I have been considerate and now am aware of the problem so I will continue to be considerate."* Another continues: *"I won't change my life-style. I won't be quiet at 9 P.M. Movies may go on until 1 A.M."* The mediator shifts to therapeutic discourse: *"But he wants to feel that you are taking his feelings into consideration. You study psychology* [in college], *you know he wants to feel he has some response from you."* This effort is to no avail. The men reply that they want to go to court: *"We need somebody with authority to hear this. If he brings us to court, he is harassing us. I will file harassment charges against him. Let's go!"* The mediator makes one more attempt: *"You are all getting madder and harder in your positions. He has agreed to this. You didn't know about the problem; now you do."*

Two of the young men now have to leave for work, and the third stays to negotiate for them. The mediator presses moral discourse further: *"If he comes to you and says it is too loud, you will know. You would then know his definition of unreasonableness. You could put things down quietly. You are dealing with a person who seems meticulous. But it takes all kinds to make a world. You have a little different kind here. If it were me—I am deaf in one ear—I wouldn't notice. But you could try to be a little more quiet. Is there anything you could sign that wouldn't mean changing your life-style but give him some control?"* The other mediator returns to therapeutic discourse: *"You study psychology. It is an attitude. It may be that he will only be happy if you take your shoes off at the door and whisper. You can't do anything then. But maybe if he feels he can have some say, he will feel better. To go to court may not get you any further."* After some further persuasion, the young man goes along with the shift in discourse: *"So it is a consideration thing, not what my friend was saying, that this is a matter of law; and in that regard, we don't have to be quiet. But this is a moral thing; I can see that. He is a different sort—and nothing against him for that."* This young man finally goes along with an agreement which says that he and his roommates are now aware of a problem of noise which bothers the plaintiff and that they will continue to be considerate of him and of the other tenants of the building. Further, the man living below agrees to contact them directly if there are any further problems and to let them know the nature of the disturbance. In persuading Fred to accept the agreement, the mediators again turn to moral and therapeutic discourse rather than to legal discourse: *"They feel that they have been careful. But now they are aware of the problem, and they weren't before. They thought the problem was their shouting up for the key. Now you can call them and tell them when you are bothered. This is really a difference in life-styles. Part of it is a misunderstanding. They didn't realize this. You never went directly to them. Now you are a human being to them. The problem is communication."* In sum, the mediators successfully shifted the discourse from a legal one, including references to rights and the authority of the court, to a moral one of consideration. The shift was aided by a few strategic references to therapeutic discourse, to understanding how the other person feels, and to implications that Fred has some psychological weakness. Comparing the initial complaint with the agreement reveals the shift in discourse, a shift which moves the plaintiff away from pursuing his grievance in court. Each side was eager to portray itself as reasonable, but each was also anxious to defend its rights. In this case, with no previous relationship to build on, the shift away from legal discourse to moral and therapeutic ones was more difficult; the mediators accomplished the shift by references to a shared moral discourse of consideration and tolerance and by psychologically diminishing the plaintiff, subtly, in order to evoke sympathy from the young men.

These discourse shifts occur as mediators and court officials try to figure out what to do with these problems. Like the respectable working-class people of Hilltowne, Oldtowne, and Riverdale, they share the feeling that bringing personal problems to court is embarrassing and humiliating. Indeed, mediators, court clerks, and sometimes judges often come from similar social backgrounds. Most are interested in providing some satisfaction, some justice for the people who bring these problems to court, and they recognize the difficulty the court faces in providing what these people are seeking. They see the problems and the pain, and they want to help. As they redefine these problems as unworthy of court attention and shift them into the discourse of morality or help instead of law, they provide help in ways which are consonant both with the capacity of the legal system as they understand it and with their own sociocultural background. They face a dilemma created by the law's offer of more help and greater protection of rights than the courts can or will deliver to ordinary citizens.

The Power of Naming

In these interactions in mediation and court, events, actions, and situations are named. The event is delineated within one or another discourse—in a sense, it is labeled, identified. Naming takes place within one of these three discourses, as the conversation circles around naming a teenager as an "acting-out adolescent," "an irresponsible kid," or a "criminal" or naming the attentions of a young boy to an older woman as "harassment," "love," or an indication that he needs help. Framing and interpreting produce different renderings and different solutions.

Naming can be considered a face of domination, a way in which power is exerted in the relations between third parties and disputants and among the disputants themselves. There is domination both in the labeling and in the consequences which flow from that labeling. The struggle to name, to establish a reigning discourse, involves all the participants in the discussions, although they have unequal resources and authority.

The pattern of defusing legal claims and shifting to moral and therapeutic discourse, of naming the problem in this framework, is common in mediation sessions, in clerk's hearings, in pretrial negotiations, and, as the next chapter shows, in trials of interpersonal cases. Indeed, this is seen by many proponents as the objective of mediation. It is advocated as a process which takes problems concerned with interpersonal dynamics, problems defined as "inappropriate" to court, and places them in a more "appropriate" process, one attentive to feelings and relationships. The language of appropriate and inappropriate is, I think, a way of talking about the discourse shift I observed—but is a way of talking about it in different terms.

Yet, ironically, in mediation this discourse shift takes place under the authority of the court and at the urging of mediators who appear to the parties to represent the court. The court mediation program in particular is defined in many subtle ways as an official, "legal" process. Mediators introduce themselves as people who work with the court and who receive an oath of confidentiality from the judge. The letters of invitation to try mediation arrive on court stationary. The mediation office is located in the courthouse, and the cases are referred by clerks, prosecutors, and judges. Sometimes mediators tell the parties that the agreements will be placed on file in the court; most mediators tell the parties that the agreement will be kept on file by the mediation program (located, as they know from the intake interview, in the courthouse itself) and that the agreement will be monitored (whatever that means to the parties) by the program staff for ninety days (a time period commonly specified by the court as well). People often agree to try mediation in the hope that it will persuade the judge of their good will and thereby strengthen their case if the agreement fails and they decide to go back to court. Half of the sixty-eight people interviewed after their mediation sessions in this program did not think they had a choice about going to mediation. Nineteen percent thought the agreement was legally binding, while 13 percent were not sure whether it was. Two-thirds said they thought it was not. The other two mediation programs I studied, although less intimately connected to the courts, also work closely with them, take cases sent by the court, and return these cases to the court if the parties fail to settle. A substantial proportion of the clients, although fewer than in the court mediation program, see the process as intimately connected to the legal authority of the court.[16]

Discussions in mediation often concern the seriousness of signing an "official" document. Mediators point out, as they did in the first case recounted in this chapter, that signing the agreement is a significant step, not to be taken lightly. Vague references to filing these agreements with the clerk, with the court, or with the mediation program encourage disputants to think of these documents as being in some way legal and official. Parties express considerable uncertainty about the kind and nature of authority that mediators exercise.

Clerk's hearings are even more clearly "official," in this sense, being held in the courthouse and dedicated to determining whether the complaint should issue. They effect a similar shift in discourse, also under the aegis of the court. Furthermore, both mediators and clerks are typically more educated, more affluent, and higher in social class than are the parties. Their words and advice carry with them the added weight conveyed by education and class in American culture.

Thus, within settings defined as connected to the symbolic authority of the court, plaintiffs are routinely told that their problems are not legal but moral or therapeutic, that they concern only social relationships and the obligations inherent in these relationships. Sometimes they concern the need of "dysfunctional" families or "acting-out teenagers" to get help from professionals. Plaintiffs find that their problems are "officially" delegalized, defined as unsuited for legal solutions. Through this process, working-class plaintiffs are discouraged from using the court for their personal problems.

Paradoxically, as ordinary people's legal claims are defused, they are given further instruction in legal discourse and in how to think about and present their problems in legal and therapeutic terms. Clerks tell them what they should have done; mediators define by implication what a "real" legal case would look like. As the previous chapters have shown, these people are primarily women and working-class people. In marital cases it is abused women, in neighborhood cases it is small homeowners, and in parent/child cases it is often single mothers working full-time trying to forge a respectable life for their children—it is these people who are discouraged from using the court for help by having their problems redefined as moral rather than as legal. Some plaintiffs, of course, are people who thrive on fighting and who relish the opportunity to take every possible insult or slight to court. Although plaintiffs endeavor to present the situation as a legal case, the court staff treats it as legally unworthy and names it as a moral problem. Once so defined, it is subject to advice, moral suasion, and therapeutic treatment.

The power of naming is a particular kind of power, different from coercive power or violence. It is a very subtle form of power (see Kapferer 1976). In mediation and lower courts, it is a power of revealing lives and of offering meaning and coherence to these lives. In mediation sessions, naming takes place in a conciliatory, participatory, and informal setting. Differences in class, education, and institutional authority all speak to this form of power as they are read by the parties through modes of speaking, dress, sense of command, and unequal revelation of the self. Similarly, in their work on vocabularies of motive that are used by divorce lawyers and their clients, Sarat and Felstiner describe the powerful processes by which lawyers make sense of and name the actions of the players in the divorce (1988).[17] This is an implicit, largely unrecognized realm of power. It is less the categories themselves, however, than the discourses in which they are embedded which constitute subtle processes of cultural domination.

7

Legal Experience and Legal Consciousness

As they spend time in court, plaintiffs discover that the courts do not take their family and neighborhood problems very seriously. The courts are not eager to handle these problems, nor do they regard them as real legal cases. Plaintiffs find that penalties are rare for the people who have injured them. Nor is there much sympathy for their plight. Instead, plaintiffs are told that these are moral problems unworthy of legal attention, that they are themselves at fault to some extent, and that they need moral advice or counseling rather than the intervention of the law.

If they do succeed in pulling their problems into the legal arena, however, plaintiffs discover that it is difficult to keep control over them and that they must struggle further to determine how their problems will proceed and be defined. This chapter describes the experiences of people in court and the ways they come to use and ultimately to resist the court's construction and management of their situation.

Experience in Court

Many plaintiffs complain that the court is rushed, that the judge is bored, that their individuality is lost. They find the experience in court to be frustrating and humiliating and that their cases are handled in a hurried and impersonal way. When a plaintiff's legal claim is rejected or sloughed off, the message is that both he and his problem are unworthy. One woman said, for example: *"The judge has seen fifty cases like this, and he sees me just as a statistic."* Another plaintiff complained: *"The court is too busy. It deals with important legal problems. I should not take my case there, and I know it doesn't belong there, but there is no place else to go."* As a third plaintiff put it, *"at the court, they have serious problems to handle. Mine is not important to them, but I didn't know what else to do."* A fourth said: *"My case is just a trivial problem to them; they have heard lots like it."*

In the neighborhood problem between the Smiths and the Browns, described in Chapter 3, Mrs. Smith was very bitter about the court's failure to do anything about her charge of assault against Mrs. Brown. She told me: *"I don't believe in law or judges or courts any more. I was raised to believe in them, but I am not going to raise my daughter that way. They are just geared to helping who they want and they didn't do anything to help me. They couldn't stop those people from driving me out of my house.*" The same lenient court also failed to act on Mrs. Brown's complaint of threats against Mrs. Smith, of course.

Another woman took a neighbor in a public housing project to court because the neighbor's daughter attacked her son. She charged the daughter with an attempt to strangle her son. Three times she made the long trip to the courthouse, paying for a taxi each time. The first two times the defendant failed to appear. The complaint was then issued. The plaintiff returned a third time for the arraignment, when the defendant finally appeared and the case was referred to mediation. After these experiences, the plaintiff said of the court (to me): "*I didn't like the court because they didn't talk to me—they were too busy. I just had to stand there and wait. The judge seemed OK, reasonably fair, but I didn't talk to him at all. The court is too busy dealing with important legal problems, and I shouldn't really have taken my case there, but there was no place else to go. I know it doesn't belong there. I did go to the manager of the project first, but I got nowhere.*"

The landlord described in Chapter 5, who was trying to persuade his ex-girlfriend to move out of his house, commented to me: "*For the court this is a small problem, but to me it is a big problem.*" A small landlord, struggling to make a living with a few rundown apartments, was angry because his tenant had moved out without giving him a month's notice and because his request for the full month's rent for the time when the apartment stood vacant was denied by the small-claims court on the grounds that he had made no effort to rent the apartment during that month. His comment to me made a veiled threat of violence as an alternative to law: "*I used to think there is justice in court, but not now. People are not going to court today—there is no justice. People are going to start taking things into their own hands.*" This theme of law as the alternative to violence, albeit a preferred alternative, appears often as these court users talk about using the law.

Although the people who bring their problems to court express anger and frustration with the court, they do not conclude that the court is illegitimate but that the court considers them and their problems unworthy of help. The experience is a challenge less to the legitimacy of the legal system than to their sense of entitlement.

Returning to Court

Some give up and do not return, while others decide to try again. Many return to court with the next problem because they have nowhere else to go. And, with experience, they are armed with greater sophistication about how the courts work, how to phrase complaints, and what to ask for.[1] They have learned some legal discourse: what charges are effective, what constitutes evidence, and what arguments are persuasive. They demand medical expenses rather than revenge, describe incidents occurring at a particular time and place even when the experience is ongoing and diffuse. The history of the conflict and the flawed character of the other person are less persuasive than are written notes of insults that the person hurled as he drove past or pictures of tire marks on the lawn. Medical bills, documents, and pictures appear as evidence.

In other kinds of legal cases, lawyers help their clients construct a case, advising them how to turn an emotional problem into a case.[2] In interpersonal cases, however, if the case passes the clerk's hearing, plaintiffs are represented only by a prosecutor, who does not and cannot devote much time to the case. Most are stalled in the clerk's hearing and/or mediation session with no lawyer at all. Women who come seeking restraining orders are also not represented by a lawyer, nor are parents who file CHINS charges against their children.

Although most people who bring interpersonal problems to court do not return soon, a small proportion come back. Some use the court very intensively. They appear in the clerk's office and mediation program over and over again, sometimes filing several complaints about the same problem, sometimes bringing new ones. Although the majority of complaints are not filed by repeat users, a small number of people do use the court frequently. Almost a third of parties with interpersonal cases who came to the Salem court in 1980–81 had appeared in court more than once during that period.[3] Of 220 interpersonal complaint-application forms[4] filed in the clerk's office during 1980–81, 29 percent (64) involved people who had already been in court during 1980 or 1981. In contrast, only 2 percent of the institutional cases (concerning bad checks, welfare, the board of health, or police officer charges) involved people with previous court contact during the preceding two years. Of the sixty-four interpersonal filings by repeat users, 13 percent were cross-complaints and 19 percent were charges filed again on the same incident. A few incidents generated a large proportion of these repeaters.[5] Repeat plaintiffs were evenly divided by gender: eight men, seven women, and one married couple appeared more than once as plaintiffs in either mediation or the clerk's office in 1980–81. These sixteen plaintiffs filed thirty-five applications for complaint. Although repeat plaintiffs were heavy users of the court, they accounted for only 6 percent of the interpersonal complaints in the clerk's office and mediation program.[6]

There is, then, a significant minority of interpersonal cases which involve people who have been to court before. Moreover, there is a tendency for a single situation to generate more than one court filing. These numbers suggest that a few people return again and again with their problems, while the large majority use the court only rarely. A longer time frame would obviously increase the number of repeat users. A cursory examination of several years of mediation records indicated that there were indeed a small number of people who appeared repeatedly in court. When I talked to mediation clients, many described histories of repeated use of both civil and criminal courts. Moreover, there are indications that people learn how to use the courts from the experience of being taken there by someone else. Ten people appeared in court first as defendants and then took someone else to court about a different problem during the two-year period. Only three were first plaintiffs and then defendants.

Individual biographies of mediation clients show that some have had intense involvement with the court. Billy and Bridget, for example, in the case described in Chapter 6, were both familiar with the court. The court clerk knew Billy's family and said that both Billy and his brother had been in and out of juvenile court for years. Bridget said he had been accused of stealing a car. According to the records of the mediation program, Billy's mother had appeared in mediation one or two years earlier as a plaintiff in a quarrel with another neighbor, Judy. Billy's mother accused Judy's ten-year-old son of inciting her younger children (five and eight years old) to fight and to set fire to a mattress. Billy's mother went to court and was referred to mediation.

Bridget also had considerable experience in court. She told me that her husband had twice been a defendant in criminal court as a result of fights with his acquaintances. The charges had all been dismissed or dropped. She once had spat on a police officer as he was putting her into a cruiser, and she had been charged with assault and battery. This case had been continued without a finding. Four years earlier she had got a restraining order from the probate court against her husband for attempting to throw her out of a window. She thought the restraining order had worked very well; the police had come up often to see how things were going and had searched the house for him. When Judy, the neighbor whom Billy's mother took to court over the mattress fire, had hit her over the head with a stick, Bridget had charged her with assault and battery and the case had gone to the judge. According to Bridget, the judge had put the woman on probation for six months. Bridget thinks that Judy was angry because the state was taking her children away because of neglect. While she lived in the Green Street tenement, Bridget's little girl, then three years old, fell off her third-floor porch and got a bad concussion. The railing was very weak, and Bridget had complained about it to the landlord many times. She stopped paying rent and sued the landlord, a notorious slumlord, for $30,000. At the time I talked to her, the case had not yet settled, but she was optimistic because her lawyer told her she had an excellent case.

Another example is the Brown family, described in Chapter 3. They were known to the dog officer, the police, the court clerk, the mediation program staff, and the prosecutor because they had come to court repeatedly in the past. The police chief knew them as complainers but did not want to talk about them. They were familiar faces around the courthouse and the town hall, and nobody wanted to tangle with them. In order to avoid an unpleasant confrontation with them, the judge postponed dismissing the case for several months. When he finally did so, the plaintiffs were not there.

The boyfriend/girlfriend case, between Joe and Mr. Lucrette, mentioned in Chapter 3 also involves parties who gradually became experienced users of the court. Here, an older man, Mr. Lucrette, wanted to keep a young man away from his daughter. The youth, Joe, was very interested in the fourteen-year-old daughter, Lynette. Over a period of three or four years, the father took this young man to court on charges of assault and battery, trespass, and threats to murder. Mr. Lucrette was dissuaded from charging the youth with yet another charge, statutory rape, only because the prosecutor told him it would take two or three years. Since the young man persisted in trying to see the daughter, Mr. Lucrette continued to press the court to keep him away. Stubborn and assertive people such as this plaintiff are noticed in court and sometimes get court officials to respond to their requests, as the description below indicates.

Joe himself was in court frequently for drug and driving charges. He did not take the court very seriously. He agreed in mediation to stay away from the girl but had no intention of following the agreement. One week after the court gave him a suspended sentence contingent on his staying away from her, he was back in front of her house. As mentioned earlier, Joe was a high school dropout, on drugs, and unable to hold a steady job. Mr. Lucrette was a man in his forties who worked as a medical technician and prided himself on the fact that his children had all finished high school.

The following detailed account of the handling of this case when it appeared as a threats-to-murder charge (the third charge) illustrates the effects of Mr. Lucrette's repeated and insistent pressure on the court and the way both of these experienced court users tried to manage the court. It shows their considerable sophistication about how to get a response from the court and demonstrates that they had some success. Court officials, on the other hand, resisted these efforts, following their own sense of a fair outcome and their assessment of the character of both Joe and Mr. Lucrette.

After the first two charges, Joe received probation on condition that he stay away from the girl's house. However, when he again came to the house and had a tussle with Lynette's brother in the street in front of the house, Mr. Lucrette filed a new charge, of threats to murder, on behalf of his son. He filed a separate charge even though this offense could have been considered a violation of the terms of probation because Joe's probation officer, convinced that Mr. Lucrette was just a troublemaker, refused to do anything about this incident or to consider it a violation of probation. The police prosecutor told me that he had signed the complaint reluctantly and only because Lucrette had put such pressure on him. The prosecutor wanted to take the case to trial because Mr. Lucrette had been pressuring him as well to do something about Joe.

At arraignment, the court appointed a defense attorney for Joe. Although this was Joe's third time in court as defendant in the same situation, this was also his third new defense attorney. Thus, the defense attorney was new to an old case well known in the oral traditions of the court. He himself knew little of its history. He knew enough, however, to urge at the pretrial conference that the case be heard before a six-man jury rather than before a judge, to bypass the judge who had heard all the previous cases.

On the day of the trial, Joe appeared with ten friends, all of equally unsavory appearance. Joe's plan was to have each testify that he was elsewhere at the moment of the alleged threats-to-murder incident. Joe had got married and was expecting a baby any minute. He brought his pregnant wife to court as well, planning to use her to prove he had no further interest in Lynette, although he confessed privately to me that he was anxious to see the baby Lynette had borne him six months earlier. He also planned to announce that he was moving to Florida soon. Joe did not want the history of the conflict to come up in the trial, since, without the history, the charge was weak and poorly substantiated. Mr. Lucrette, on the other hand, told me that he wanted the trial to consider the history and context of the present incident, including Joe's failure to abide by previous court decisions. He made a special visit to the prosecutor to explain his view of the situation but did not hire an attorney.

The prosecutor knew that there was an error in the complaint application (the charge was threats to murder, and the description of the incident was that the young man threatened "I'll punch you in the mouth"). He appealed to the judge to have the complaint application amended, to change the charge to "threats to do bodily injury." Joe's court-appointed attorney opposed the change. He argued that the complaint should be dropped because of the error. The judge responded: "Let's consider this in my lobby. We will recess."

He met for 15 minutes in chambers with the prosecutor, the probation officer, the director of the mediation program, and the defense attorney. He also invited me to attend. Only the defense attorney and the judge were ignorant of the long history of the problem. The other participants explained that this was not a single incident of threats but a long, ongoing battle in which the father had brought repeated charges to court and in which the young man had ignored the court's orders. Further, they explained that the father himself was a difficult, unstable person and that there was an element of mutual fault in the case. They pointed out that the two families lived a few blocks apart and that they would have to live together in the same town for the rest of their lives. The judge's reaction was that this case was like the Hatfields and the McCoys, that it was a no-win case: "What can we do?" He compared it to the case of the lawn mower running over the neighbor's feet described in Chapter 4. He wanted to refer the case to mediation, but the mediation director refused since they had already tried to mediate the case a year and a half ago and had reached an agreement which the young man subsequently had broken. The judge consulted the probation files and discovered that the defendant was already on probation for a previous charge of assault in the same situation. The judge concluded: *"This is a tough case, but it is not worth doing time. I will put an extrastringent probation on him, with the condition that he stay away from the house. I will extend it until winter time, in the hope that this will at least get them past the hot time, and maybe when the snow flies, the case will cool down."*

When the prosecutor, an old hand in the court, told the judge that the father was very difficult and was waiting in the courtroom for the outcome, the judge offered to give a stern lecture to the young man to satisfy the father. The defense attorney readily agreed, noting apologetically that he had not known of the history of the dispute. The judge returned to the courtroom and formally announced that the probation was to be extended and made more stringent and that the defendant must stay away from the girl.

Technically, the complaint application was invalid and the amendment procedure was inappropriate. It should have been dismissed, as the defense attorney argued. But the judge made a decision based on his knowledge of the history of the problem, his sense of fairness, and his assessment of the most effective way to manage the situation. He recognized the difficulty of dealing with a stubborn and persistent plaintiff and a resistant defendant.

Both Mr. Lucrette and Joe seemed to be familiar with the way to generate action from the courts. Joe knew that his job, marital status, and promise to move were important and that the history of the conflict stood against him. Mr. Lucrette knew that it was critical to introduce into court information on the boy's persistent and flagrant violation of court orders in the past, as well as evidence about his character.

When Joe violated the terms of even this probation, however, he was given a suspended sentence of ten days in prison. When he violated the terms of the suspended sentence, the court converted the penalty to twenty days in a mental institution, since the court psychiatrist and other court officials felt that Joe was not a real criminal. They categorized Joe as "not a bad kid, but one with problems with sex and drugs." After twenty-four hours in the mental institution, however, he was released. The mental institution claimed that he did not have mental problems.

Thus, despite Joe's repeated violation of court orders and despite the inevitable escalation of punishments he earned, court officials still did not consider him or his actions in this situation as deserving jail time. They subverted the escalating-punishment system in order to avoid sending him to jail. Jail is a penalty within legal discourse, while Joe's behavior had been defined within moral and therapeutic discourse. Although Joe encountered the pattern of threatening to act but postponing the action, he refused to change his behavior under these threats. Consequently, the court was forced to carry them out. At the last minute, however, court officials managed to avoid imposing the threatened penalty of jail, which seemed inappropriate. Here, as in other cases I have described, court officials were guided by a sense that justice was promoted by removing the case from legal discourse despite the plaintiffs' assertions that the problem is legal. However, judges are sometimes forced to return to legal discourse when they have been unable to move a case into other discourses, as occurred in the case with the jealous landlord described in Chapter 5.

The individuals described are not unusual in their return to court, although they do so more often than most. A substantial proportion of the plaintiffs who bring interpersonal problems to court have had previous contact with the courts in some form or another. Among seventy-one plaintiffs interviewed from the first two mediation programs, forty-one (60 percent of those who answered) had had previous experience in court.[7] Among the families in the parent-child mediation program, almost one-third (31 percent) had already had other children involved in CHINS ("Children in Need of Services," the Massachusetts term for status offenders) proceedings. One-third of the youths said that they had friends who had been to court on a delinquency, 12 percent had friends in court on a CHINS, 27 percent had friends in court on both, and only 25 percent knew no one who had been to court. Twenty-five percent of the young people had friends who had been to the same mediation program. In the follow-up interviews, 49 percent of the children, 35 percent of the mothers, and 29 percent of the fathers said that they knew other CHINS children. Five percent of the children themselves had been involved in a previous CHINS charge, and 18 percent had been involved in a delinquency charge. One had been involved with an abuse or neglect hearing. Another study of 150 youths in court for status offenses in New York City reported that 37 percent had had previous court appearances and that 19 percent had had a previous delinquency charge filed against them (Block and Kreger 1982: 39–40).

People who repeatedly use the court usually acquire a reputation for being "court happy" and are shunned. Some of these frequent court users are suspicious of others, afraid that they will become victims, anxious to protect a self which seems vulnerable and subject to oppression, and angry at the way other people treat them. Some are exhilarated by the excitement of battle. The Brown family, clearly experienced in the use of both town government and other official agencies as well as in the use of the courts, had become repeat users for whom the court is a logical and often a reasonable first step in a problem or a complaint. In her study of a mediation program which handles neighborhood cases in suburban Philadelphia, Jennifer Beer observes that there is a rare type of disputant whom she labels as the "difficult" person, the person who refuses to give in and who wishes to continue to fight. "They are often articulate and smart people, but they seem to crave the excitement of a good fight too much to actually end it. A few have been unable to trust anyone; they claw at everyone around them like a cornered cat" (1986: 48). These people tend to have firm and unyielding ideas about what they expect of "good" neighbors, what constitutes "quiet," and how people should be "considerate" (Beer 1986: 49).

Some of these repeat users are socially isolated, lacking informal networks of friends and relatives but heavily dependent on government services and benefits. Whether this situation reflects a progressive alienation from friends and relatives because of court use or the fact that isolated people turn to court because they lack networks of family and friends I do not know. I suspect, however, that court use is a slippery slope which tends to alienate others, leading to an isolation which furthers dependence on the court for future problems. But only a longitudinal study could shed some light on the interaction between social networks and court use over time.

In sum, a small minority of people who go to court with interpersonal problems use it repeatedly and stubbornly, refusing to give up when it seems that the court is not taking their problems seriously as legal cases. These people, with their recurrent appearances and demands, probably contribute to court officials' feeling that interpersonal problems are frivolous, unending, and unsolvable. Yet, through their persistence, these stubborn plaintiffs sometimes receive the help they are looking for.

Awe, Fear, and Play

First-time court users tend to see the court as awesome and fearful. Naive court users often feel scared about appearing in court, afraid of talking, and anxious simply about being in the courthouse. They fear that they or their enemy will be sent to jail. Teenagers brought to juvenile court as status offenders worry about being sent away from home; women bringing their boyfriends or spouses to court fear that the latter will be sent to jail. In juvenile cases, parents often go to court in hopes of scaring their children, and sometimes it works. One mother, for example, reported that her son started coming home on time at night after he learned she was considering taking him to court to force him to do so. Another girl went to school regularly because she was afraid of a residential placement by the court.

But teenagers are infrequently placed outside the home. Judges in status-offender cases bemoan their lack of power to do anything about these cases. Defendants in interpersonal cases are very rarely sent to jail. Court users who return repeatedly with personal problems discover that very little happens. Court becomes a less frightening and less humiliating experience. Experienced repeat users sometimes think of the court as a site for sparring and contest. Some regard its power lightly and flagrantly ignore its orders. One probation officer complained that defendants who have been to court often treat it as a joke.

With experience, the court gradually ceases to be a place for awe and fear, one which imposes harsh penalties with inexorable firmness, and becomes a somewhat pliant, if excruciatingly complex, institution which, with pressure and patience, can sometimes be made to yield help. It comes to seem like a flawed instrument which must be played with skill and finesse. Some plaintiffs come to use the law as an arena for manipulation and play, a place to toy with enemies and to gain strategic successes by pummeling one's opponents with legal charges and summonses, even if no serious penalties are forthcoming. Some come to regard the court as entertainment, as a place to try out dominance games with others and to see what will happen. The following case illustrates the way an experienced court user, here the defendant, ignores the commands of the court, without much consequence to herself.

In this neighborhood case, a teenage girl, Jean (pseudonym) allegedly broke a window in a neighbor's house where another teenage girl, Mary (also pseudonym) lived. Mary accused Jean of breaking the window, a charge leading to several serious fights in school and to Jean's threats that she would attack Mary if she caught the latter without her mother around. Mary came home once or twice covered with bruises. Her mother filed a charge of assault against both Jean's mother and Jean. She wanted protection for her daughter, to feel that her daughter was safe in the afternoons when she had to work.

Jean and her mother ignored the court, however. As I reconstructed the course of events, after the application for complaint was filed the case was referred to mediation and was scheduled for a session. But Jean's mother refused to come. Then the clerk scheduled a hearing to determine whether the complaint should issue, but Jean's mother failed to appear. The plaintiffs, Mary and her mother, came. Faced with a defaulting defendant but not wanting to issue the complaint, the clerk tried to send the problem back to the mediation program or to the diversion program. Diversion sent it back to mediation, which refused to hear the case because Jean's mother had already refused mediation of the problem. Jean's mother said that she had tried mediation for another problem and did not think it worked.

The clerk scheduled a second hearing three weeks hence. Mary and her mother again appeared but Jean and her mother did not. This time the clerk issued the complaint and sent it to the juvenile court for a hearing two weeks hence. When Jean and her mother failed to appear for the juvenile-court hearing (Mary and her mother again came), the judge issued a warrant for Jean's arrest.

A police officer who knew the family told Jean that there was a warrant out on her and that she had better go to the courthouse and look into it. A date was established for an arraignment before the juvenile judge. At the arraignment three weeks later, Jean and her mother did appear and the judge gave them a stern lecture about the seriousness of the charge and the risk that Jean could be sent away to a reform school or to a similar program. Then he referred the matter to mediation, telling Jean and her mother that they had better get together with Mary and her mother and talk to them. Jean and her mother did come to a mediation session, held a week later, where they met with Mary and her mother and reached an agreement. The mothers had not known one another before, since Mary's family had recently moved into the neighborhood. I observed this mediation session.

When the case returned to juvenile court a week later, the judge, rather than dismissing it, continued it for ninety days because the school principal had requested him to keep tabs on the problem. The school feared it would boil up again. The original incidents occurred in April and May, the application for complaint was filed in early July, the mediation session was held at the end of September, and the final juvenile-court session took place in early October.

Mary's family expected the court to provide protection for Mary. Her mother arrived in mediation with a thick sheaf of documents, pictures, and notes about specific incidents and dates. Jean's family, it seems, took court more lightly. After refusing several times to appear, they came in only under considerable pressure. Mary had had no previous legal trouble beyond some truancy. Jean's family had far more experience with court. Her brother had been on probation as a juvenile and was, in early September, in the local jail. Two years earlier her mother and her husband had been defendants in another mediation case, initiated by one of their tenants who charged them with pushing her down the stairs. The family had a reputation, in the court, as being one with problems.

Thus, the more naive court users, Mary's family, took the court more seriously than did the more experienced court users, Jean's family. Indeed, the latter's assessment was more realistic, since the court sought continually to divert the case to nonlegal forums—mediation and diversion–rather than to handle it as a crime. Mary's family framed the problem in legal discourse, but Jean's family seemed fairly confident that the court would consider it only in moral terms and would impose no legal penalties. They had apparently discovered that the court shifts discourses in this way and that, consequently, they did not need to take seriously the charges filed by Mary's family (see Merry 1986).

Malcolm Feeley's description of the handling of regular criminal cases in the lower criminal court in New Haven, Connecticut, similarly indicates that lower courts impose lenient penalties and that the judges feel relatively powerless to do anything (1979). All they can do is ratify decisions made by prosecutors and defense attorneys or impose sentences (1979: 69). One judge asked: "What do you do in these petty cases? They're not serious enough to put a person in jail; yet you want to do something to show society's disapproval. Normally a fine would be appropriate, but so many of these people don't have any money. So we end up giving meaningless conditional discharges or probation, and it becomes something of a joke. It's frustrating; there's little we can do" (1979: 69). Furthermore, in cases in which there is prior acquaintance between the parties, the court is likely not to prosecute at all (1979: 132).

Feeley notes that, for many of the people brought into court, the fear of arrest and conviction is not as great as it is for middle-class people. He observed frequent lack of concern about the stigma of conviction; instead, there was concern about getting out of court. Many of those he studied were experienced court users: at least 50 percent had already been arrested before, and many had been convicted (1979: 200–201). One symptom of their casual attitude was a failure to come to scheduled court appearances. One-third of the defendants in his sample missed one or more of their scheduled court appearances, and one in five never returned despite letters of warning (1979: 224). But the court was casual about those who failed to appear, generally taking no action unless they were arrested again on another charge, at which point the court usually dropped the failure-to-appear charge. For those charged with a minor offense and released on a low bond, failure to appear means that the bond is forfeited and the case is closed. Prosecutors are usually happy when this happens. Feeley's data show that one in every eight or nine cases is not resolved in any way but is left outstanding until the person is rearrested on another charge (1979: 224). He concludes that failure to appear is likely to depend on how well defendants understand the operation of the court, how much respect they have for it, how seriously they take it, how aware they are of their scheduled court appearances, and what they believe will be the consequences if they fail to appear (1979: 232).

If the criminal defendants Feeley describes discover that the court is lenient,[8] it is even more likely that litigants involved in personal problems will learn this as well, since their difficulties are generally regarded as even less serious. Plaintiffs are frustrated that they can get no satisfaction, but defendants are pleased that they have escaped the court. Plaintiffs discover that their rights to protection of property and person are weaker and more erratically enforced than they had expected. They do not necessarily abandon the idea of rights and entitlement, however, but sometimes become more sophisticated and persistent in using the law as a tool in struggles with neighbors, friends, and relatives. Rights come to be opportunities for action, not guarantees of protection.

It is not that the legal system loses legitimacy altogether, since these people did not expect that the courts would be that different from all other institutions, that the courts would treat everyone the same, or that money and education would not matter.[9] On the other hand, they do see themselves as entitled to help and to protection of the basic rights they hold as members of American society. When the court fails to protect these rights, they come to see the particular court and its personnel as corrupt and flawed and accept the fact that extracting this help from the courts is a complicated, frustrating, and unpredictable process. They retain a fundamental notion of society as legally ordered but come to see that their entitlements are not taken as seriously as are those of other people. At the same time, they gain a growing practical knowledge of how to get things done within the institution.

And of course, sometimes court officials take personal problems seriously, and sometimes they provide the help that plaintiffs seek. As they try to scare plaintiffs away and press defendants to change, court officials often indicate that these are serious offenses with heavy penalties, thereby endeavoring to frighten defendants into changing their behavior. They may deliver stern lectures in legal discourse, as the judge did to Joe for the benefit of Mr. Lucrette. Indeed, often the moral lecture delivered by the clerk-magistrate sufficiently intimidates the defendant that he leaves his ex-girlfriend alone. Sometimes the court evicts the violent husband from the house, forces the tenant to leave despite the "love note," or sends the desperate lover away (if only for two days in a mental institution). The legalistic written, signed, and witnessed agreement provided in mediation sometimes ends a neighborhood feud. Ironically, although the substance of mediation agreements is generally written in moral or therapeutic discourse, the form of the agreement and the discussion about what will be done with it puts a final legal frame around the problem.

Resistance and Emotions

Some plaintiffs begin to resist the court's efforts to ignore and discard their legal claims. They return to court with new charges or new problems. When they are urged to see the problem as a moral one, they insist that it is a legal one. Referrals to mediation programs are refused; instead they talk of seeing their opponents in court. Plaintiffs insist on legal meanings, while defendants counter that the problem is one of mutual fault and of moral rather than legal importance. Some plaintiffs, fearing that their case is in danger of being ignored or discarded, become emotional, shouting at the clerk or weeping in the courtroom. Perhaps these emotional outbursts are a form of manipulation; but at least some of the time they appeared to me to be genuine.[10] These efforts can be considered a kind of resistance to the cultural domination of the court and its efforts to control the discourses and to name the problems it handles.

There is a considerable and growing literature on resistance, much of which locates resistance in covert, subtle, and symbolic actions as well as in more tangible and collective political actions. For example, Jean Comaroff talks about the symbolic resistance to South Africa inherent in Zionist cults which portray a different vision of society and healing than that of the white South African state (1985: 262–63). In South Africa, where explicit, direct resistance is suppressed, resistance takes place in domains other than political action and consciousness. Comaroff shows how under these conditions "a subtle but systematic breach of authoritative cultural codes might make a statement of protest which, by virtue of being rooted in a shared structural predicament and experience of dispossession, conveys an unambiguous message" (1985: 196).

James Scott describes the everyday acts of resistance by peasant farmers in Malaysia, who challenge the class system by small acts of passive noncompliance, foot-dragging, subtle sabotage, evasion, and deception (1985: 31). Resistance here consists of assaults on the claims of superior groups. David Lan describes the collaboration between the spirit mediums of Zimbabwe and the more direct resistance of the guerrillas (1985). Clearly, these studies see resistance as encompassing a wide range of actions, from symbolic ones to direct acts of violence (see Bourdieu 1977). The more subtle, symbolic forms of resistance emerge, in particular, in settings where severe repression prevents more direct political action.

It is with qualifications that I adopt the language of resistance for the situation of working-class plaintiffs in court. This is obviously a different context: these people are not fighting against a repressive regime but have themselves gone to that regime to ask for help. They have submitted their problems voluntarily for the court's consideration, suggesting a willingness to accept its authority. But the choice of court is not unconstrained: virtually the only alternatives are violence and enduring the situation. Local authorities are absent or ignored. These people are resisting in the sense that they are trying to control the course of their problem in court. They are resisting the court's claim to determine the nature of the problem and its outcome. This is resistance to authority—but in a different sense than that of the Malaysian peasant or the South African Zionist.

Here, resistance consists of challenges to the court's efforts to determine which discourse frames the problem at hand. Plaintiffs resist this cultural domination by asserting their own understanding of the problem, usually by insisting on talking about it in legal discourse. For example, when mediators, clerks, or judges say that the problem is really one of not taking sufficient care of one's children or of drinking too much, plaintiffs retort that it is a problem of harassment, of being hit and injured, or of destruction of property for which they are entitled to damages and medical expenses. When the case is dismissed for lack of probable cause, they file new charges on another, more promising incident. When the criminal court refuses to help, they turn to small-claims court. When the criminal court tells plaintiffs that their problem really belongs in mediation, they refuse to accept this interpretation, insisting on going forward in the court. In mediation, some plaintiffs, when asked to reveal themselves, either respond with silence or talk only in legal discourse. They insist on legal claims and refuse to settle. A few walk out of the room.

Another form of resistance is to abandon all three discourses and to become emotional. The three discourses of mediation and the lower courts are all rational, calm, and orderly forms of talk. Participants are expected to present reasoned arguments and to move logically toward a synthesis. Yet, some participants refuse to handle their problems rationally and calmly. They may refuse to talk at all, insist doggedly on following their own line of argument, or continue to repeat the same demands or positions over and over rather than move toward compromise. Instead of progressing from proposals to counterproposals, they snipe, raising allegations of wrongdoing at other times and places. References to past events, charges of other nasty things done and of insults delivered, constantly bubble up in mediation and, to a lesser extent, in court.

The most chaotic element of mediation and court hearings is talk of feelings—of anger, misery, pain, and injustice. Although the court attempts to squeeze out talk of these feelings and although mediators endeavor to contain and suppress them in order to arrive at a settlement, they constantly threaten to break through, to undermine the rationality of the talk. The mediators beat back the shouting match between neighbors, shifting to discussions of property lines and of neighborly behavior, only to have these feelings reemerge in a new round of accusations of raised fingers, late-night phone calls, egg-smeared cars. In mediation sessions, order is always tenuous and fragile; the disorderly feelings constantly threaten to take over the session and to carry it in new directions which cannot be anticipated.

Such volcanic feelings are more contained in the lower court, which has developed an elaborate array of techniques for controlling and managing feelings, for avoiding the pain, anger, and outrage; but they still break out from time to time, disrupting the process. Clerks see their mandate as filtering out disorderly problems. One said, for example: "If I let this go upstairs, and they start to go on and on, the judge will say: 'Who let this in?' " Prosecutors feel a similar responsibility. One said, for example, "I don't want to take this case to trial, because if I put this witness on the stand, who can tell what he will say? He will go on and on, and the judge will turn to me and say: 'Who brought this here?' " If a case progresses to a pretrial conference or to a trial, the prosecutors and defense attorneys play a critical role in translating complex, emotional problems into narrow legal cases. They serve as the front line, cleansing problems of their emotionally chaotic elements and reducing them to cold, rational issues. If the parties shout in anger or burst into tears, the judge will not have to hear it; it will take place in the halls of the courthouse. Indeed, it is likely that the clerk-magistrate has already heard the tears and rage and has tried to calm and deflect these feelings in his office. If he sends the case to the mediation room, the feelings are elicited and channeled under the supervision of people whose background and training is more in the area of feelings than of law. Thus, mediation adds another arena where these feelings can be expressed and therefore contained by the court.

It is possible to see much of the contemporary American social order as directed toward displacing, controlling, and taming feelings, teaching people to "be nice" and to let feelings out in small doses at appropriate moments and in settings where they will not be disruptive or troublesome to the smooth functioning of institutions. The processes of case handling in mediation and in the lower court are a small part of this general social move toward domesticating feelings in order to contain their chaotic potential.

The assertion of feelings, the insistence on having them heard, is, then, a form of resistance to all three discourses, to the requirement that talk be calm and rational. People who feel strongly push against the system, demanding to be heard, insisting on the issuance of a complaint by yelling at the clerk, calling up the prosecutor over and over and demanding justice in an angry voice, calling the judge to complain about his decision. The woman appearing in court covered with bruises and crying in the corner is confronting the court with feelings. These people are regarded as difficult and troublesome by the court officials, but they cannot ignore them. They often get heard and sometimes get what they want. Despite the range of devices for containing and deflecting feelings, they sometimes break through and assault the court with their reality and power. The hegemony of the rational legal order is not complete; those who refuse to be ordered, who resist behaving calmly, who insist on being disruptive and chaotic, get some response.

As F. G. Bailey discusses in his analysis of political tactics, within a world of rational discourse the person who appeals to passion plays a trump card that is often decisive in winning the battle (1983). He argues that there are fundamentally two forms of persuasion: one based on rational argument, including a delineation of the consequences of following one or another course of action, and one based on passion (1983: 22–23). Appeal to emotion as a form of persuasion can create trust, since it reveals the sincere inner self, but it can also create mistrust, since passion obstructs access to reason, generally considered the better route to reality. Bailey points out that in certain settings, such as bureaucracies, committees, parliaments, and so on, Anglo-American political culture denies that passions have a significant part to play. Here, rationality is the proper mode of conducting business, while passion is "officially submerged but lived out in action" (1983: 25). In these settings, when the proper cultural rules for the display of passion are followed, emotion can excite trust and be persuasive—although, if mishandled, it awakens mistrust and derision. Thus, we find a paradox: "in debates and arguments reason must ultimately be trumped by emotion, but at the same time it is upheld as the superior mode . . . . in competition for power, those who know when and how to penetrate the outer cover—the normative integument of culture—win the day. Third, it seems that the passions are tools both for the maintenance of this integument and—paradoxically—for its penetration" (1983: 7).

Courts are clearly one of those settings in which rational discussion is valued above emotional discussion. Emotion in court is troublesome, out of place. Its expression can lead to disdain and derision, but it can also be powerful if it is used in the right way at the right time. Conversely, in mediation the discourse is frequently highly emotional, and the person who plays the trump card of rationality wins the day.

Two Problems in Mediation and in Court

The following detailed descriptions of two problems handled in both mediation and court illustrate the effects of experience on legal consciousness and suggest some of the forms that resistance to the court's management of these problems can take. In both cases, the plaintiffs are experienced court users who are assertive about their rights. In both cases, the plaintiffs were very persistent. In the first, because the plaintiff was so insistent and because the defendant was afraid to compromise, the case came to trial. While the case was in court, the plaintiff clearly learned how to put a case together, although he also noticed that the court did not take his problem seriously. He regarded the court as a place for contest and play. In the end, he says he enjoyed the experience. There are strong emotions in this case, feelings of hurt and insult, but although they seem to be a large part of the reason why the parties resist settling, they do not surface in the court process. The plaintiff in the second case is also emotional, and she seems to have discovered how to use her emotions to good effect in the court.

More generally, these two cases illustrate the arguments of the book as a whole. Both are somewhat unusual in the extent of court involvement but are typical in the issues involved, in the kinds of people who bring these issues to court, and in the dynamics of the problem itself. One is a neighborhood problem, one a marital problem. The characteristics of the parties and the neighborhoods they come from are similar to those described in earlier chapters. The people in each are economically marginal but striving toward a respectable status. One of the plaintiffs is a woman and one is a man, but both feel vulnerable and powerless in the relationship which brings them to court. The problems involve mutual accusations and are embedded in complex social relationships with long histories.

As they move into court, the problems are interpreted and handled as cases, but their definition as problems remains very much in evidence. The parties in both cases assert legal interpretations of the problems, while mediators and court officials see them as relationship problems and endeavor to reinterpret them in moral discourse. In both cases there are struggles between parties who insist a problem is a legal one and judges and clerks who see it as a moral one. Both plaintiffs persist in legal discourse despite the efforts of the court to reinterpret their problems in moral terms. And despite the repeated efforts of court personnel in both these cases to get the parties to settle, they refuse. In the second case, the plaintiff becomes emotional when she has trouble persuading the court to listen to her, and she finds that she gets what she wants.

One can sympathize both with the parties and with the court in these cases, as I did while I watched them unfold. To the parties, these are serious legal problems about the protection of themselves, their property, and their social position. To the court, they are struggles within private, personal relationships whose legal significance is trivial and whose central issues are both unworthy of the court's attention and impossible to resolve. Moreover, some plaintiffs pressed their demands incessantly and remained unwilling to compromise or give in. Court officials nevertheless generally tried to respond with what they saw as fair and just solutions. For the parties, however, these solutions were generally inadequate, since the problems themselves were deeper and more complex than any solution the legal system had to offer.

A Neighborhood Problem

In the early 1980s, individual rooms in a shabby rooming house on a busy street in Cambridge rented for $15/week. Seventeen people lived in the two adjacent buildings sharing two bathrooms, a shower, and a pay phone by the front door. At the time of the incident, Zoar, an aspiring poet, had been in the rooming house for eight months, having moved there at the invitation of his friend, Mischa, a machinist. They had met at a poetry reading three years earlier. Zoar, although born in the area and a graduate of a local high school in a working-class section of the city, had assumed a pen name and English ancestry, hiding his real name and origins from his friends. Mischa's father is American, and his mother is from India. She is a teacher of Oriental religion and philosophy. Both Mischa and his mother live in separate rooms in the rooming house and have been there for three years. Zoar is twenty-seven years old, Mischa thirty-six. A woman, Jean, another resident of the rooming house, is also important in the protracted conflict between Zoar and Mischa which pulled both men into court. She is about twenty-five years old.

Zoar considers himself a struggling artist and is anxious to be more than the down-and-out resident of a rooming house. Although he finished high school, he has not attended college. He wants to go to school and get an associate's degree in accounting. He is small and thin, about five feet four inches tall, and speaks with a high, wheezing sound. According to Mischa, he once drank lye; Zoar says that he has had fifteen operations on his throat. Zoar aspires to move in educated circles and is very concerned about his reputation. He fears that a criminal conviction would prevent his moving into a nice neighborhood with respectable people. He has worked as a mail clerk in the past but has been unemployed for thirteen months. Mischa is a large, dark-skinned man with a substantial belly and a strong, assertive manner. He seems very dominant in the relationship with Zoar. He works on and off as a machinist but apparently is not greatly concerned with either his job or his self-presentation. Jean, a white woman from New Mexico, is hostile to courts and to the "white male hierarchy which runs things around here." She used to be friendly with Mischa but has now broken off that relationship and sides with Zoar. She has lived in the rooming house for two yeas. She has a history of mental problems but has never been institutionalized—unlike, she says, all her friends. She is now in charge of a mental patients' liberation front and is on general relief, but when that runs out she may apply to Social Security for disability status. She hates to do that—to claim that she is too mentally disabled to work—because it stigmatizes her reputation, but she may have to. Along with Zoar, she claims she is about to move out of the rooming house and is interested in artistic things. She has worked temporarily as a waitress and as a secretary. She has a social worker to whom she turns in crises.

In May, Mischa either sold or loaned a tape recorder to Zoar (a point of dispute between them). When Zoar failed to pay for it, Mischa followed Zoar into his room and demanded the money, $50. Zoar refused and, according to Mischa, pulled a knife on him. Zoar denies the knife but claims that Mischa pushed him against his bed. The next day, Mischa came back to the room demanding his money, and Zoar yelled at him through the door: "I don't talk to niggers." Furious, Mischa went to court and charged Zoar with assault with a dangerous weapon. At the clerk's hearing, which Jean also attended, the complaint was issued, despite the fact that Zoar had hired a lawyer.[11] Mischa said that he told the clerk that he had feared for his life. Apparently Jean talked too much in this hearing, according to Zoar's lawyer, and he told her not to come next time. Zoar immediately filed a cross-complaint against Mischa for assault and battery.

Mischa also filed charges in small-claims court against both Zoar and Jean, for money owed. He sued Zoar for $50 for the tape recorder and Jean for $65 for a previous loan. Zoar says he has been in court only once before, on a shoplifting charge as a juvenile. He is very concerned about the criminal charge and fears it will be a smear on his reputation. Mischa says he himself was in court only once as a defendant and was put on probation. His mother, however, said that Mischa's father was always going to court and enjoyed it. She fears that Mischa has some of his father in him; she herself thinks that going to court is a stupid waste of time. Indeed, while Zoar appears to dread and fear going to court, Mischa regards it with enthusiasm and anticipation, as a challenge and a form of entertainment.

After the complaint was issued, the court clerk referred the case to mediation. My observation of the case began with the mediation session held at the end of June. Mischa begins the mediation session by describing his court complaint of assault with a knife. He describes the situation as follows:

> *The circumstances behind the complaint were the $50 he owed me for the tape recorder. He refused to give me the tape recorder back or the money, and he sold it to someone else. He pulled a knife on me. I went to grab him but decided to take him to court instead. It would have looked bad if I had grabbed the knife, because I was in his room. I have known him for three years. I felt bad about this because I brought him into the house. The incident happened on Memorial Day. I said: "Why did you do this to me?" and he said: "I don't talk to niggers." So I figured he wouldn't apologize, so I went to court.*

Zoar's initial statement, framed in legal discourse, constitutes his defense: "*We are not friends. Mischa thinks I owe him $50, but there are no witnesses. I borrowed it from him. I will pay if he will show me an I.O.U.*" Mischa replies that his mother saw Zoar take it. Zoar responds: "*I borrowed it. The tape recorder is not the issue; the assault is the issue. If you want money, go to small-claims court.*" Mischa retorts: "*I am not going to waste these people's time if you are going to sit here and lie.*" He asks for a lie detector test, locating himself squarely within legal discourse.

As the argument continues, Zoar demands payment of his legal fees, about $150, and refuses to pay the $50 unless Mischa can produce a written receipt, while Mischa claims that in the past he has loaned Zoar money without receipts and wants the $50, in addition to an apology for the racial slur and for threatening him with a knife. Both agree that they do not want to be friends any more.

Mischa says that Zoar's pulling the knife on him destroyed his trust in Zoar, while Zoar says that Mischa's bringing charges in court has ended their friendship. Zoar would like an agreement so as to stay out of court, which is damaging to his reputation, but Mischa thinks they might as well go to court, since mediation is getting them nowhere. When the mediator asks Mischa what he hopes to get from court, he replies: *"I want to see just how just it is, if it really works, because I think they can get away with murder in court. I wouldn't mind paying his $150 legal fees just to see this."* Zoar retorts: *"Your charges are stupid. I didn't touch you."* He wants to avoid going to court again, since it will cost him an additional $100 in legal fees each time his lawyer appears. He points out to Mischa that he has also filed a serious charge against him, a charge worth three months in jail.

In his private caucus with the mediator, Mischa tells the mediator that Zoar is lying, that Zoar had a knife, and that he would like to see whether the court believes him. He also points out that Zoar has some kind of a psychiatric record which the mediator should look up. Thus, he draws on therapeutic discourse— but to condemn, not to excuse. He describes this as a "test case." Although he has no actual witnesses, he does have a witness who will say that Zoar owns a knife. He insists on an apology for the knife. When the mediator urges him to make some concession, he resists, saying that Zoar is "perjuring himself" (thereby returning to legal discourse) and asks: "Am I supposed to deny the reality I experience?" After Mischa describes some of his previous conflicts with Jean and his theory that Jean has put Zoar up to this, the mediator asks him whether he is willing to pay $150, Zoar's legal fees (the mediator thinks that the clerk will require Mischa to pay these fees), just for the chance to go to court. Mischa responds: *"Yes. Just the experience—to see what happens in court. I'll never know unless I try. See, he took the tape recorder, didn't give me $50. What am I supposed to do? Go down there to his room, have him call me 'nigger'?"*

In Zoar's private caucus, Zoar says he is willing to apologize for the racial comment but not for the knife. He also refuses to pay for the tape recorder unless Mischa can produce a written I.O.U. from him. When the mediator asks again whether there is anything Zoar can propose as a settlement, he replies *"Well, if he has any record of the sale, I will pay; but it is hearsay. There are no witnesses. He knows that if he takes me to small-claims court he has no proof. It is the $50 he really wants. That is why he is trying criminal court—but this affects my reputation. That is worth a lot more than $50. He is a poor businessman if he expects more."* In making his defense Zoar relies on legal discourse: the requirement of a receipt (when they have not usually dealt in receipts) and talk of witnesses and proof.

The mediator calls both parties back and admits he is stumped. He urges them to talk about the comments that each has made to the other and about their hurt feelings, endeavoring to shift to a therapeutic talk of feelings and apologies; but Mischa insists on an apology for the knife threat, and Zoar continues to refuse to admit he had a knife. Both continue to frame the problem in legal discourse. Zoar says, in a clear use of legal discourse: *"I came in the building, he followed me up the stairs, and I showed him the tape recorder with my name on it. You* [Mischa] *followed me in, forced your way in. You were annoying me, technically. That was forcible entry. You came over, knocked me over against the bed—I didn't fall. You did push me."* Mischa responds: *"You didn't go to the hospital. You weren't hurt. I am wasting my time here. I will see you in court."* The mediator acknowledges an impasse and, after one hour and forty-five minutes, ends the mediation session. The case returns to court. Mischa requests that the small-claims cases be postponed until mid-August, the day scheduled for trial for his complaint, against Zoar, of assault with a dangerous weapon.

The clerk's hearing on Zoar's cross-complaint is scheduled for mid-July. On the morning of the clerk's hearing, however, no one appears. The clerk calls the names several times and, when no one responds, dismisses the complaint. The parties are indeed in the courthouse—but on another floor. They are involved in a conference with the prosecutor, who is urging them to settle. I did not attend this meeting but heard several reports of it. Zoar did not bring his lawyer, since he did not want to pay an additional $100. Mischa brought four witnesses, including his mother and a woman who said that she knew Zoar had a knife. The prosecutor urged the parties to make a deal, but Zoar refused to negotiate anything without his lawyer's presence. The prosecutor told me that, although he had promised Zoar that if he would apologize for the knife the case would be handled noncriminally, Zoar still had refused.

When Zoar discovered that his complaint application had been dismissed by the clerk's office, he hurried back to the clerk's office and demanded that it be reinstated. The clerk rescheduled the probable-cause hearing on the complaint application for the same day as that for the trial on the cross-complaint; he planned to hold this hearing before the trial. Thus, on the day of the pretrial conference with the prosecutor, both Mischa and Zoar resisted a great deal of pressure, from the prosecutor and from the clerk, to settle. Zoar, an inexperienced court user, was afraid of the consequences to his reputation if he admitted that he had had the knife. Mischa was looking forward to the trial.

Three days before the trial I discussed the situation with the prosecutor, a young attorney. He said that, in general, this is the kind of case that the court likes to handle simply. No one except the parties wants to get into it very deeply. The parties keep bringing up a lot of other issues and problems, but no one else wants to deal with them. In this case, he figures he will just have to leave it up to the judge, since it is a case where one party says one thing and another says another, and there is no way to tell whom to believe. He prefers to handle these problems by letting the parties settle it themselves, and he has already spent a long time talking to them, trying to get them to settle. But he could not do so, because one party refused to admit something that the other wanted. He does not think that it will be much of a trial. He plans to talk to the lawyer for the defendant to see whether they can arrange some kind of an agreement before the trial. He adds: *"This kind of case doesn't really belong in criminal court. It is just one person wanting something out of the other. One person wants some kind of specific remedy, and none of the remedies which are available through the court are what they want. I know the people in this kind of a case will be dissatisfied, and I have to deal with their dissatisfaction and explain to them what the court can do. They don't really want a jail sentence—or whatever the court can provide—but something more specific."*

Meanwhile, anticipating her small-claims case in three days, Jean spent two hours talking to the staff in the mediation program about her fears of court. She is convinced that she will be handcuffed and locked up if she fails to appear in small-claims court and to pay the money she owes Mischa. She had called the court and her social worker, who all had assured her that this would not happen, but she is still upset. Later that day, she called to say she had a statement from a doctor that she was on Valium and that she did not have to appear in court. As an inexperienced court user, she expressed much of the fear and anxiety common among people who have had little previous contact with the court.

The day of the trial, in mid-August, I arrive in court about 9:30 A.M. Mischa is talking to the prosecutor, who again urges him to settle. Mischa replies that he will drop all charges if Zoar will simply apologize for the knife. Since Zoar will not do so, the prosecutor reluctantly agrees to go forward with the trial. Mischa insists that it is a matter of principle to him now, not a matter of $50. The money is not worth the time he has to take off from work. Zoar tells me that he is concerned about his reputation and is here to defend it. To him as well, the case is about more than money; it is a matter of his reputation and sense of self. He thinks that it will look very bad if he has a record. It is now a matter of pride. He says he needs a lawyer because these people are scum, criminals, and because he cannot bear to deal with them directly. He wants his lawyer to serve as a go-between. He also says that he belongs to a religious group which uses knives ceremonially. I interpreted this as a tacit admission that he did possess a knife, whether or not he actually used it to threaten Mischa. The charge against Zoar is a felony with a maximum five-year sentence in prison, and Zoar is a little nervous about doing time.

The clerk brings the cross-complaint (Zoar's against Mischa) to the trial courtroom to be handled at the same time, without a prior clerk's hearing. The clerk asks me whether I will try to mediate the case, as a person loosely associated with the mediation program and hanging around the courtroom. I explain that I cannot, that I am a researcher, and that mediation has already failed to settle the case. At the same time, the clerk tells Mischa to settle his small-claims case with Jean, since no judge is going to make a person on general relief pay a debt.

I spoke to Zoar's lawyer before the trial, and he described this case as a "pile of shit," "garbage," "excrement," and with a string of similar terms. He adds: "I think the D.A. smelled it too." He knows that the prosecutor does not want to bring it to trial but cannot settle it. The lawyer is confident that one of the judges in the court, who knows him, is fair and would just let it go. But he is unsure about what the sitting judge will do. He expects that there will be a continued-without-a-finding disposition with court costs but that Zoar may be found guilty.

At 9:30 A.M., Jean and Zoar are in the small-claims courtroom, and Mischa, Zoar's lawyer, and the prosecutor are in a courtroom two floors below. The prosecutor says that the case is about to come to trial, so they should table the case in small-claims and come down for the trial, which is to begin about 10:00 A.M. Mischa rushes up and informs Zoar, and the clerk agrees to hold the small-claims case until the end of business. When the criminal case is called, however, Zoar's lawyer says that he is at the same time handling another case, which has been transferred to another courtroom; could they transfer this one as well? The court clerk says no but tells the lawyer to go to the other courtroom for his other case. Mischa and Zoar go back to the small-claims courtroom where Jean is still sitting, but now their case is at the end of the list, and the clerk will not move it up. The clerk also tells Mischa to settle with Jean, because the court will not make her pay. Jean agrees to pay the $65 she owes Mischa but does not want to pay the $14 court costs. Since Mischa insists on this money as well, the case has to wait for a judge.

Meanwhile, the prosecutor has worked privately with Mischa to prepare his testimony, asking him to specify where the knife was, what kind of knife it was, and when and where the incident took place. He has tried to prepare Mischa for the kinds of questions he is going to ask and for the specificity of answers he expects. In the middle of this process, however, the prosecutor has been called away on another case. However, in the course of this discussion, Mischa has learned a good deal about what constitutes evidence and how one constructs a case.

It is not clear where the case stands when the court calls a lunch recess until 2 P.M. Just before the lunch break, the criminal case is reassigned to a different judge on the floor above, and Mischa is taken to the courtroom.

At 2 P.M., Mischa and his mother (the other witness left after an hour) are waiting in the new courtroom along with the prosecutor, but neither Zoar nor his lawyer is present. The prosecutor searches all over for them, insisting that he told Zoar's lawyer where they were to be. At 2:15 P.M. the judge arrives and asks where the other parties are. The prosecutor replies lamely that he does not know but has been looking. The judge says without much conviction that he supposes the defendant is in default. The prosecutor replies that the defendant was in court all morning. The prosecutor then explains that there is a small-claims matter which is being heard in the civil-motions room upstairs. The judge suggests that the criminal matter be handled there at the same time. The prosecutor cannot go upstairs, however, since he has another trial now in front of the same judge. Someone asks Mischa whether he agrees to move the case to the small-claims room, and, after checking with the prosecutor, he acquiesces uncertainly. Zoar's lawyer has now arrived, complaining that he was in another courtroom because he had been assigned there with another case and that he had requested that both cases be sent to the same court. Zoar has now arrived as well, and all troop up to the small-claims courtroom. It is now about 2:30 P.M., and Jean is still in the small-claims courtroom; but almost no one else is left there. Two other long small-claims cases are heard, and the courtroom is now empty except for the participants in this trial. Mischa tells me that he is enjoying the court experience.

When the judge is informed that a criminal complaint is to be heard without the presence of the prosecutor, he refuses to hear the case, saying that the charge is a felony, an assault with a dangerous weapon, and that he is sure that the chief of the prosecutor's office would not like it handled without a prosecutor. He then considers the small-claims cases. While these are being heard, two different individuals arrive for restraining orders in domestic violence cases (209A orders) and are immediately brought to the bench, thereby interrupting the small-claims proceedings. There is no word of explanation to the parties.

The first small-claims trial concerns Mischa's complaint against Zoar for $50. It commences at 3:10 P.M. The judge asks Mischa for any record or receipt. Mischa replies that he has none but that he and Zoar have always used word of mouth. After asking a few more questions about the tape recorder and what happened to it and after acknowledging that the price seems reasonable, he swears in Mischa's mother, who corroborates Mischa's story although she did not see any of the exchanges take place. Zoar says that it was his tape recorder all along and that he sold it to someone else. The judge concludes that he will take the case under advisement. The trial lasts nine minutes. The trial between Mischa and Jean lasts three minutes. The judge asks Jean why she came to court when he has a letter that says that she cannot, and she replies that she changed her mind. She says she owes Mischa the money and just wants time to pay, maybe two months. The judge gives her two months, then tells her she must also pay $14.50 in court costs. She resists, saying she is on welfare and cannot pay; but the judge simply gives her two months to pay this as well.

At this point the prosecutor, having finished the other trial, appears in the courtroom. The criminal trial begins at 3:28 P.M. It consists of both the complaint against Zoar and an application for a cross-complaint against Mischa. The judge suggests putting over the cross-complaint for another day, but Zoar's lawyer says that it has already been put over for today. The judge tells the prosecutor to excuse himself from cross-examination on the cross-complaint, as it would mean he was prosecuting both sides and wearing two hats. The following is a rendition of the trial, according to the notes I took as it took place.

After placing Mischa on the stand and asking him to name his address and place of employment, the prosecutor begins:

> PROSECUTOR: *I would like to direct your attention to May 25 at 12:30 P.M. Where were you at this time?*
> MISCHA: *Outside my house.*
> PROSECUTOR: *What happened?*
> MISCHA: *I saw Zoar with the tape recorder and asked for the tape recorder back.*
> PROSECUTOR: *What kind of tape recorder was it? What did you know about it?*
> MISCHA: *It is mine; it is a GE something or other.*
> PROSECUTOR: *What did you do after this?*
> MISCHA: *I went up the steps behind him to his room.*
> PROSECUTOR: *Did you have any conversation at this time?*
> MISCHA: *I said I wanted the tape recorder.*
> PROSECUTOR: *What happened then?*
> MISCHA: *I sat down in his room. I said I wanted my tape recorder back. I thought he should give it to me.*
> LAWYER: *Objection.*
> JUDGE: *Keep to the facts.*
> MISHCA: *I said I wanted the $50. Then he pulled out a knife.*
> PROSECUTOR: *From where?*
> MISCHA: *From his pocket.*
> PROSECUTOR: *How long was the knife?*
> MISCHA: *About four inches, a typical blade with a switch.*
> PROSECUTOR: *What did you do?*
> MISCHA: *I left the room. I thought if I did anything there in his room, it would look bad.*
> JUDGE: *We don't want your thoughts, only what you did and he did— not what you thought about this. Stick to the point.*
> PROSECUTOR: *What did you do then?*
> MISCHA: *I walked out of the room.*
> PROSECUTOR: *Is Mr. Zoar here today?*
> MISCHA: *Yes.*
> PROSECUTOR: *Could you point him out, please?*
> MISCHA: *He is sitting next to Mr. Jones* [the lawyer].
> PROSECUTOR: *No further questions.*

Zoar's lawyer asks for a directed finding of not guilty, claiming that the Commonwealth has not proved that this incident has the elements of assault as they have been defined in a series of cases. The judge ignores this argument. The lawyer points out that Zoar is substantially smaller than Mischa, to which the judge replies that the same was true of David and Goliath. The judge denies the directed finding, and Zoar takes the stand. He also describes the tape recorder and the incident in the room, ending with the following discussion:

LAWYER: *Then he came into your room? How?*
ZOAR: *He barged in, opened the door.*
LAWYER: *Did you ask him to leave?*
ZOAR: *Yes.*
LAWYER: *Did he?*
ZOAR: *No.*
LAWYER: *What did he do?*
ZOAR: *He came at me, pushed me.*
LAWYER: *You heard him testify that you pulled a knife. Did you?*
ZOAR: *No.*
LAWYER: *Are you likely to have any knives lying around your room?*
PROSECUTOR: *Objection. Leading the witness.*
JUDGE: *Sustained.*

The prosecutor asks Zoar about how well he knows Mr. Mischa and about the tape recorder and its ownership. The judge stops this line of questioning, urging the prosecutor to stick to the point:

JUDGE: *The essence of this case is what happened in the room.*
PROSECUTOR: *Has he been in your room before?*
ZOAR: *Yes. I just didn't want him in.*
PROSECUTOR: *How long was he in there?*
ZOAR: *Ten minutes. He came over to me.*
PROSECUTOR: *How did he knock you down?*
ZOAR: *He looked like he was trying to punch me in the stomach.*
PROSECUTOR: *What did you do?*
ZOAR: *I backed off.*
JUDGE: *How large was the room, and what kind of furniture?* [Zoar explains.]
(Then, shifting gears) JUDGE: *What school did you go to?*
ZOAR: *X High School and then Y Community College.*

After pursuing this line of questioning briefly, the judge asks the prosecutor and defense attorney whether they have any further arguments. When they do not, he concludes: "*In my view, this is not an assault with a dangerous weapon, this is not a five-year felony as the law intends. I find the defendant not guilty and the cross-complaint will not be issued.*" The trial lasted twenty-six minutes, with two interruptions for restraining orders. The proceedings themselves took about twenty minutes.

Zoar left quickly with his lawyer. Mischa stopped to tell me that he was not displeased, that it was an experience, and that he was glad that Zoar had to pay all those legal fees. Mischa's mother again said that she thought it was a stupid waste of time and that he should just forget the money and drop the whole thing. Jean said that she was very relieved that there were no handcuffs. In two months, she will go back to court and say that she needs more time to pay, and she thinks that they may not make her pay for a while. She seemed fairly satisfied with the process.

Three months later, no one had paid any of the money owed to Mischa. Nor had anyone moved out of the rooming house. Jean said that she was angry when the decision arrived from the small-claims court stating that Zoar had to pay Mischa $50 for the tape recorder and court costs. Since there were no witnesses and no records, so that it was a matter of one person's word against another, she assumed that the decision reflected some kind of undue influence on the judge by Mischa. She thought Zoar's lawyer was only interested in money. She thinks the whole system is that way and wants to move to another state, but right now she is still living in the same rooming house. As she put it: *"All the people in this state are corrupt, and so are all the people in the courthouse."* She recalled a past incident when Mischa had hit her and she had called the police, who had suggested that she take him to court; but her social worker had said that he was just trying to get her emotionally engaged, so she had dropped it. (Here, the social worker shifted the problem from legal to moral discourse.) She feels that the courts will not help her unless she has a lawyer. Nevertheless, she says: *"The next move Mischa makes, I will go to the courts. I didn't want to engage him, I wanted to keep it out of court if possible. If I take him in for hitting me, it will be in the criminal division."* I was unable to locate Zoar for a follow-up discussion. Mischa, three months later, said he had enjoyed his experiences in mediation and court. His real interest in the case was the money owed him—not the knife—and he assumed that, since the court had made a judgment that he was owed the money, he only had to wait and it would appear. He was pleased that Zoar was humiliated by having to pay his lawyer and by having his real name and origins revealed. Mischa was taking some satisfaction in spreading this around among their friends. The experience was, for him, educational and fun. He enjoyed watching Zoar lie in court. He regarded the outcome as a victory. So, apparently, did Zoar. Zoar and Mischa no longer talk to each other.

This case illustrates the continuous pressure on litigants to settle and drop out of the process, but it also shows that people can and do resist this pressure. All three parties resisted constant pressure to settle before trial. In mediation, in the conference with the prosecutor, and in discussions with the clerks, various third parties urged Zoar to admit having the knife and urged Mischa to drop his case against Jean and Zoar. When Zoar's cross-complaint was dismissed, he rushed back to the clerk's office and had it reinstated. Because he refused, despite considerable urging, to admit to having wielded the knife, Zoar had to go to trial; but he succeeded in clearing his name, his fundamental objective. Mischa's persistence won him the chance to bring the case to trial and the opportunity to humiliate Zoar, which was one of his objectives. The parties' intransigence about settling repeatedly pulled the case back into court when it teetered on the brink of dismissal.

Court officials did not simply dump the case, however. They invested considerable time and energy in efforts to settle it. Their strategies suggest that they were convinced that settling between the parties was the fairest and most appropriate way of dealing with a problem of this sort. Most interpersonal cases are settled through negotiations of this sort; Mischa was unusually stubborn, and Zoar was unusually afraid of compromising.

Throughout the process, both Mischa and Zoar persisted in using legal discourse. During the mediation session, the mediator managed to elicit a discussion of hurt feelings and their previous friendship, but Mischa and Zoar quickly returned to a conversation about evidence and receipts. Zoar insisted on a written document stating that he owed Mischa money before he would repay the debt, although he acknowledged that they had never used written documents before. Mischa talked about perjury. At the first clerk's hearing, he said he was in fear for his life. In the public court hearings, court officials maintained strictly legal discourse, but behind-the-scenes discussions concerned relationships and the need to settle. The prosecutor raised the issue of the existence of a relationship between the parties but did not use it as a basis for settlement. Whereas mediators attempt to bypass legal discourse to arrive at a settlement which takes account of relationships, court officials attempt to circumscribe the problem, minimizing the relationships behind it, to reveal its insignificance as a legal case.

These litigants emerge from their court encounter with a curious combination of cynicism, triumph, and eagerness to try the court again. Their consciousness has been subtly changed. Jean and Zoar had been relatively naive users of the court who regard it with fear and awe. Mischa had been a more experienced user who has seen it more in terms of play, as a game which he could master. Jean seems to feel less fear afterward. Mischa's sense of mastery is simply enhanced. All three discover that their cases are shuffled from one court to another, suggesting that neither they nor their problems are taken seriously. All three learn a good deal about how the court works. The prosecutor teaches Mischa to present his case as an incident located in time and place and stripped of social and personal meaning. Jean discovers that it is easy to get more time to pay her debts and is now willing to ask for even more time. She thinks the courts are places of influence and that Mischa has some "connections," but she is nevertheless ready to go back to criminal court against Mischa for his next violent assault. Mischa is willing to try mediation again as well as to return to court.

The legal consciousness of these people is shaped by encounters such as this one, which shows that the court can be a place for getting what they want and that there is a level of chaos to its operation. After their experiences, the participants in this case do not believe that law treats all equally, that it can uncover the truth, or that everyone has equal access to the courts, but they see themselves as possessing some entitlement to use the services of the court, recognizing that, if one is poor, it takes persistence, skill, and a great deal of time to assert this entitlement. Their sense of entitlement, then, is refracted through their own recognition that they live at the bottom of a stratified and hierarchal society. All persons have legal rights as citizens, but that does not create a society of political, economic, and social equality; nor does it mean that poor people's problems will be taken as seriously as are those of rich people.

A Family Problem

A second case, a stormy struggle among spouses and siblings over a deteriorating marriage, involves people who return to court repeatedly in efforts to deal with the same tangle of relationships.[12] The barrage of accusations and counteraccusations flies between Mary, a young woman twenty-three years old, and her sister-in-law, Joan, eighteen years old and married to Mary's younger brother, Joe, who is twenty-one years old. All are white and live in Salem.

Joan became pregnant with Joe's child, married him in July, and moved in with Joe's parents. Joe was twenty years old at the time. After some months of living with Joe's parents, during which time Joan stayed in bed in order to protect her pregnancy and Joe's mother felt that she was lazy, Joe and Joan moved into an upstairs apartment, owned by Joe's mother, which cost $30/week. Joe's parents bought the newlyweds new living-room, dining-room, and bedroom furniture and a washer/dryer. Joe's older sister Mary lived in the downstairs apartment with her husband and two-year old daughter while Joe and Joan lived upstairs. In March, the baby was born, but conflict between Joe and Joan became more intense, and new strains developed between Joan and Mary, living in the same house. They had at least one fist fight. Joe worked as a truck driver and came home, after a twelve- to thirteen-hour day, to stories of the fights between the two women. Mary's husband was also a truck driver. Both women stayed with their children. Mary is a high school graduate, and Joan dropped out in eleventh grade. Both claim a family income between $16,000 and $20,000.

In April, Joe decided to leave Joan, to move out of the apartment and back to his parents' house. In early May, Joan scheduled her son's christening for the same day as Mary's daughter's birthday party, which infuriated Mary. In May, Joe hit Joan, and she called the police, who advised her to go to court and get a restraining order against him. She did so and was referred by the judge to mediation. Joan thought this was because the judge did not want to make a decision. In the mediation session, held in the program's office and attended by Joe, Joan, Mary, and Joe's mother, Joe and Joan arranged a separation and division of property. According to the mediator, Joan was "climbing the walls," screaming, and in tears much of the time. I did not observe this session. Joan said that she cried when she told her story because it seemed so final, the end of their lives together. They agreed to go to a regularly scheduled mediation session with community mediators the next week to decide support and visitation questions, but neither of them showed up for it.

The day after the mediation session, Mary called the mediation office to complain that Joan had already violated the agreement and was upstairs banging on her door. Joan went back to court for a two-week extension of the restraining order, but, when this expired Joan and Joe had reunited. They returned to tell the judge that all was now fine. Joan thought the judge was pleased.

The problem was soon back in court, however. In June, according to court records, Mary charged Joan with "assault, threatening to blow my car up, and threatening to kill my two-year old daughter." At the same time, in a cross-complaint, Joan charged Mary with stealing her bike from the shed behind the house. She said Mary had admitted that she stole the bike in retaliation for Joan's theft of her gold necklace, but, when Joan called the police, Mary would not admit taking the bike. A clerk's hearing was scheduled on both charges, but neither party appeared. In July, Joan filed a complaint against Joe for stealing her diamond ring and wedding ring. This was reported as settled before they came to the hearing. Sometime in the spring, Joan went on welfare. In early July, the welfare department charged Joe in court with nonsupport of his wife and minor child. Joan was on welfare, receiving $314/month. The welfare department requested dismissal of this case when Joe moved back in with Joan during the summer.

Thus, although the fight began outside the court, by the summer the battle was gradually moving into the courthouse. It was the police who initially suggested that the parties take their problems to court. At this point, the parties are still using the power of the court in limited ways: they file charges, but they fail to appear to press them further. Legal action is still primarily a threat.

Joan's account of the situation indicates a more extensive involvement of the law in the family struggle. When Joe moved out and into his parent's house, he had his lawyer contact Joan about a divorce. She went to a lawyer herself, but since the lawyer wanted $700 in advance and since she had no job, she did not pursue the matter. After Joe moved out of the apartment, his parents contacted an attorney and went to court to evict Joan from the apartment, which, after some time, they succeeded in doing. They also got a restraining order against Joan. Mary too got a restraining order against Joan. About the same time, Joan asked for a restraining order against Mary. According to her account, the judge was influenced by her tears. When she did not think the judge would give her the restraining order, she got angry, burst into tears, and marched out of the courtroom. The court officer sent her back in and told her to apologize. The judge then gave her the restraining order, so she figures that making a scene works. The next day, according to Joan, Joe called the Children's Protective Service to report her as an unfit mother. Joan was very depressed at this time and tried to commit suicide, but a friend called the police and she went for counseling to an agency she called "protective services" which, she said, helped out by listening and supporting. She also talked to a woman in another district court. Thus, the problem was heavily involved with other social services as well as the court. The parties used legal resources as weapons against each others.

During this period, Joe was jealous because Joan had other boyfriends, and

Joan was jealous of Joe's girlfriends. As Joe and Mary watched Joan go out with friends—including male friends—one night, there was another punching and shoving fight. Joe then had the apartment's gas, electricity, and phone turned off. The welfare office called Joe, asking him to pay $75/week in child support. He was furious, according to Joan.

But, as Joan planned to move out of the apartment, Mary became more friendly. One evening Joan recommended a baby-sitter to Mary. When the baby-sitter had to leave briefly, Joan went into Mary's apartment when her phone rang; it was Mary calling the baby-sitter. Mary claimed that an emerald ring disappeared that night and accused Joan of stealing it. At this point, Mary took Joan to court for assault and battery, threats, trespassing, disturbing the peace, and violating the restraining order. Both Joan and Joe thought that Mary took her to court for larceny of the ring as well.

After Joan moved out of the apartment and back to her parents' house, Joe decided he wanted to live with her again, and at the end of July they reunited and moved into a new apartment in the next town. But conflicts continued. Joe's parents refused to give him their phone number, arguing that Joan's threats against Joe's father were aggravating his heart condition, giving him palpitations, and threatening his death. Joan says that by this time she has been in court so many times that the court officials know who she is.

In the meantime, Mary's complaint against Joan was issued by the clerk's office. I did not observe the hearing. According to Mary, the clerk issued the complaint because Joan had started making death threats against Mary's father in the clerk's presence. According to the mediation program staff, the complaint was issued because Joan had failed to attend the hearing. The complaint was for assault and battery, disturbing the peace, and trespassing, although Mary told the mediation program that it was for harassment, threats, trespassing, and larceny of a ring. The prosecutor told my research assistant that the charges were harassment, threats, and trespassing. In individual conversations with me and my research assistant, Mary said she had taken Joan to court "just to teach her a good lesson," to give her "a good scare" and something to think about. She hoped Joan would get probation or a fine, not jail. She wanted to have nothing more to do with Joan. Joan told us that she wanted Mary to leave her alone as well and that she did not want to go to court and have a record. Each women told us that the problem was almost entirely the other one's fault. Mary thinks Joan was raised differently from her family and that her parents do not help her out much.

Although the mediation program sent Mary and Joan an invitation to try mediation for this charge, they failed to respond. They said that they had received the invitation too late, although the letter was sent well in advance of the hearing date. Both expressed some dissatisfaction with the previous mediation— Joan because she had felt pressed by the mediator and because she thought Joe had been better treated than she, Mary because Joan did not follow the agreement. Thus, after trying mediation once, they avoided it whenever it was offered again. But they did not stop going to court. By this time, both women were becoming experienced court users.

When they appear in court for the pretrial conference on the issued complaint in mid-August, the attorneys—the prosecutor and a court-appointed defense attorney—again urge mediation. My research assistant observed these events. (It was the same day as the trial between Mischa and Zoar so I was in another court). Joan had been assigned a court-appointed attorney who had not spoken to her before the conference date. After waiting some time for Joan to appear, he finally asks a line of women sitting in the courtroom whether any of them were Joan. All say no. He asks whether any of them know what she looks like. Mary, sitting in the line, says she does, and he asks whether she could go get Joan. Mary says no, and the lawyer asks whether she is the opposite party. Then he asks her to describe Joan and he himself goes off to look for her. He discovers her in the clerk's office. They discuss the case briefly in the crowded hallway of the courthouse while the attorney says hello to his friends and colleagues and lets his eyes wander around. At one point, Joan asks him if he is listening to her, and he responds with a quick recap of what she had said. He asks her for more details only of the night of the ring incident, not of the surrounding social relationships. When he asks her whether there was a clerk's hearing, she says no, that it went right to court, that she received a paper saying that there was a hearing. At this hearing, she stood in front of the microphone (probably referring to the arraignment). He asks whether she got a letter from mediation, and she says yes, but she adds that when she called they told her it was too late and that Mary had not called anyway. Then she shows him the restraining order, pointing out, in the hallway, the police officer who helped her and who had said that this was a family feud and that he did not want to get involved.

It seems that, despite her extensive experience in court, Joan is still somewhat confused about the stages of the court process and about the relationship between mediation, clerk's hearings, arraignments, pretrial conferences, and trials. Although this courthouse is smaller than that in Cambridge and although there is not the confusion of multiple floors and courtrooms, there is still no one who is likely to explain the whole process to the parties. The mediation program office here is on one floor, the clerk's office is on a second floor, and the courtroom is on a third floor.

In a private conference in the hallway, both attorneys agree that mediation is where the case belongs but they recognize that the parties may not want it. The prosecutor suggests that she will see whether she can get the judge to tell the parties to go to mediation. The mediation program agrees to take the case back with "forceful direction"—that is, direction by the judge. To persuade Joan, the defendant on this charge, to go to mediation, the defense attorney tells her that the charges are serious and that the two women should go to mediation and "talk it out like adult women." He says that enemies put a strain on a marriage, that they both have families and a lot to lose, and that he thinks mediation might help. At the same time, he assures her that going to mediation does not mean that she has psychological problems. He concludes by telling her that she should stay away from Mary and that "you're wasting all of our time." When she agrees to mediation, the defense attorney says that he will move to have the charges dismissed, saying: "*There* are *grounds for these charges. Next time you could do time, or worse. It could be the end of everything—the marriage, children. Be a bigger person than she is. The point is to take a step back here, realize what's at stake. It's hard, because she is your sister-in-law. You can pretend she doesn't exist. Maybe when it's all talked out, it'll all be rectified. Just don't call her or talk to her*" [emphasis is speaker's]. He goes on: "*This is the last step, the court. The alternatives to mediation are pretty severe: fines, jail, extended probation.*" As Joan protests that Mary may not agree to try mediation, the attorney replies: "*I think she'll agree. I think you can both be logical.*" Here the lawyer uses two strategies to pressure Joan to go to mediation. First, he draws on legal discourse to emphasize the severity of the charges she faces. Second, he uses moral discourse to frame her resistance to mediation as meaning that Joan is not being "a bigger person than she [Mary] is" and as not being logical. Her resistance is interpreted as indicative of her emotionalism and her uncooperativeness. Thus, the advice to try mediation is accompanied by a subtle slap against both participants, an insult which seems to me to have gender overtones. My research assistant did not observe the prosecutor's efforts (going on at the same time) to persuade Mary to go to mediation.

The problem was described both by the attorneys and by the police liaison officer as a "family matter" and a "family feud," and all said that they did not want to get involved. The defense attorney was concerned about his reputation with the judge if he let the case proceed. The mediation staff talked about it as a case between sisters-in-law but privately described it as a garbage case because the people involved lie all the time and have no interest in settling the case.

After both Joan and Mary agree to try mediation, a court officer takes them downstairs to the mediation office. In her private mediation intake interview, Mary describes the problem as breaking and entering and theft of an emerald ring. She wants the ring back. She trusts the baby-sitter and does not think the baby-sitter took it. She does not want mediation because Joan broke the last mediation agreement. But she says that in court Joan also got away with everything. Mary hopes that the court will give Joan probation or something so she will not bother Mary again. In her private intake interview, Joan says that things have quieted down since the last mediation but that the court business is putting a strain on her marriage: "*This has got way out of hand. Mary had a lot to do with breaking us up and wants to see us divorced.*" Joan says she wants mediation. Her lawyer has told her that she could get into serious trouble on these charges. "*That's all I need. I never did anything when I was young. Now, they're going to slap charges on me."* She reports that he has told her that the judge will only take so much before he gets mad at both of them. She then complains that she does not feel comfortable with her lawyer and that she can't talk with him or cry in front of him: "He's too cute."

Both women appeared for a mediation session at the end of August. Joe came as well. I observed this session. The mediators began this session by asking what the complaints were and saying that they would start with these complaints, thus framing the event as a legal one. Mary said that Joan had threatened her daughter and her father and that Joan had said that if Mary did not drop the charges, "I will see your father dead and walk on his grave." Joan denied threatening Mary's daughter and presented her side of a series of incidents. She pointed out that Mary, despite knowing about Joan's temper, makes comments for Joan to hear about Joe's new girlfriend: *"She knows once I get going, I don't stop. She doesn't get mad so quickly."* She bursts into tears, saying that she is grateful to her husband's family for all they have done for her and that she has thanked them but that suddenly the whole family wants nothing to do with her. Joe, in his initial statement, says that the situation has nothing to do with him. He is disturbed that his sister called the police when he parked in her driveway for a few minutes. He continues *"Mary has done things for us, it is true, but this is so stretched out now, everybody hates everybody else; everything I do gets hated. Joan did say she would kill my father next time. I could have punched her. She says things like that. They are still my parents."* He goes on: *"There is so much hatred, I can't say anything now. I am right in the middle—I can't say anything to make things better. She is my wife, that is what I know—but they are my parents too."* The mediators see the solution as a separation of the two women while Joe maintains contact with his parents. They say privately to each other that he is in a difficult situation and needs counseling. In the session, they focus on restructuring the relationships but feel stumped by the problem of the ring. In the private session with Mary, they again ask for clarification of the charges, and Mary insists on the importance of having the ring back. At the same time, she complains that she used to be very close to her brother but is now angry with him and has no relationship with him at all. The mediators ask again: "So, is the larceny charge still on the books?" Mary says that she asked about the larceny in court and that they told her to come back to mediation and raise it again, but she thinks the court is more concerned about the assault and battery. She asserts that the ring is worth $1,000, although it was purchased for $300. Mary says she is determined to go back to court over the ring. The mediators fear that a new court action will destroy the fragile peace currently existing as a result of Joe and Joan's moving away.

Joan spent much of her time in this mediation session in tears. The mediators recommended counseling, but she was not interested. After about three hours, Joan and Mary agreed to continue to have no contact with each other and to have no threats or other forms of communication.

The confusion over the larceny charge, which was never filed, is puzzling. One possible explanation is that Mary, as plaintiff, presumes that she will get more response from the court about a stolen ring than about harassment and disturbing the peace. She says the police told her to take Joan to court and she thinks that there is enough evidence against Joan in the stolen-ring charge for a good case. However, court officials, such as the clerk, seem to have dissuaded her from filing this charge, focusing instead on the more diffuse relational charges. Thus, it seems that Mary persists in raising the ring complaint despite the court's efforts to drop it. Or, perhaps Mary thought of adding the ring charge after the clerk's hearing. It seems to me that the ring complaint provides a legal framing for the problem and that, in persuading the plaintiff to shift to moral discourse, the clerk encouraged her to drop the charge, thus moving the case away from legal discourse.

A subsequent court hearing in mid-September considered whether the case should be continued or dismissed. Mary appeared briefly, Joan not at all. The defense attorney argued that the case should be dismissed, but the prosecutor insisted on continuing it for three months. The two attorneys privately agreed that both women were nuts, crazy, and that there was a long history to the conflict. In arguing for a continuance, the prosecutor pointed out that the mediation program usually monitors cases for ninety days and that, given the long history of difficulty between these women, it would be good to maintain some supervision to be sure that the problem was over. Joan was furious, since she felt that now Mary had something over her head for the next three months. The ring was never mentioned in court.

When Mary first came to court, she had some faith in the power and effectiveness of the judge, although she observed that Joan ignored some of the court's demands. She thought that Joan could "sweet-talk" the mediators, but "What the judge says goes, and she can't say no to the judge like she can to the mediator." After her experiences in court, she still thinks courts are generally fair and that in court something gets done, but her expectations are more limited.

Joan, on the other hand, thinks that the legal system is pervaded by influence, that it is not fair, that it hinders rather than helps personal problems, and that one does not have to go along with the orders of the court because it is always possible to appeal to a higher court. And she thinks that domestic problems are shunted to mediation. But she has also discovered that the court responds to a scene and that she can get what she wants by turning on the tears. For example, she attributes her success in getting a restraining order against Mary to her throwing a scene in the courtroom. She thinks that she is better off in court than in mediation— "especially if I turned on the waterworks" (resorted to tears)— because she knows Judge "Jones." She also cried through much of the mediation session, although whether deliberately or because she was genuinely upset I could not tell. After her extensive experience in court, however, she concludes, in a pithy phrase: "The law don't mean pickles."

These people are experienced and heavy users of the court and of other services: Joan had been to another local court asking for help as well as to a counselor at a battered-woman's shelter. Both are clearly using the court as a resource in their struggles with each other, both in filing charges and in following through with them. But they are not entirely comfortable in this arena. Despite their experience, the defense attorney managed to scare Joan into thinking that she faced serious legal charges, although she was beginning to be skeptical of these fears. Both Joan and Mary are still confused about the stages of the court process, although they are growing more sophisticated. They also experienced continuing pressure to settle, which they resisted by asserting, in various ways, that they had a real legal problem. I think Mary's continued assertion of the larceny of the ring may reflect this strategy. Joan has discovered the power of emotion in court, but, as her attorney showed when he urged her to try mediation and be logical, her emotions can also be used against her. Throughout this case, there seems to be an underlying assumption that these are women's problems—and that they are therefore not worthy of real concern.

The parties' extensive experience in court brings with it a paradox: on the one hand, Joan and Mary are known in the court and have learned how to elicit a response, but at the same time, as the court officials see them over and over, they become less interested in helping them. The parties acquire reputations as being crazy and as being involved in an interminable and insoluble feud. The mediation program too came to regard their problems as unworthy of attention. On the one hand, court officials minimize the case, handling it superficially, pressing for early settlement, refusing to prosecute, and discouraging the parties by rudeness and long waiting periods and by telling them they are wasting the court's time. On the other hand, because the parties are persistent and emotionally intense, the court does handle their cases. They have, indeed, received extensive services from the court and other government agencies. Many experienced court users, such as Joan, have discovered and use the trump card of passion, but it is one which simultaneously wins and loses as the person gets some results but also acquires a reputation for being crazy.

This is an unusual case in that it involves so many charges in court. As we have seen, there are a significant number of such cases in court every year, although they are only a small proportion of the total caseload. But several themes appear in this case which are characteristic of most interpersonal cases in court. The police are important sources of referral to court. They urge people to go, tell them that they have cases, and suggest asking for restraining orders. There is continual pressure to settle rather than to go forward to trial. The court officials view the parties as troublesome and mutually at fault. The problem is classified as a family matter or as a family feud, and the attorneys and judges are anxious not to get too deeply involved with it. As with most of the interpersonal cases I observed, as a case it is trivial but as a problem it is excruciating. As a case, the conflict is vague, with multiple charges and countercharges. But as a problem involving jealousy, money, early marriage of a favorite brother and son, and subtle class differences between a more settled-living family and a more hard-living daughter-in-law, it is sharp and painful. Joe, the center of the struggle, complains that all there is in his family is hatred. He is in the middle and cannot do anything.

Conclusions

These encounters with the legal system shift plaintiffs' consciousness of law. The people involved come to think of the courts as ineffective, unwilling to help in these personal crises, and indifferent to the ordinary person's problem. They discover that one need not fear the court; one need not even appear. Areas of resistance to the authority of the court open up. If the court says it will not deal with one's problem, one can burst into tears or scream in anger. Even if the prosecutor tells someone she is wasting his time and the court's time, she can still go back and file another application for complaint. Despite the court's ex-pectation of rational talk limited to the elaboration of specific incidents and buttressed by evidence of some sort, one can talk about being in fear for one's life or repeatedly bring up the time when he hit you or when she stole the ring. One can insist on retaining legal discourse and block the shift to moral or thera-peutic discourse. The court turns out to be different, in some ways, than what it seemed from the outside; but the reward of experience is greater skill in wrest-ing help from the court.

The categories and procedures of the law are hegemonic, but not entirely so. Plaintiffs take for granted that courts are places where they can get help. They premise their demands on the hegemonic legal categories of property and con-tract, but they do not accept that the system is always fair, just, or even-handed.[13] Experience in court leads them to think that the institution is erratic, unreliable, and sometimes ineffectual. For many, a sense of legal entitlement coexists with cynicism about power and influence within the government and the court system. When they do not succeed in court, plaintiffs are quick to charge that there is personal influence. Ironically, plaintiffs' experience of the ineffectiveness of the court derives from court personnel's recognition that they are faced with problems rather than with cases and that they are unable to handle problems of this kind. Yet, many court officials and mediators do make con-certed and extensive efforts to provide some kind of help for these problems.

The puzzle here, as throughout this book, is why these people come back to court despite the efforts of court personnel to persuade them that their problems do not belong in court. I believe they return because there is nowhere else to go for "justice," however that is conceived, and because the law is preferable to violence. Moreover, the court does, from time to time, provide help, even if this help is simply a summons mailed to the opponent's house or a lecture delivered by a judge, a clerk, or even a defense attorney. These actions are clothed in the symbolic power of the court, making them more than they would seem from the perspective of case processing in the court itself. Even though people who fail to appear in clerk's hearings seem to be people who have not taken advantage of the court's help, the filing of the complaint and the receipt of a summons often makes a large impact, even if no one comes to the hearing. What the courts provide is often symbolic rather than directly coercive. In many cases, the critical role of law is its symbolic presence in the battle rather than its active intervention.

Although the consciousness of legal entitlement is pervasive and powerful and draws ordinary people into court, with experience they reinterpret that entitlement as something to be won with struggle. Some demand that their feelings be recognized, some continue to insist on legal claims and entitlements, some begin to regard the court as an arena for contest. A few shout and complain, charging the system with injustice, demanding that their misery, their outrage, their anger, be recognized. Others, of course, give in and go away, frustrated or disillusioned. These cases are burrs in the court, unsettling and disquieting to the normal order of things. They demand recognition of another view of the world, a view which says that some people live in dangerous housing, that some people face daily violence from their spouses, that some neighborhoods are rife with violence and anger.

Thus, the garbage case is a site of struggle: the court endeavors to manage chaos, to contain emotion, to blunt the impression of injustice by providing some service, while the plaintiff fights for recognition of his problem as he or she experiences it and for the legal relief to which he or she feels entitled. The court tries to manage and eject the case while still providing some form of justice. The plaintiff, as she resists conversion of the case to moral discourse, discovers how to use the court for her own purposes.

These cases pose difficult dilemmas for American society, dilemmas inherent in its liberal legal order and in its widespread consciousness of legal entitlement. They pit the ideals of equality before the law and equal access to justice against the danger of the expanding and intrusive state. To ignore or refuse to act denies citizens their sense of entitlement, but to intervene encourages dependence on state ordering of family and neighborhood life. Moreover, as courts fail to intervene in legal terms but attempt to convert problems to moral terms—a move reflective of more general tendencies within American culture—courts risk enhancing the image of ineffectiveness and powerlessness that they have among the working-class and the poor, groups which have traditionally been the subjects of control by state legal authority. A diminishing legitimacy and diminishing appearance of power by the courts could require a greater expenditure of state resources in the apparatus of sanctioning and punishing. These are fundamental dilemmas in the intersection of culture and law in American society and are not susceptible to easy resolution.

8

Conclusions: The Paradox of Legal Entitlement

This journey into the social and cultural worlds of working-class plaintiffs suggests that these Americans turn to the courts with problems they consider legal in an effort to get help and to establish the truth of the situations they confront. But they enter the courthouse neither eagerly nor quickly; it is typically a last resort, a desperate move when all else seems to have failed. Turning to the court is symbolically a very serious step, one which inflames the other side and rapidly escalates the conflict. People hesitate to turn to court unless they feel that important principles are at stake. The plaintiffs in this book endured problems for a long time before resorting to the court. When they finally did so, they were searching for an authority who could determine who was right and who was wrong.

Litigiousness, Court Use, and the Escape from Community

In trying to understand what it means when people bring personal problems to court, some commentators have blamed it on an American tendency toward litigiousness. They hypothesize, as I discussed in Chapter 1, that Americans are ready to sue at the slightest provocation, their desires unleashed by the breakdown of community and the erosion of authority. By the end of the 1980s, the theory of the litigious American was widely accepted, occupying the status of common sense (see Hayden 1989). Implicit in this theory is the assumption that community has broken down, that the traditional authorities of family, church, and community have weakened so that people go to court rather than rely on these authorities, and that Americans generally regret this change and bemoan the loss of community (e.g., see Lieberman 1981: 186.) With the decline in commitment to family and neighborhood life, people pull the government—the police and the courts—into their squabbles. They do so because they no longer feel either the same loyalty to these institutions or the same willingness to defer to the wishes of others. Now it is every man and woman for him- or herself as the modern citizen focuses on his own self-interest rather than on a greater communal good. Since the willingness to compromise and settle differences depends on the existence of social relationships which people wish to preserve, those who fail to settle must be people who put their personal interests above their social relationships.

This way of understanding the role of state law and community social order grows out of a general theory of the relationship between formal and informal social control and of the conditions under which one or the other predominates (see, generally, Wirth 1938; Schwartz 1954; Black 1976). According to this theory, formal and informal social control exist in inverse relation: the more formal social control, the less informal, and vice versa (Black 1976). Informal control exists only under conditions of stability, intimacy, and normative homogeneity. As society becomes more functionally specialized, mobile, and differentiated through the effects of urbanization and industrialization, these conditions tend to disappear. The normative homogeneity and social linkages which provided for effective informal social controls within local communities dissipate. Gossip, scandal, and other forms of social pressure fail to produce an orderly society. Because informal social control has collapsed, formal social control expands. Donald Black (1976) is careful to point out that this is a correlation, not a causal relationship. Yet it is often taken to be a causal relationship, with the implication that, as community collapses, the state is forced to expand into the vacuum.

I argue, however, that the expansion of formal social control is not caused by the collapse of community but by American individualism and egalitarian values and by the expansive efforts of the state. It is a result of ordinary citizens' desire to escape from community and, at the same time, of the legal system's invitation to them to bring their neighborhood and family problems to the courts. Individuals turn to the law to escape from the bonds of community and to construct a preferred mode of social ordering within families and neighborhoods. They often use the law to challenge the social hierarchies in families and communities which control their lives. Yet, in doing so they also respond to the entitlements and services offered by the state. Thus, the behavior I am describing is not so different from that claimed by proponents of the litigiousness and community-breakdown theory, but my interpretation of this behavior is different.

The theory of litigiousness and of the breakdown of community misunderstands the contemporary American attitude toward community. As long as community is conceived according the romantic American folk vision of a warm, intimate, and supportive social group, it is hard to understand why anyone would give it up. But the very intimacy and totality of such a social world make it miserable for the person who cannot or will not go along.[1] It is not clear that urban Americans truly regret the loss of an intimate, consensual community. Proponents of community portray the alienated urbanite forced to sacrifice the close social world of his ancestral village, but it often seems that he or she wanted to leave. For example, those who lived in the small towns of America during the nineteenth and twentieth centuries left the country for the city, in droves. Obviously, the pull of jobs and the push of rural poverty are critical to rural-to-urban migration, but the attraction of a social life more free of gossip and of the informal surveillance of neighbors, family, and friends also has an appeal. Even eighteenth-century New England communities were constantly changing as discontented people and segments of the community moved away in order to deal with their differences (Bender 1978: 73). The United States, unlike Europe and many other parts of the world, lacks a tradition of settled peasant villages in which restrictions on mobility create enormous pressures to compromise interests and to settle. Even American immigrant communities, in which such village-like social structures are recreated, rarely last more than two or three generations, unless they are replenished by new immigrants. For much of American history, the frontier provided, for people enmeshed in conflicts, opportunities to move away. Perhaps the original decision to come to the United States was a similar strike toward freedom. Indeed, historian Robert Wiebe argues that it is a fundamental cultural logic in America to deal with difference by living apart (1975). "What held Americans together," he says, "was their ability to live apart. Society depended on segmentation (1975: 46)."

In the postwar period, the suburbs have offered the possibility of a more private, autonomous life, regulated less by convention, by gossip, and by local leaders. As the working-class adolescent from an inner-city, close-knit neighborhood put it: "I want to get out of here, away from the people here. I want to get to a place where you can decide for yourself how you want to live. In Cityville, you have to be what others want (Steinitz and Solomon 1986: 50)." Other adolescents from this neighborhood want the peace and quiet of the suburbs, their spaciousness, the opportunities that they think the suburbs provide to be oneself and to be free of conventions, although they also fear that life there will be lonely and isolated (Steinitz and Solomon 1986: 17–62). Such suburban neighborhoods provide more freedom of individual expression, self-fulfillment, and individuality in private life—as long as one does not park an unregistered car in the driveway, make noise after 11 P.M., allow a dog to run free, build a structure too close to the property line, or in other ways violate the elaborate set of local regulations and zoning restrictions which are typical of suburbs.[2]

Insofar as contemporary Americans are voting with their feet rather than with their rhetoric, they are continuing to move to suburbs, to choose privacy, separation, and, for social ordering, dependence on the law rather than the intimacy of community.[3] In the postwar period, Americans in large numbers left the urban ethnic villages of the inner city to move to the suburbs. Three-quarters of all American housing has been built since 1940, a period in which the single-family detached home, produced in vast numbers, became the norm (Hayden 1984: 12). By 1980, two-thirds of the American housing stock consisted of single-family, detached homes (Hayden 1984: 12). Increased affluence has been translated into more widely spaced homes, reduced dependence on neighbors, smaller networks of kinsmen in which reciprocity prevails, and fewer people living in the same household, whether through elimination of older relatives, through divorce, or through restriction of the household to the nuclear family. As Americans have moved up, they have moved apart.

In addition to the flaws in the argument that the litigious American has been unleashed by community breakdown—an argument premised on a romanticized vision of an intimate, orderly community lost—there are other reasons to doubt the picture of the litigious American. A significant body of careful empirical research casts doubt on the existence of a litigation explosion at all.[4] We do not know whether there has been any increase in the number of interpersonal disputes in court during the massive urbanization and industrialization which have swept American society in this century, nor whether there are more interpersonal cases in court per person now then there were in the more rural eighteenth and nineteenth centuries. Historical comparisons are very difficult, since, before the court reforms of the early twentieth century, these problems were typically handled by local magistrates and justices of the peace in informal and diverse ways (Friedman 1973; Harrington 1985). There has been very little historical research on caseloads in these lower courts of the eighteenth and nineteenth centuries, and we know little about how the myriad and diverse local courts operated (Daniels 1985: 391). Some historical research on this question, research on early modern Europe and the United States, has produced interesting but spotty data, based on the limited documentary evidence which is available (e.g., see Auerbach 1983; Bossy 1983). So we really do not know whether, accompanying the urbanization of the late nineteenth and twentieth centuries, there has in fact been an increase in the amount of interpersonal disputing which takes place in the courts.

Yet, the notion of the litigious American, in a cultural and psychological sense, remains popular. Its continuing appeal suggests that, in addition to conforming to the political interests of federal judges clamoring for more resources and to the economic interests of insurance companies eager to charge higher premiums while passing the blame on to lawyers (see Sarat 1985), this theory resonates with our cultural myths about American society. It is, as Carol Greenhouse points out, a way of understanding American society and the behavior of individual Americans, a cultural interpretation of our motivations for turning to the court (1989).[5] Moreover, the story fits with broadly accepted understandings of the social effects of urbanization and industrialization.[6] In contrast to rural communities, the city appears to be fractured by a diversity of religions, moral codes, and ethnic and racial heritages, a diversity which leads to disorder and the need for more formal social control. People take personal problems to court instead of taking them to community or religious leaders. Thus, litigiousness has been added to the catalog of urban ills.

But this theory of urbanism looks only at one side of the social life of cities: it focuses on features of disorganization but overlooks the freedom and tolerance of the city, often popularly considered the hallmarks of urban life. It is precisely the diversity and disorder which creates spaces for freedom and tolerance. By comparison, the life of the small village is often oppressively narrow, limited, and confined. The theory of the litigious American ignores the ways in which litigation serves to challenge existing hierarchies of power, to make spaces within established social orders. It ignores the desire to challenge the control inherent in village or neighborhood life that law use represents as well as the greater authority it makes possible.

I argue that people turn to the courts as an alternative source of authority as they seek to escape the supervision of local political authorities and to avoid recourse to violence. Plaintiffs go to court as part of a search for a new kind of community: they aspire to neighborhoods such as Riverdale, relatively free of confrontation and conflict, in which neighbors are remote from one another and in which conflicts are governed by avoidance or law, not by violence and angry shouting matches. These neighborhoods, epitomized by the spreading suburbs of the postwar period, have far greater privacy and less gossip than the older, denser neighborhoods. Neighbors are no longer relatives or friends; they are people known in an affable way on whom one can call for help in an emergency. But suburbanites often call the police instead. From zoning to leash laws regulation by town officials and by law, provides the order within which these private neighborhoods can exist, an order established by the legal authority of town government and courts rather than by ward bosses, local merchants, or the cop on the beat. In this kind of social order, weaker parties can use the law to challenge the domination of stronger parties. For example, women use the courts as they struggle to define a more autonomous role with relationship to their husbands and boyfriends, one in which they need not endure violence or abuse.

In sum, in searching for the meaning of the use of courts by plaintiffs with interpersonal disputes, one cannot stop by labeling it a cultural pattern of "litigiousness" or by attributing it to the breakdown of community. It is part of an effort by working-class Americans to escape from the control of local political authorities and from dependence on violence to a less violent, more autonomous, more legally regulated social life. It expresses a desire for privacy and peace. And among some subordinate groups, such as women, it expresses a desire for greater equality.

The Invitation

Further, the law has invited citizens to bring personal problems to court. Laws enacted by legislatures, legal services policies, and some actions of the courts themselves encourage citizens to bring their problems to court. Statutes have been passed which assert the obligations of the law to supervise aspects of family and neighborhood life (e.g., see Donzelot 1980; Teitelbaum, n.d.). The government subsidizes legal services for the poor. The courts have been reorganized to be more accessible to all social classes. The courts have on occasion intervened powerfully on the side of the disadvantaged, as in the famous *Brown v. Board of Education* case in 1954.

Four periods are particularly noteworthy in the extension of the invitation to use the courts: (1) the Progressive Era in the early decades of the century, (2) the New Deal programs in the 1930s, (3) the legal rights activism of the 1960s, and (4) the extension of therapeutic services attached to the courts in the 1970s and 1980s. All have been periods of liberal reform in which the state expanded its role in order to provide improved benefits and services, new rights and protections, and a more accessible and efficient legal system. Progressive Era reforms changed the municipal courts, probation, and juvenile courts; New Deal reforms offered insurance for unemployment and old age, along with federal protection of unions and the right to organize; the aggressive legal rights movement of the 1960s and 1970s created new rights for the poor, minorities, and consumers and provided legal services to implement these rights; and the 1970s and 1980s reforms brought a wide range of social services intended to promote social adjustment to the criminal courts. The following discussion examines some of these periods in more detail.

Early in the twentieth century, new criminal justice institutions such as juvenile courts, reformatories, probation, and reform-oriented prisons emerged to provide therapeutic services designed to facilitate the adjustment of immigrant populations to the American mainstream (Rothman 1980; Kett 1983: 275). These reforms in the criminal justice system pulled more people under its supervision (Rothman 1980). The legal rights activism of the 1960s and its associated legislation concerning individual rights further involved poor people with the law. It encouraged minorities, prisoners, welfare mothers, consumers, and other disadvantaged groups to turn to the courts for protection. The movement fostered a vision of the law as the ally of the powerless and provided a cadre of energetic and accessible lawyers who encouraged poor people to use the law to improve their lot, efforts funded by the federal government (Handler et al. 1978).[7] Handler et. al. maintain that aggressive legal rights organizations functioned very differently than the traditional legal aid provided to indigents since the beginnings of the twentieth century, helping to create a revolution in legal thought on behalf of the poor and unrepresented and changing the legal consciousness of our society (1978: 13–14, 46).

I argue that this legal rights activism affected the poor and unrepresented themselves, suggesting to them the possibility of seeking the court's help in dealing with their problems.[8] Even earlier, however, the new stance of the government as the ally of the little person, a stance taken during the Progressive Era and strengthened during the Depression, encouraged the average person to think of the law as a source of help rather than as an alien institution. Celebrated cases which began to chip away at the structures of privilege in the area of union recognition and civil rights intensified this feeling. Together, as Friedman observes, these changes contributed to the creation of a new understanding of the relationship between the legal system and the disadvantaged and, more broadly, between the lower-class individual and the state (1973). These changes created a new ideology of the state as friendly and supportive, as the protector of the poor and weak and as the regulator of the strong. In the era of liberal legal reformism, old concerns about the tyranny of the state disappeared. Americans in the eighteenth century feared state domination; twentieth-century Americans look to the state for protection against the giant corporations (Friedman 1973). During the twentieth century, the law has gradually taken on a new face as the protector of the weak and vulnerable, as a tool for achieving social justice, and as a weapon against big business and corporate power.

Thus, the government has in a sense invited ordinary people to bring their problems to the courts. It has fostered an image of helpfulness and has provided legal assistance. Since the Second World War, there has been a general increase in the accessibility of the law.[9] Some people think this invitation has worked too well: bar associations and judicial leaders complain that too many people are using the courts. The current interest in alternative forms of dispute resolution seems to invite these users out of the legal system, encouraging them to turn elsewhere with their problems (Nader 1980; Auerbach 1983). At the same time as the working class has taken on the pervasive legal ideology of American society, middle-class Americans are promoting reforms based on an antilaw ideology.

Women have responded in particular force to this invitation, disproportionately using the courts for personal problems. It represents for them a resource in relationships of unequal power, a way to deal with abusive husbands and lovers as well as with difficult neighbors and children. Women's use of the courts is another aspect of the general pattern of relatively vulnerable and powerless people turning to the courts for help in those relationships in which they feel at a disadvantage. Not all court users fit this pattern, of course: some are the more powerful members of relationships who are calling on yet another ally to buttress their control. But many do fit. Turning to the court requires moving outside a relationship and one's private world, and this is not something anyone does readily or without paying a social price. Those who do not need to call on this form of power tend to do so less frequently. Men very rarely take their wives to court.

I have not explored here the institutional sources of the discourses I describe, nor the reasons they have emerged in American courts in the 1980s. And I have not described the groups which have constructed and promoted them. These are important questions, alluded to in the earlier discussion of the development of the juvenile court and of a more therapeutic notion of legal intervention. These questions are beyond the scope of this book, but they are questions which are important to ask. If there is a power to naming, to framing experiences in one or another discourse, it is critical to examine both how the names and discourses are formed historically and which groups promote them and impose them on others.[10]

Paradoxes

The Denial of Legal Entitlement

One result of this invitation is the widespread use of law for personal problems. Poorer as well as richer citizens feel entitled to use the courts. The law serves as a source of secular moral authority, defining everyday social relationships and promising protection in a society which eschews the religious authority which in other societies typically governs interpersonal relationships. Plaintiffs in interpersonal cases see the law as a source of authority in a society organized by rules, not by violence, and dedicated to mythic ideals of equality, even if these are rarely achieved in practice. The law is a valuable resource because it is symbolically powerful and because it expresses a pervasive pattern of social ordering.[11] Legality, in this constitutive sense, is part of the taken-for-granted world of the white working-class people I talked to.[12]

The people who go to court in these communities do so not out of an eagerness to use the court but out of a sense of entitlement, a sense that the courts are a resource which they, as citizens, have a right to use. They go with problems framed within their consciousness of law, problems presented in terms of fundamental rights to protection from violence, in terms of defense of property, in terms of assertion of the authority of parents over children, in terms of new ideas about the rights of women to security from violence by the men in their lives. They are angry at injuries to themselves and to their property and think that they have the right to protest. Some go because the law is more civilized than violence. Their consciousness of legal entitlement conforms to fundamental categories of the law itself: protections for property and persons, control over children, management of the marriage relationship, and increasingly, more therapeutic kinds of help available through the court.

But, as these plaintiffs arrive in court, they discover that their legal consciousness differs in subtle ways from that of the clerks, prosecutors, and mediators they meet there. The problems they think are legally serious are interpreted as trivial in a legal sense although important in terms of the morality of interpersonal relationships. Their demands to be heard as plaintiffs with a case are typically rejected, but they receive consideration of their problems in a social sense. Court officials, endeavoring to provide what they consider justice, convert these problems from legal to moral or therapeutic discourse. They send them to mediation or handle them themselves, providing advice and refusing to go forward with criminal charges. Juvenile-court proceedings represent another example of a legalistic setting in which law is rarely raised and in which problems are converted to moral discourse.

This analysis explains why these problems are matter out of place in the courts. They are both invited and encouraged into the court and, at the same time, denied legal handling. Incorporating them into the legal arena is important because they are potentially disruptive to the large social order. But they need only to be framed and contained, not to receive the full panoply of litigation which brings with it an invitation to assert rights and to demand change. Because these problems are handled in a blend of discourses rather than in legal terms alone, the legal claims can be deflected, transformed, extinguished while tensions ease. Problems become rephrased as cases which are then rejected as inappropriate; plaintiffs' efforts to master legal discourse and to demand satisfaction are undone as their problems are named in moral and therapeutic terms, terms which deny them access to legal remedies.

Thus, as these working-class court users seek to assert their sense of entitlement to legal relief for these problems, they find that it is denied by the courts. The court does not reject their requests out of hand but subjects them to periods of monitoring, to probationary supervision, to social services. The problems are denied as legal cases but receive continuing supervision and management as moral or therapeutic problems.[13] The plaintiffs do not find their rights protected, but they do receive lectures, advice about how to organize their lives, encouragement to come back for mediation, and promises that something will be done to the defendant if the problem recurs: the complaint will be issued, the problem will go back to court, perhaps the defendant will be fined or imprisoned. This can be seen as a form of cultural domination in that the court uses its legal authority to frame the problems in other discourses, to offer nonlegal solutions, and to deny the forms of protection and help promised by the legal system itself. But it is cultural domination exercised on those who have chosen to come to the court in the first place.

Yet, there are forms of resistance. Even within this relationship of domination, plaintiffs struggle to control their problems, to shape the legal system to their needs rather than to be shaped by it. Despite the efforts of lower-court personnel to convert these legal claims to moral discourse and to send them out the door, plaintiffs struggle to keep the legal issues in the forefront, to assert their claims for protection of their rights. Plaintiffs come back, renewing their demands, learning to use legal categories with more sophistication, mastering legal discourse, asserting their problems in their full complexity and emotional power, demanding recognition in their own terms. This is a continuing struggle, a pull between plaintiffs who wish to harness the power of the law for their own ends and those who would use it to control the weaker and subordinate members of society.

Indeed, the ideological face of law is a form of domination, but it is not complete. Experience challenges it, evokes resistance, teaches its use against those who control it. The relationship between the mythic vision of law and subordinate groups is not simply a story of imposition but is one of struggle: of penetration, reformulation, and resistance.

Entitlement and Dependency

There is a fundamental paradox to the consciousness of legal entitlement. The use of law by those at the bottom of the social hierarchy empowers the individual with relation to his or her neighbors and family members. On the other hand, it increases his dependence on the institutions of the state. The plaintiff draws on the symbolic power of the law to gain strength in fights with those he or she knows, but he or she loses control over this power when the problem moves into the courts. As the working-class citizen turns to the courts for protection against spouses, friends, and neighbors, he or she becomes vulnerable to the intervention of the rules and practices of the legal system and to the groups with the power to generate them. Thus, the use of the courts furthers the subordination of the working class to those who manage and dispense court services. The more that working-class people become conscious of their legal rights and use the legal system to assert them, the more they can challenge traditional hierarchies which control their lives. But, at the same time, they become more dependent on the laws to mount that challenge and to define its terms.

This is the paradox of going to court: freedom from the control of the community comes at the price of domination by the state, in the form of the courts. To return to court again is to offer the court the opportunity to shape the problem in *its* discourses, to name it, and to point toward its solution. As the average person returns to court with new demands, he strengthens the power of the law over his life, both its direct coercive power and its ideological domination, its capacity to interpret and make sense of his problems. The use of the law challenges existing social hierarchies, but the discourses of the courthouse continue to constrain and restrict the way these problems are understood. Plaintiffs rebel against the social order, but their complaints are held within a framework established by the law, by traditions of social relationships, and by the language of therapy and help.

The consciousness of legal entitlement and the consequent turning to the law are profoundly democratic, radically egalitarian, and fundamentally American. This legal entitlement is an outgrowth of faith in the law, a faith observed early by Tocqueville and other commentators on the American scene. Cultural values of autonomy, self-reliance, individualism, and tolerance have led local courthouses to become the nearest moral authority for dealing with family and neighborhood problems. The roots of this legal consciousness lie, I believe, in the historical American demand for tolerance and pluralism, which pressed toward a public life governed by codes of law and science rather than by religion or local morality. As the discourses of law and therapy spread into popular consciousness, they fostered the transformation from a local, exclusive, morally closed society to an open, incorporative, secular, and individualistic one, a society better equipped to absorb culturally diverse groups. One mode of incorporation was to increase reliance on those national discourses which stretch beyond local places: the discourses of the helping professions and of the law. These discourses rise at the expense of idiosyncrasy, localism, religious authority, and prejudice.

But, the irony of court use for these working-class plaintiffs is that as they seek to use the law to establish a more autonomous life, one regulated by law rather than by violence, they become more dependent on the law to order their lives. There is, in this sense, a new relationship forged between the individual and the state. The individual seeks to construct a social world of autonomy and individualism, a vision deeply entrenched in American culture, by establishing closer ties to the state as a way to order family and neighborhood life. The individual allows the institutions of the state, in this case the courts, to expand their supervision and governance of his intimate world of neighborhood and family. These plaintiffs free themselves from the control of their neighbors and spouses but tie themselves more closely to the state.

Thus, the paradox of legal entitlement poses a fundamental dilemma for American society and for its legal order founded on liberalism. This is a society which celebrates individualism and equal access to the due process of the law. Yet there are some problems which seem less worthy of this equal access and less appropriate for legal intervention. This book concerns an arena of behavior which lies in the gray area between that traditionally regulated by the state and that which is private and beyond state control. The location of this boundary between public and private is now recognized as a profoundly political boundary and is being hotly contested, particularly by feminists (e.g., Minow 1990). To see family and neighborhood problems as being within the scope of the law is to expand that boundary and to increase government supervision over areas of life long defined as private; to deny access for these problems is to violate the expectations of relatively powerless citizens that the authority of the law is available to them as well as to the more privileged. This paradox is inherent in the legal order of contemporary America itself.

Appendix: Other Studies of Court Users

In order to examine to what extent the people I studied were typical of court users in other regions of the country, I examined existing studies of mediation program clients and court clients for information on the kinds of people who bring interpersonal cases to court. The following summaries indicate that such information is sparse but that, insofar as it exists, it shows that the social characteristics of court users are roughly the same as those I observed in Cambridge and Salem.

Kansas City

Christine Harrington's thorough and detailed study of both the Kansas City Neighborhood Justice Center (a mediation program) and the Kansas City Municipal Court describes a similar clientele (1985). She examines 591 cases referred to mediation between March 1978 and January 1979 and a matched sample of 545 related party cases filed in the prosecutor's office of the Kansas City Municipal Court over ten months of 1977 and 1978 (1985: 108).

The cases referred to mediation were similar in composition: 194 (34 percent) were domestic 206 (36 percent) were neighbor, 47 (8 percent) were friends, 42 (7 percent) were merchant/consumer; 66 (11 percent) were landlord/tenant, 11 (2 percent) were employer/employee, and 9 (2 percent) were other kinds of cases; the remaining 16 cases (3 percent) were unclassified because of missing data (1985: 135). Two-thirds (67 percent) of the cases were referred from the criminal justice system (1985: 112). Sixty-eight percent of the complainants were female and 32 percent were male, while the respondents were 40 percent female and 60 percent male (1985: 111). The most common pattern was female complainant–male respondent (41 percent).[1] In the two largest categories of disputes referred to this mediation program, harassment and assault (46 percent), women are typically complainants against men. These are generally the kinds of problems I have labeled "marital" and "boyfriend/girlfriend," which tend to have assault and harassment charges. The racial composition of parties was about half black, half white; 49 percent of the plaintiffs were blacks, 46 percent were whites, and 4 percent were Hispanic. The racial composition of plaintiffs and defendants was almost the same (Harrington 1985: 134–35).[2] Only 12 percent of cases involved interracial disputes; the rest occurred within racial groups (1985: 111). The majority (56 percent) of plaintiffs reported an annual income under $6000, and 94 percent reported incomes under $18,000.[3] Many were unemployed. The majority of people referred to the Neighborhood Justice Center, both complainants and respondents, were between the ages of nineteen and thirty-nine years (1985: 111).

The court comparison group had a similar social composition in terms of age and gender (1985: 149), but it had twice as high a proportion of cases with female plaintiffs and male defendants (see note 1, on gender). There were also more assault cases (56 percent) and vandalism cases (16 percent) and fewer disorderly conduct/harassment cases (14 percent) (1985: 150). It seems likely that the court caseload had a higher proportion of domestic cases and a lower proportion of neighborhood and small-claims cases than did the mediation program, which would explain this difference in gender. Although Harrington was unable to extract further information from the court records, her summary, based on observations and interviews with court personnel and mediation program staff, is worth quoting in full:

> The lower criminal court and the neighborhood justice program share a common class clientele and lower class status. Prosecutors and judges defined a specific community that both the lower court and the neighborhood justice program serve. This community is described by one prosecutor as "agency abusers," comprised largely of unemployed women with children. Another prosecutor's description captures an attitude toward this group that is pervasive among prosecutors and judges in the lower court: "poor white trash; not the black community or the Mexican-American; not even good blue collar." The Neighborhood Justice Center staff describe the people they serve in similar terms and agree that the Neighborhood Justice Center draws on a similar pool of lower class people. Prosecutors, who have private practices in addition to working for the municipal court, said they would never refer their own clients to the Neighborhood Justice Center because of its lower class status" (1985: 149).

The comments of the prosecutors and the mediation program staff seem consistent with the demographic characteristics of the court-using population described in the Kansas City study.

Dorchester, Massachusetts

One of the earliest court-affiliated mediation programs was the Dorchester Urban Court, a program established in 1975 to serve a low-income, racially mixed neighborhood of Boston. Based on mediation program case files, William Felstiner and Lynne Williams's detailed study of the first 500 cases in this mediation program (1975–77) indicates that about 64 percent of the plaintiffs were women, 28 percent were men, 3 percent were boys (under seventeen years old), and 2 percent were girls (1980: 20). These cases were almost all referred from the criminal justice system—60 percent from the court, 29 percent from the clerk, 4 percent from the police, and 7 percent from other sources (1980: 14). These were to a large extent family and neighborhood cases: 25 percent were between spouses and ex-spouses, 14 percent were between lovers and ex-lovers, 9 percent were parent/child, and 23 percent were between neighbors (1980: 21). Although this study did not provide demographic data on the parties, notes from observations of thirty-four mediation sessions in this program, which were provided to me by William Felstiner, indicate that in this randomly selected group of cases, twenty-seven (79 percent) of the plaintiffs were women, eighteen (58 percent) were black, eleven (36 percent) were white, and two (7 percent) were Hispanic (for three cases, racial identity was not specified). The average age of the plaintiffs was thirty-five years, with half being in their thirties and forties. These cases were typical of the program caseload overall: 30 percent were marital, 29 percent were between neighbors, 12 percent were boyfriend/girlfriend, 6 percent were parent/child, and the rest were primarily landlord/tenant, merchant/customer, acquaintances, and employer/employee cases. As for the charges, 58 percent were assault, 18 percent were harassment, 9 percent were larceny, and the rest were breaking and entering, receiving stolen property, nonpayment, property damage, and trespassing.

San Francisco

According to a study by Judith Rothschild (1986), the Mediation Program (a pseudonym) in San Francisco handled only cases which were not referred directly from the criminal justice system. Half of the cases involved neighbors. Despite this program's different referral system and caseload, however, its plaintiffs were still more often women than men and its defendants were more often men than women. An examination of the 1,402 cases referred to the program between its opening in 1977 and about 1981 showed that 56 percent of the plaintiffs were women, 34 percent were men, and 10 percent were couples or families. Men were more often defendants. In a smaller sample of forty cases studied intensively, 58 percent of the plaintiffs were women, 33 percent were men, and 10 percent were couples, while the people complained about were more men (50 percent) than women (23 percent). In general, the parties tended to be relatively poor and not highly educated. Many of the plaintiffs were single women complaining about their neighbors, whom they knew only tenuously, about boundaries, noise, retaining walls, and so forth (1986: 119). In the forty cases studied intensively, women were more likely to complain about neighbors and roommates than were men, while men complained more often about landlords and tenants (1986: 245–47).[4]

Since the proportion of women plaintiffs is about the same in this program as in all the others I have looked at and as in the studies of cases which go directly to court, it seems that women are more likely to seek the help of an outside legal or quasi-legal third party than are men, particularly in situations in which they are trying to establish greater control over men. Many of these women, as is the case with the parent/child cases, are also single women and relatively poor. These observations suggest that this is a way in which weaker parties are using mediation programs and the court to control more powerful parties.

Delaware County, Pennsylvania

As documented in Jennifer Beer's study (1986: 176), an independent mediation program in suburban Philadelphia received three-quarters of its mediated cases from the courts. It handled primarily neighborhood cases: most of the problems concerned noise, dogs, rude children, property damage, name-calling, threats, and harassment (1986: 34, 40). This program received very few referrals for assault, landlord/tenant, and consumer disputes and refused to handle domestic violence or substance abuse cases (1986: 43). Although Delaware County is a highly diverse area with half a million residents ranging widely in income, race, age, and proportion of owner occupancy, an area which includes prestigious college towns as well as desperately poor areas, the mediation cases tended to come from middle-income and poorer sectors of the county and almost never from the professional and wealthy sectors (1986: 188). Most disputants lived in the crowded, poorer neighborhoods which stretch along the city boundary and around the factories along the Delaware River (1986: 33). Many came from areas of changing neighborhoods as new people move in.

The disputants were often blue-collar and clerical workers, housewives, nurses, and people who own small businesses. These are the same kinds of people I saw with neighborhood problems. A few managers, teachers, and other white collar professionals also came. In a survey of people who went through mediation (in the early 1980s), twenty-seven reported their family incomes; the average was $26,6000, in comparison with the 1980 Delaware County median family income of $23,105 (1986: 34). However, Beer notes that this figure may be skewed upward toward the more affluent, who are more likely to return surveys and to report their income. Forty-two disputants provided information on education: seven had less than a high school education, eighteen had a high school diploma, nine had some college, six had a college degree, and two had a master's degree (1986: 34). As in the neighborhood cases I studied, over half (59 percent) had a high school education or less. On the basis of her observations, as well as on the basis of these statistics, Beer concludes that the program is not primarily for the poor and unemployed but for lower-income middle-class households. Beer's research supports my argument that the people who bring neighborhood cases to court tend to be better educated and more affluent; marital, parent/child, and boyfriend/girlfriend cases are more often brought by the poor and the unemployed. The mediation programs which handle a higher proportion of marital and boyfriend/girlfriend cases, such as Kansas City and Dorchester, tend to have poorer, less educated clients.

Suffolk County, New York

The Suffolk County Community Mediation Center handles primarily neighborhood cases (62 percent) and marital cases (13 percent), plus a few boy-
friend/girlfriend cases (4 percent) and parent/child cases (3 percent), according
to an evaluation study based on 515 cases handled in 1978 (1980). This is a
predominantly white, middle-income suburban area outside of New York City.
The fragmentary information available on complainants indicates that they are
disproportionately female (58 percent) rather than male (34 percent) (6 percent
of cases are initiated by groups), predominantly white, with incomes generally
between $11,000 and $20,000, and in their thirties, with the second largest
group being in their twenties. Most of these cases were referred by the police or
the district attorney. In about two-thirds of the cases the charge is harassment,
and in about 5–10 percent it is assault. Thus, these users constitute a lower-
middle-class or working-class clientele.

New York City

A study of 153 cases referred to a mediation program for parent/child cases
from Manhattan and the Bronx in New York City in 1981 and 1982 suggests that
the people who bring their children to court in New York are similar in many
ways to those I observed in Boston (Morris 1983). All these cases were referred
from Family Court, three fourths of them after the plaintiff had filed a petition
for a PINS (person in need of supervision) status and one fourth of them at the
probation intake interview (1983: 16). The mother was the plaintiff in 86 percent of the cases; in the rest the plaintiff was another relative: a father, a
grandparent, or an aunt or uncle (1983: 18). In only nine cases (6 percent) did
both parents participate in mediation, but this is not surprising considering that
an earlier study of 150 PINS youths showed that fewer than one quarter of the
PINS children lived either with both of their parents or with a mother and with a
father surrogate (Block and Kreger 1982: 40). This is far fewer than in the general New York City population (ibid.).

The problems described by the plaintiff are again similar to those in the
Boston parent/child mediation program: 61 percent mentioned truancy, 51 percent running away, 37 percent staying out late, 28 percent incorrigibility, and 20
percent associating with undesirable companions (Morris 1983: 19). The figures exceed 100 percent because during the intake interview three-quarters of
the plaintiffs mentioned more than one problem. More than half (58 percent) of
the defendants were girls. The defendants ranged in age from ten to eighteen
years, but the majority were between fourteen and sixteen years old. The racial
composition of the group was 55 percent black, 37 percent Hispanic, 7 percent
white, and 1 percent mixed. Twenty percent of the youths had had one or more
previous court appearances, with 9 percent having had a previous delinquency
charge and 13 percent (three of whom also had had a previous delinquency

charge) having had a previous PINS (1983: 24). Fewer than 10 percent had a history of placement, but 48 percent had had some kind of psychological counseling already (1983: 25–26).

This study provides no further information on the social class characteristics of the status offender population, but it does suggest that in the highly varied boroughs of Manhattan and the Bronx, it is primarily nonwhites who are bringing their children to court. Since other studies show that it is primarily whites who use court services, I suspect that, in determining who goes to court with personal problems, the critical variables are income and social class, not race. An earlier (1981–82) study of 150 PINS cases in the same area found that the group as a whole was "economically disadvantaged" and had inadequate resources in the areas of recreation, education, and health care (Block and Kreger 1982: 46–47). Income figures, available for only half of these families, indicated a median family income of $9,088. Interviews with forty-eight families who agreed to enter mediation showed a median income of $10,004. Welfare was mentioned as a source of income in 38 percent of the families, suggesting again that this is not primarily a population of welfare poor, despite their low incomes.

Court Studies

There are few studies reporting the social characteristics of parties who bring interpersonal conflicts to court. One of the few, on nonstranger violence in four lower courts in Charlotte (Virginia), Minneapolis, Los Angeles, and Brooklyn, indicates that the majority of the plaintiffs were women and that 35 percent reported having financial difficulty (Smith 1983: 89). These cases tended to involve assaults in which the perpetrator was most often a spouse, lover, or member of the victim's nuclear family. Twenty percent were marital problems, and many others were between lovers and ex-lovers. Over two-thirds of the victims sustained injuries.

Mary Pat Baumgartner's research on the social order of a relatively affluent suburb of New York City indicates a substantial difference in court use between the upper-middle class residents of the town and its working-class residents (1985). Citizen-initiated complaints are brought to court far more often by working-class residents (1985: 14). Of the 44 cases she observed in the municipal court involving interpersonal problems, 70 percent involved two working-class people, 9 percent involved a working-class plaintiff and a middle-class defendant, 11 percent involved two middle-class people, and 7 percent involved a middle-class complainant and a working-class defendant. Yet, only one-third of the population of the town is working class. Cases handled informally by the court also involved predominantly working-class people. Working-class people also were far more likely than were middle-class people to take problems to the police, to the zoning office, to the board of health, and to the mayor and six town council members (1985: 14–17).

Notes

Chapter One

1. Problems between people who know one another appear regularly in the lower courts. Indeed, a substantial proportion of cases which seem to be crimes actually involve fights within interpersonal relationships. According to a 1978 study in Kansas City, prosecutors, defense attorneys, and judges estimated that 40–60 percent of the municipal court cases on the general ordinance docket were interpersonal cases (Harrington 1985: 146). A 1977 study of felony arrests in New York City by the Vera Institute of Justice found that a prior relationship existed between defendant and complainant in 36 percent of fifty-three cases studied in detail (1977: 19). In these arrests, of those charged with violent crimes, 56 percent involved prior relationships (1977: 19). Five of the defendants were relatives, lovers, or former spouses of the complainant, eleven were friends or neighbors, two were prostitutes versus client or pimp, and one was a friend of a friend. Many robbery cases turned out to be personal conflicts, susceptible to being defined as robberies in only a technical sense (see Black 1983). The complainant in these cases generally wanted the court to "lecture" the defendant to get him or her to stop some form of undesirable behavior, but the complainant had little desire to follow through on the criminal court process. To the prosecutors, the complainant is bringing a trumped-up story of robbery to the police in order to settle interpersonal conflicts (1977: 70). These cases receive less serious treatment in court than do cases involving strangers: about one-third resulted in a conviction of any kind, in comparison to 88 percent of the cases involving strangers (1977: 65).

One study of nonstranger-violence cases found that these problems also arrive in criminal court as misdemeanor assaults. In this study, which covered four cities—Charlotte (Virginia), Minneapolis, Los Angeles, and Brooklyn—perpetrators in nonstranger-violence cases were most often spouses, lovers, or members of the victim's nuclear family (Smith 1983). Over two-thirds of the victims sustained injuries, and a quarter of them required hospitalization. The majority of the victims were women. They had usually had previous conflicts—some of them violent—with the perpetrator. Going to court was often the culmination of a long history of conflict between the disputants. In Dorchester, Massachusetts, another study found that 39 percent of the assault cases in court involved people who knew each other (Felstiner and Williams 1980: 16).

Cases between people who know each other appear in other lower courts as well as in the criminal court. A study of a Manhattan small-claims court found that approximately 40 percent of the cases surveyed involved partners who had known each other for at least one year or who had an expectation of continuing interaction (Sarat 1976). Juvenile courts regularly handle cases brought by parents against their children which charge these teenagers with disruptive and disobedient behavior, truancy, and running away from home. A New York City study, for example, examined the cases of 150 teenagers charged as status offenders who were sent to mediation by the court (Block and Kreger 1982). Seventy-nine percent of these cases were initiated by the mother, and most of the rest were initiated by some other household member. The petitions filed in the court mentioned problems with incorrigibility (84 percent), truancy (70 percent), staying out late (62 percent), running away (55 percent), and undesirable companions (50 percent) (1982: 41). Boys and girls were equally represented, in contrast to juvenile delinquency cases, which tend to be overwhelmingly male (1982: 42).

During the 1980s, an increasing number of these cases have ended up either in alternative dispute-resolution programs such as community mediation programs or in specialized domestic-relations courts. By the late 1980s, the move to create alternative processes for handling these problems was moving in the direction of creating mandatory procedures, outside the regular judicial process, for handling interpersonal conflicts (Goldberg et al. 1985). There are now as many as 400 mediation programs in the United States. In 1986, the mediation programs of New York State alone processed eighty thousand cases.

2. This is a different kind of entitlement than that used in constitutional law discussions about statutory entitlements and "new property" (Brigham 1988). "Entitlement" in the literature on constitutional law refers to statute-created government benefits, such as Aid to Families with Dependent Children or survivor's benefits, which have been viewed as a kind of new property deserving some of the same legal protections as the old property. Defined more broadly, this new property has come to refer to expectations created by the actions of government (1988: 412). (See also Rosenblatt 1987.)

3. See Laura Nader's valuable discussion of problems of access to law in the consumer field (1980).

4. In Massachusetts, as Felstiner and Williams point out, it is important to remember that a clerk is not a clerk (1980). Clerks usually have law degrees, are politically appointed, and, in some local courts, can become as powerful as the presiding judges. In Massachusetts, they perform an important intake role of screening citizen complaints, a task which is carried out by prosecutors in other states. During a court reorganization effort in the late 1970s, they were renamed clerk-magistrates to reflect their broad responsibilities.

5. By "working class" I mean relatively poor, relatively uneducated, relatively unskilled workers who earn hourly wages and who most of the time are not on welfare. But many go on welfare from time to time when between jobs.

6. Thus, consciousness incorporates what Ann Swidler calls "strategies of action" (1986). Social life, she argues, is organized not only around normative rules and values but also around familiar, repeated ways of doing things, or "practices," which may not be the result of conscious choice or preference but simply what seem the natural or normal ways of doing things. Swidler suggests that culture can be understood as "a 'toolkit' of symbols, stories, rituals, and world-views, which people may use in varying configurations to solve different kinds of problems" (1986: 273). Individuals develop particular "strategies of action" which are based on culturally shaped, repeated chains of practices linked together over time, not on choices made singly and independently. Culture consists of repertoires of skills, styles, habits, and techniques which explain patterns of action. People pursue those values which they have the cultural competence to pursue, not simply those which they consider the most desirable. Since any individual possesses more of a cultural repertoire than he or she actually uses, a person has some flexibility to adapt or change patterns of action depending on circumstances and constraints. Further, individuals constantly possess the capacity to learn new repertoires and competencies, particularly when the existing ones prove inadequate or when more promising ones become available. Situations of contradiction are, she argues, particularly likely to lead individuals and groups to abandon habituated and familiar repertoires for new ones.

7. There is a growing literature on consciousness and resistance, some of which I am drawing on here. Jean Comaroff's study of both the consciousness of the Tshidi in South Africa and the impact of the missionary efforts on this consciousness is of particular importance (1985). In a similar vein, in two recent papers Comaroff and Comaroff have developed and expanded conceptions of consciousness (1986; 1987). In other examples of recent work on resistance, James Scott discusses the concept of resistance in the context of peasant reactions to the Green Revolution in Malaysia, (1985) and David Lan describes the role of spirit mediums in resistance movements in Zimbabwe (1985).

8. This survey revealed widespread consultation with lawyers, among blacks as well as among whites, among poor as well as among rich. Seventy percent of those interviewed had consulted a lawyer at some time. The poor consulted lawyers less often than did the rich, but since most consultations (69 percent of all visits) concerned property, the authors conclude that it is the possession of property, rather than social class, which determines frequency of consultations. For nonproperty problems, the proportion was much more similar: 34 percent of the poorest group saw a lawyer, 42 percent of middle-income groups did, and about the same proportion of the higher-income groups did. In other words, for nonproperty problems—such as domestic problems, neighborhood problems, car accidents, personal injuries, problems with public authorities, and problems with expensive consumer goods and car repairs—the use of lawyers does not increase with income, although for property problems it does increase with income (Mayhew and Reiss 1969: 312). This finding, based on research in Detroit twenty years ago, accords with my observations during the early 1980s.

9. The study of legal effectiveness also lacks attention to legal consciousness and action. This research presumes that a law can be measured in terms of the effect it has on society. Analysis of the effectiveness of law has animated the law-and-society tradition for two decades, yet there is now a clear recognition of the inadequacy of this way of framing the question of the relationship between law and society (Silbey and Sarat 1987, 1988; Trubek and Esser 1989). It tends to posit two separate entities, law and society, each of which affects the other. The current move is to see law and society as the same phenomenon, each forming and constituting the other, such that what law is depends on how it is understood, interpreted, and used (see Nelken 1986; Brigham 1988; Harrington and Merry 1988). By looking at questions of legal consciousness and legal action inside and outside (but attached to) court settings, I hope to move beyond the dichotomies of law and society and of attitude and behavior to see both how action is constituted by consciousness and how consciousness is formed through experience.

10. A recent *Law and Society Review* Special Issue on law and ideology edited by the Amherst Seminar explores, from several vantage points, law as ideology (1988). The introductory essay to this volume briefly describes the theoretical shift produced by a focus on law as ideology (Amherst Seminar 1988: 1). (See also Larrain 1979; Hunt 1985.) For another perspective on popular consciousness of law, see Macaulay (1987).

11. Comaroff and Roberts suggest a synthesis of this kind in their argument that an adequate analysis of conflict and social order should encompass attention both to rules and to processes of conflict (1981). They argue that in order to understand Tswana legal and political life it is necessary both to analyze the form and content of disputes and to examine Tswana ideology itself, since it is this which gives meaning to Tswana experience and to the Tswana dispute process (1981: 20). Consequently, they locate the Tswana dispute process within the logic of the encompassing sociopolitical order.

12. John Brigham, in his analysis of three social movements, takes this approach as he shows the different ways in which the law provides symbols which are mobilized to oppose pornography, to assert gay rights, and to promote alternative dispute resolution (1987b). In Harrington and Merry (1988), we argue that the symbols of consensus and

community are symbols subject to contest by the various political factions within the community mediation movement.

13. Frank Parkin argues that it is important to distinguish between (a) those who accept a social order as being just and (b) those who acquiesce because they have no choice, regardless of whether they believe it is just (1971).

14. According to the theory of hegemony as developed by Antonio Gramsci (1971), the ruling class imposes ideas on subordinate groups, ideas which make the system seem inevitable and/or just to these subordinate groups. The debate over hegemony concerns the extent to which elites can impose their own image of a just social order not only on the behavior of nonelites but on their consciousness as well (Scott 1985: 39).

15. Sally Humphreys also suggests analyzing law as discourse in an interesting but slightly different way (1985). She argues that law is a part of a discourse about good and bad states of society, a debate over alternative views of rights which has both utopian and polemical elements (1985: 251). Law is then a discourse about what society should be. My use of the term *discourse* is more similar to Martha Fineman's (1988). She compares the competing discourses in child-custody decision making: the adversarial model populated by judges and attorneys and the therapeutic model populated by social workers and mediators (1988: 731).

16. As Bourdieu points out, the conception of things arbitrary and cultural as being natural and normal provides a particularly powerful form of domination (1977).

17. Other studies have argued that talk in legal contexts constructs particular interpretations of actions, governed to some extent by the third party, the audience for the presentations. In Mather and Yngvesson's model of dispute transformation, the audience to the dispute plays a critical role in shaping and structuring the account of the dispute (1980/81). Barbara Yngvesson describes the role of the clerk of courts as he performs this function in a lower court (1988). William O'Barr and John Conley's studies of small-claims court talk reveals differences—in terms of the fit between the way the parties present their cases and the way the court is prepared to hear them—in the legal adequacy of litigants' presentations of their cases (1985). They conclude that, without the help of the magistrate, parties tend not to produce legally adequate narratives because they fail both to develop a theory of responsibility and to present it in the deductive, hypothesis-testing form common to most decision makers (1985: 697). In his study of forms of conflict talk in Fiji, Donald Brenneis examines the way village leaders orchestrate public mediation sessions as a way of constructing a public definition of a dispute (1984). These sessions develop shared accounts of the events but reach no solution and do not end with the pronouncement of a judgment (1984). Indeed, the way accounts are presented—the form of speech itself—may be determined by the task of the third party in the conflict. Robert Hayden argues that when the task of a judicial process is to find facts, the ordering of speaking turns is important and that cospeech, or overlapping speech, is problematic, while in judicial settings in which the objective is to determine the normative value of known fact situations, turn taking is not so strictly ordered or structured (1987). (See also Arno 1985; Weissbourd and Mertz 1985).

18. Similarly, Comaroff and Comaroff (1987) analyze the competing meanings of work and custom in South African and Tswana society. They describe the coexistence of two competing systems of meaning in a single social field.

19. As third parties talk about cases, they present particular visions of the law. Sarat and Felstiner have shown how divorce lawyers present a picture of the law to their clients to persuade them to go along with the way they are handling their cases, often presenting the law not as rule governed, impersonal, impartial, predictable, reliable, and relatively error free but as a system in which rules are of limited relevance and not always uniformly applied, decisions are situational and personally formed, private influence affects

outcomes, and mistakes are made (1986). I have argued elsewhere that in interpersonal cases court officials, when they are trying to persuade either a plaintiff to drop charges or a defendant to comply with a plaintiff's request, endeavor to present the law as absolute and unyielding whereas to one another they discuss these cases as being trivial in importance, unworthy of serious penalties, and subject to the application of law depending on the case's situation, history, and the parties' characters (1986).

20. For a further development of this perspective, see Silbey and Sarat (1987).

21. In his analysis of the role of law in eighteenth-century England, Douglas Hay argues that the law exerts control not just as a set of rules and practices but also as an ideology (1975: 26). During this period, the courts imposed, in public occasions of great ceremony, an enormous number of death penalties on the population yet carried out relatively few of them. Hay suggests that through this process the aristocrats elicited consent from the poor, who came to see the law as powerful, just, and merciful. Others have criticized Hay's analysis, however, arguing that there was a great deal of popular discontent and rebelliousness in this period (e.g., see Linebaugh 1975). It is possible that the ideology of law induced some compliance but that its reach was only partial, leaving space for resistance.

22. For a further elaboration of this argument, see Greenhouse (1982). Brigham (1987: b) has discussed the way law serves as a set of symbols which can be drawn on by social movements such as the antipornography movement. For a further elaboration of the use of symbols and their interpretations within the community mediation movement, see Harrington and Merry (1988).

23. As Engel and Steele show, the boundary between civil and criminal cases is similarly arbitrary, with the same problem possibly being susceptible of being handled in either system (1979). Several of the cases people brought to criminal court were diverted to civil court, for example; and some of the small-claims cases could have been defined as criminal cases.

24. Barbara Yngvesson (1988) explores the processes by which this public/private boundary is constructed by focusing on the role of the court clerk, a person on the boundary between public and private, between court and community.

25. Laura Nader points out that historically, the boundaries between private law and public law have shifted (1980: 69–70). Consumer problems, for example, are now considered private problems and are handled case by case rather than collectively as public problems which are the responsibility of the state. She argues that there is a tendency in American society to privatize interpersonal complaints which reflect public wrongs such as those occasioned by dense housing, alcoholism, industrial work situations, changing roles of women, participation outside the work force, insufficient resources, and so forth. Instead of aggregating patterns and seeing them as indicative of larger social problems, society treats consumer problems as private, interpersonal grievances. On the other hand, Donald Black notes that behavior which is treated as a crime, a public concern, often involves fights within personal relationships, which are private concerns (1983).

26. Along this frontier there is a rich ethnographic literature on law, a literature which examines the police, the lower courts, and the communities from which problems arise. The police have often been described as combining peacekeeping, service delivery, and family management with rule enforcement and crime control (e.g., see Bittner 1967; Wilson 1968; Black 1980). More recently, there have been studies of other gatekeepers to the legal system, such as court clerks (Yngvesson 1985a, 1988), community courts and nonjudicial conflict management (Auerbach 1983; Greenhouse 1986), community mediation programs (Harrington 1985), prosecutors in the lower courts (Feeley 1979), and private lawyers (Blumberg 1967; Sarat and Felstiner 1986). Studies of conflict in

American communities and of the cases which arrive in court from them include research on rural counties (Engel 1980, 1984), Southern towns (Greenhouse 1982, 1986), urban neighborhoods (Merry 1979; Buckle and Thomas-Buckle 1982), and New England towns (Yngvesson 1988).

27. In his study of a similar court in New Haven, Connecticut, Feeley (1979) observes that the court is sensitive to its political context and that the personnel in the court are appointed and linked to local political authorities, just as in the courts I studied.

28. Richard Hofrichter explains this inaction by the court by arguing that, although the state does not wish to intervene in these disputes and attempts to sluff them from the system, at the same time it wishes to avoid their politicization (1982, 215; 1987); consequently, it provides a minimum level of service to limit the development of dissatisfaction and discontent. These cases are of little importance to the court, he argues, but are dangerous to the social order if they are totally ignored.

Chapter Two

1. For an historical background linking the development of the working class in the early twentieth century and legal consciousness, see Haydu (1987).

2. It has been well documented that negotiated settlements, often encouraged by judges, are the way most cases are handled in both civil and criminal courts (see *Law and Society Review* Special Issue on plea bargaining 1979; Mather 1979; Trubek et al. 1983) There is now a growing body of research on judicial settlement conferences as well.

3. There are over eighteen thousand limited-jurisdiction, first-instance courts in the United States. Such courts constitute over 90 percent of all state trial courts, are staffed by 81 percent of all judges, and hear over 80 percent of all trials, excluding those for traffic violations (Silbey 1979).

4. In a study of two Massachusetts clerks' offices, Yngvesson found that 33 percent of citizen-initiated complaints were issued in one town and that 27 percent were issued in another (1985a: 75).

5. For a further discussion of the role and practices of Massachusetts clerks, see Yngvesson (1985a, 1988).

6. In its first three years of operation, 1979–82, it received 587 referrals and held mediation sessions for 308, i.e., 54 percent of those referred.

7. For further discussion of small-claims court procedures, see O'Barr and Conley (1985) and (1988).

8. The cases Rocheleau and I studied had been in court an average of six times, and the families themselves had appeared an average of four times. It generally took an average of two to three weeks to move from court application to arraignment and one and a half to three months to move from court application to arraignment and the issuing of a petition. On the average, these cases stayed in court an average of five to six months before dismissal and an average of eight months if they were not dismissed. Some cases are quickly dismissed, however, while others remain under the supervision of the court, in various stages, for one, two, and even three years (see Merry and Rocheleau 1985).

9. In his detailed study of criminal (nontraffic) cases in a lower criminal court in New Haven, Feeley finds a similar pattern of lenient sentences and pretrial settlements (1979). For example, in the closed cases in his sample of cases in the Court of Common Pleas, 96 percent received a guilty plea or were not prosecuted: of these, 50 percent pleaded guilty, 38 percent were not prosecuted, 8 percent forfeited bonds without an appearance, and 4 percent received other dispositions (1979: 127). Not one case went to trial. Of a sample of 1,648 defendants, slightly over half were eventually convicted. Of these, only 4.9 percent were sent to jail, mostly (75 percent) for ninety days or less, and 43 percent were fined $50 or less. Thirteen percent of all sentences involve some combination of proba-

tion and suspended jail sentences (1979: 137–8). Fewer than 1 percent of all criminal cases went to trial in the New Haven court; nationwide, 90–98 percent of all cases are settled by some means other than trial (1979: 184–85). Thus, Feeley observed a pattern of leniency in all cases in the criminal court, not just in the interpersonal cases.

10. The practice of negotiation and settlement rather than trial has been widely documented in both civil cases and in regular criminal cases as well as in these interpersonal cases. Plea bargaining is widespread in criminal courts as a way of settling cases before trial (see Feeley 1979; *Law and Society Review* special issue on plea bargaining 1979; Mather 1979; Buckle and Buckle 1977). According to Galanter, in almost every American jurisdiction, nontrial dispositions account for 80–90 percent of criminal dispositions (1983). Most civil cases are also settled, some before they become lawsuits, but, even of those which become lawsuits, most are settled. Galanter reports that in the major study of civil litigation, the Civil Litigation Research Project, 88 percent of the cases filed (those under $10,000 in value) were settled and only 9 percent went to trial (1983). He concludes that "the master pattern of American disputing is one in which there is actual or threatened invocation of an authoritative decision maker. This is countered by a threat of protracted or hard-fought resistance, leading to a negotiated or mediated settlement, often in the anteroom of the adjudicative institutions" (1983: 27).

Chapter Three

1. Cases of these four types make up the bulk of the nonproperty caseload of most community mediation programs. In the court-connected mediation program in Salem, they made up 64 percent of program referrals: 25 percent were neighbors, 19 percent spouses, 11 percent boyfriend/girlfriend, and 9 percent were parent/child. In the independent mediation program in Cambridge, they were 31 percent of referrals: 18 percent were neighbors, 6 percent were spouses, 4 percent boyfriend/girlfriend, and 3 percent were parent/child. The juvenile mediation program handled only parent/child problems, categorized as "truants," "stubborns," and "runs" on the the basis of the charge in court. Almost all involved conflicts between parents and children.

2. For further discussion of neighborhood conflicts, see Baumgartner (1988) and Perin (1988).

3. I consulted the following sources for information on the social class composition of the people who bring interpersonal problems to court in other areas, but I found little on this topic: Buckle and Buckle (1977), Eisenstein and Jacob (1977), Mather (1979), Sheppard et al. (1979), Tomasic and Feeley (1982), Boyum and Mather (1983), Feeley (1983), Lipetz (1984), Coates (1985), Silberman (1985), and Umbreit (1985). There is far more information on the clients of community mediation programs. However, there are drawbacks to using mediation program data to draw inferences about the kinds of people who bring their personal problems to court. Not all interpersonal cases which arrive in court are referred to mediation, nor are all mediation cases necessarily referred from courts. Courts vary greatly in the kinds of cases they refer to mediation and in the frequency with which they do so. Court-affiliated mediation programs, which tend to have the largest caseloads and the most direct referral networks, provide the best approximation. The appendix summarizes the information I was able to collect on this point.

4. The exact proportions were as follows:

Plaintiff/Defendant	N	(%)
Male/Male	6	21%
Male/Female	3	10%
Female/Female	13	45%
Female/Male	4	14%
Couple/Couple	3	10%

5. Ten were in their thirties, one was in her forties and one was in her sixties. One involved a younger person against an older person.

6. The median family incomes for Salem and Cambridge, according to the 1980 census, were $17,845 and $19,138, respectively. The interviews were mostly done in 1981 and 1982, and the census data are from 1979, so these figures slightly exaggerate the affluence of these families.

7. Of the twelve for whom I have information, five have a high school education or less, four have some college, and three have a college degree. The ten defendants for whom I have information have about the same pattern: five have a high school education or less, three have some college, and two have a college degree.

8. In her discussion of neighborhood disputes in suburban Philadelphia, Beer observed similar kinds of parties and similar themes in dispute (1986: 40–42). There, as here, the disputants are often upwardly mobile homeowners with their first piece of property for whom the house is a means to safeguard this fragile status.

9. Unraveling the histories and settings of conflicts is a complex task. In this and subsequent cases, I have gathered information from several sources, constantly cross-checking to determine accuracy. Particularly in situations of conflict, parties will present themselves in the most flattering light, omitting or distorting information which puts their actions in a more questionable light. Furthermore, parties may simply hold different interpretations about what happened and what it meant. In this case, as in others, I observed as much of the court and mediation processing as I could, talked to the parties themselves as the case progressed, visited the neighborhood, and talked to the officials involved in the court and mediation: the prosecutor, mediation staff, mediators, clerk, police officer on the scene, and police liaison officer. As the case developed, I gathered further bits of information from people in the courthouse and from the parties themselves. I also consulted records about the case that were kept in the courthouse and mediation program. I am grateful to Susan Silbey and Barbara Yngvesson, who gathered some of the material on this case. Here, as in all the other cases, I have changed the names to protect the privacy of the people involved. I did not tape-record mediation sessions, interviews, or court sessions. Although I asked to tape-record mediation sessions, the mediation programs uniformly prohibited taping. Consequently, the dialogue I present is based on my detailed notes and reconstructions rather than on verbatim transcript.

10. In her study of a suburban town, M. P. Baumgartner similarly describes the critical meaning of homeownership to identity (1988).

11. After the session, the older woman paid for a survey, which revealed that all the houses on the street were off four feet. She then did another survey, which confirmed the man's point that between each house there is an old twelve-inch easement belonging to the city, which had been created to allow people in the last century to walk between the houses on their way to work in the tanning factory nearby. This did not leave her enough room to build a fence, and at last contact she had not done so.

12. Alan Stone describes property and contract as the essential legal relations of capitalist society, relations which are set and nearly universally accepted, part of the taken-for-granted world within which children grow up (1985: 50–58). Stone argues that these legal relations are simply accepted, without demands being made for their moral justification, thus helping to establish and maintain a hegemonic form of social conformity (1985: 60).

13. The nature of the rights included under the domain of property is changing within the law (Brigham 1988). For example, the concept has recently been expanded to include welfare and other benefits as part of the "new property" also protected within the law.

14. See Pierre Bourdieu for an analysis of the power inherent in the rendition of things cultural as natural (1977).

15. Lillian Rubin describes a similar acceptance by working-class women that violence is part of family life (1976).

16. Ten of twelve earned under $20,000 one earned between $20,000 and $25,000, and one earned between $25,000 and $35,000.

17. In the mediation session, they agreed to see a marriage counselor, to get together calmly and without violence, and to share the use of their common car.

18. Lillian Rubin describes a similar difference, within working-class families in the mid-1970s, between women's new views of a marriage of communication and sharing and men's concern with authority in the marriage (1976).

19. I refer here to that law known as section 209A, passed in 1979, which provides a temporary restraining order in emergency situations.

20. Fifty-one cases were studied in the status-offender mediation program. This represents almost all of the cases in the program over an eighteen-month period in 1981–83, excluding a few Hispanic cases and one Portuguese case because of translation problems. In addition, information is available on two comparison groups: fifty cases referred to mediation but which did not reach the stage of a mediation session (nonmediated cases) and fifty cases in court which were not referred to mediation (court cases). The information on the social characteristics of the plaintiffs and defendants in mediation and nonmediation cases is more complete than that for court cases, since it is based on intake interviews. In addition, the researchers observed the mediation session in each case and interviewed almost all the parties in mediation (114). Information on the court sample is based on court records (Merry and Rocheleau 1985).

21. The fifty-one cases studied in this mediation program were primarily those involving stubborn children (43 percent) and runaways (33 percent), with fewer truants (24 percent).

22. At the intake interview for the mediation program, the most commonly mentioned issues (and the percent of the fifty-one cases in which these issues were raised) were as follows: curfews (61 percent), school attendance (45 percent), the teenager's friends (45 percent), chores (41 percent), where the teenager goes (41 percent), fighting with siblings (29 percent), parents' yelling or nagging (28 percent), teenager's disrespectful attitude (28 percent), drinking and drugs (26 percent), and punishment (26 percent) (Merry and Rocheleau 1985: Table 65). In both court and mediation discussions of these problems, truancy, running away, and curfews were most common (for variations within each of these forums, see Merry and Rocheleau 1985).

23. Among the mothers of the fifty-one young people who went through mediation, 32 percent expected the court to scare their child, 18 percent expected the court to change the child, 5 percent expected the court to place her in a residential facility or foster home, and the rest sought some other kind of help (Merry and Rocheleau 1985: 172). Fathers were a bit more severe: 46 percent hoped to scare the child, 15 percent hoped to change him, and 23 percent hoped to place him. In 19 percent of the thirty-nine mediated cases referred from the court the child was eventually placed in either a residential facility or a foster home, and in the comparison group, which did not go to mediation, 20 percent were placed.

24. Three-fourths (thirty-nine) of the mediated cases were referred by the court. (All but nine of the mediated cases had some involvement with the court, however.) Three quarters (twenty-seven) of the plaintiffs in the court-referred cases were parents, one quarter (nine) were the school, and one was the police department. In a comparison sample of fifty court cases not referred to mediation, fewer than half (twenty-one) were brought by the parents and over half (twenty-eight) were brought by the school. Cases referred to mediation tended to involve issues of family conflict rather than simple truancy, while cases not referred were mostly truancy cases. Since I could not separate the

cases with parent plaintiffs from those brought by the school or by the police, the following description refers to all parents. Parents who were not plaintiffs were similar to plaintiff parents in the characteristics described here, however.

25. Another study of 150 status offenders brought to the family court of the Bronx or Manhattan in New York City in 1981–82 reported that mothers were most likely to bring their children to the court: 79 percent of the plaintiffs were mothers (Block and Kreger 1982: 39).

26. The racial and religious composition of the three groups was as follows:

A. Race

	% (no.)		
	Mediated (N=51)	Nonmediated (N=50)	Court (N=50)
White	78 (40)	74 (37)	84 (42)
Black	22 (11)	22 (11)	16 (8)
Hispanic	0	4 (2)	0

B. Religion[a]

	% (no.)		
	Mediated (N=50)	Nonmediated (N=31)	Court (N=16)
Catholic	70 (35)	77 (24)	81 (13)
Protestant	24 (12)	13 (4)	19 (3)
Other	2 (1)	3 (1)	0
No religion	4 (2)	7 (2)	0

[a] This section of the table has considerable missing data.

27. The nonmediated sample was 72 percent female, and the court sample was 58 percent female. The age breakdown for the three groups is as follows:

	% (no.)		
AGE (years)	Mediated (N=51; mean age 14 years)	Nonmediated (N=50; mean age 14.5 years)	Court (N=50; mean age 14 years)
13 and under	26 (13)	20 (10)	30 (15)
14	31 (16)	20 (10)	28 (14)
15	26 (13)	36 (18)	38 (19)
16	18 (9)	24 (12)	4 (2)

28. Other studies report a similar distinction. In Boston, Sheehan talks about the Irish homeowners in comparison to the "little guys," the renters (1984). The term "blue-collar aristocrats" describes a segment of the working class which has secure, unionized jobs with good pay, benefits, and union protection for grievances and which comprises skilled craftsmen who enjoy their jobs and who experience loose supervision (Mackenzie 1973; LeMasters 1975). In Pappas's study of a working-class community in Ohio, he describes the widely acknowledged benefits in pay and security of a union job in a large factory (1989). Wives of these men may work as clerical and sales workers. Over

half the women who work as clerical or sales workers, including telephone operators and cashiers, are married to working-class men and identify themselves with that class (Levison 1974).

But other segments of the working class have far more marginal, low-paying, and unstable jobs, often in the service sector. Jobs such as janitors, waiters, and guards, all of which fall into this category, are described as lower class by some, as working class by others (Levison 1974). These jobs are often temporary or part-time, and wives usually work as do husbands. Some people find themselves working two jobs in order to survive. Women in this group find they need to depend on a combination of insecure and low-paid service jobs and public assistance (Susser 1986). To the working-class elites, these people are viewed as the lower classes, people who are not quite respectable: "They are always fighting and getting drunk" (Berger 1968: 81).

29. In her study of a working-class neighborhood in Brooklyn, Susser describes the close relations between working-class homeowners, who maintained their houses themselves and were always close to the line financially, and the tenants in their buildings (1982: 87–102).

Chapter Four

1. These numbers refer, of course, to mediation program referrals, not to court filings. But, because the mediation program inspected the cases filed in the clerk's office every day for interpersonal disputes, these numbers represent a close approximation of the number of interpersonal cases which arrived at the court under citizen initiative.

2. The six precincts with the highest rate of cases per capita, ranging from 16.5 per thousand to 9 per thousand, fall into two census tracts. According to the 1980 census, these tracts had median incomes below the city average of $19,138; that for the Green Street area was particularly low ($13,000); that for the other tract was $17,953. In these two census tracts, a higher-than-average proportion of young people aged sixteen to nineteen years were neither in school nor high school graduates (36 and 23 percent for these two tracts, respectively, vs. a city average of 9 percent) and a higher proportion of housing units were rented (84 and 63 percent, respectively, in comparison with a city average of 58 percent). In 1970, these two areas had the highest proportion of female-headed households with children under eighteen years of age.

Residents of the census tract which included Green Street had less education, with almost half (48 percent) of the adult population (over twenty-five years of age) not high school graduates, 28 percent high school graduates, 8 percent with some college, and 16 percent college graduates. In comparison, 33 percent of the adult population in the city had less than a high school education, 37 percent had a high school diploma, 15 percent had some college, and 14 had a college degree or more. In this census tract, over half (52 percent) the employed residents older than sixteen years were service or skilled and unskilled manual workers.

3. To do the ethnographic study of these three neighborhoods, I talked informally to several residents in each neighborhood for about twenty to thirty hours. I read about the history of each neighborhood and talked to older residents who remembered its past. I did general ethnographic observation and interviewing in all three neighborhoods. In addition, I worked with neighborhood residents and student research assistants to carry out a survey of neighborhood problems, reported in more detail in Merry (1987). In this survey, we interviewed in person ninety-three people, roughly divided between the three neighborhoods, about their neighborhoods, their problems, and what they did about them. A student lived in one of the neighborhoods for a summer while doing ethnographic research and completing the survey. I interviewed in detail people who came

to mediation from these neighborhoods, asking each about his or her case and about the neighborhood it came from. I recorded extensive accounts of particular problems in all three neighborhoods. The names of the neighborhoods are pseudonyms to protect the privacy of their inhabitants.

4. I examined the records of the mediation program, looking at all the cases referred to mediation, and at the records of complaints filed in the clerk's office. Although I examined the records of cases in which complaints did not issue, I could not track those with issued complaints. Cases with issued complaints which were never referred to mediation are therefore not included here. But there are very few such cases.

5. A questionnaire of eighty-eight items asked neighborhood residents about the problems they had and what they did about them, about the social organization of the neighborhood, about the extent of informal neighboring, about their perceptions of the neighborhood, and about their ways of handling problems. This questionnaire was administered to ninety-three individuals in the three small neighborhoods: thirty-six in Riverdale, thirty-two in Oldtowne, and twenty-five in Hilltowne. In all three neighborhoods, the interviewer left a letter describing the study and then a few days later knocked on the door and requested an interview. Interviews were all in person and typically lasted between forty-five and ninety minutes. In the survey, each respondent was presented with a list of the problems which I had seen most commonly in mediation and was asked whether he or she had experienced these problems, how long they had gone on, and what he had done about them. The forty-one problems were divided into four categories: neighborhood problems, family (marital and parent/child) problems, friendship problems (including boyfriend/girlfriend), and consumer and services problems. For a more detailed description of this survey and the results, see Merry and Silbey (1984) and Merry (1987).

6. For a detailed analysis of a similar community, see Warner and Srole (1949) and Warner et al. (1963).

7. According to the report of one participant, she was found guilty by a judge but appealed the case to a six-person jury, which acquitted her. After this victory in court, the young woman returned home saying how easy it is to win in court.

8. The 1980 census tracts do not follow the lines of this development. According to this census, 71 percent of the households were nuclear families and 62 percent of the families owned their own homes, but some neighboring areas are included in these figures.

9. According to the 1980 census of this and adjacent neighborhoods, of those over age eighteen, 77 percent had finished high school and 12 percent had four years of college or more.

10. There is a rich and valuable literature on the way outsiders and strangers use the courts. Some argue that outsiders are more likely to use the courts in a community than are insiders, as Todd (1978) describes in Bavaria and as Engel (1984) describes in the American Midwest. On the other hand, the court may be a resource used by insiders to eliminate outsiders. Of course, the role of insider and outsider is ambiguous. In a community in which court use is not accepted, to use the court may consign the user to the status of outsider, for example. For further discussion of these issues, see Yngvesson (1976, 1988) Greenhouse (1986), Baumgartner (1988), and Perin (1988), and more generally, the studies in Nader and Todd (1978).

11. This is, of course, a well-established theory within social anthropology. Gluckman (1955) argued that conflict reflects structural tensions, and Turner elaborated on this point in his analysis of the relationship between social dramas, or conflicts, and the underlying strains of the kinship system of the Ndembu (1957).

Chapter Five

1. For further discussion of this perspective, see Yngvesson (1988).

2. Yngvesson and Hennessey make a similar argument about small-claims courts (1975).

3. The people who brought their personal conflicts to court rarely referred to them as disputes. One of the mediation programs I studied was called the Dispute Settlement Center, and its advertisements claimed that it helped people with their "disputes." Yet, many people brought difficulties to this center which were not the kinds of things the center staff meant by disputes. The staff spent a great deal of its time fielding calls and questions from people with problems which were not appropriate for mediation. Almost half of the cases (i.e., 44 percent of fifty-five cases over ten months) which arrived at the center through individual initiative were judged inappropriate by center staff, while only one-tenth (14 of 138 cases) of those which were referred from the court were considered inappropriate. Inappropriate cases included consumer complaints against large companies, tenants complaining about the public housing authority, employers who were unhappy with their workers, people angry at teenage gangs whose names they did not know, and divorces. Many of these cases were referred to legal services. I began to suspect that the general public had only a remote idea of what a "dispute" was.

4. This will probably change, of course, as the movement to create alternative dispute resolution expands and, as it does, introduces the concept of dispute to popular consciousness.

5. For a thorough and valuable analysis of the concept, see the introduction of Nader and Todd (1978). The case studies in this book provide a good illustration of the richness of dispute analysis. Monographs taking this approach include those of Koch (1974) and Starr (1978).

6. For an extensive discussion of both the development of dispute analysis and the controversy surrounding it, see Silbey and Sarat (1988: 38–69).

7. Among the numerous critics of the concept, Cain and Kulscar have argued that it is difficult to compare disputes between capitalist and precapitalist societies, for example (1981–82). Other critiques of the concept of dispute include Kidder (1980/81), Lempert (1980/81), Chanock (1983), and Merry and Silbey (1984). (See generally, Snyder 1981.)

8. Comaroff and Roberts suggest that in certain kinds of disputes, those concerning the nature and quality of a social relationship, parties may engage in an effort to establish the definition of that bond (1981: 235). Thus, these disputes hinge on the interpretation and ordering of a range of events, a process in which the litigants construe the history of the interaction both between the litigants and between themselves and other people involved in the situation, in particular ways designed to persuade.

9. The idea that "facts" exist separate from law is fundamental to the contemporary culture of Anglo-American law, although it is not a distinction shared by other legal systems (Geertz 1983). As carriers of the Anglo-American culture of law, the plaintiffs I studied tended to see mediation and court as places to argue about "facts" by presenting evidence. This is, however, their cultural construction of the scene and, as we will see, is not the way mediators and court officials interpreted the meaning of the conversations about conflicts.

10. The overall analytic purpose of *Rules and Processes* (Comaroff and Roberts 1981) is to show how a rule-centered approach to the anthropology of law can be combined with a processual approach. Instead of seeing these as two competing paradigms within legal anthropology, they demonstrate how dispute processes can only be understood

within the logic of a particular sociocultural system and how the process of dispute itself transforms that system. Disputing is not a matter of the simple application of rule to situation but is a complex negotiation in which a number of rules and norms of equivalent importance are relevant to the particular situation. These authors emphasize, as do I, the critical role played by the litigant who, choosing one or another way to frame the problem he or she brings to the court, thus shapes the discussion which follows.

11. Felstiner et al. describe this quality of disputes as the "pandora's box" problem (1980/81). See also Bumiller (1988).

12. Studies of warfare in small-scale societies have analyzed these interactions in terms of triggering mechanisms as well (e.g., see Chagnon 1969; Meggitt 1977). Here, particular incidents signal to both sides that the level of fighting has changed: as the Yanomamo switch from chest pounding to spear throwing, for example, they escalate the level of the fight (Chagnon 1969).

13. Most of the plaintiffs in mediation think that these problems are primarily the fault of the other side. Interviews with sixty-eight plaintiffs from the first two mediation programs, after their cases were mediated, indicated that almost half (thirty-two) thought the other side was completely at fault, over a third (twenty-six) thought the other side was mostly at fault, nine thought both sides were equally at fault, and only one person said that he or she was mostly at fault. In other words, 85 percent said that the problem was largely caused by the other side. The defendants thought almost the same thing: of forty-seven defendants interviewed, one third (fifteen) said that the other side was completely at fault, a little over one third (eighteen) said that the other party was mostly at fault, eleven said that both were at fault, and only three said that they themselves were partly or wholly at fault. In other words, 70 percent of the defendants said that the problem was largely the fault of the other side as well.

14. Of 110 people interviewed after their mediation session, three quarters (81) said that they were upset in the mediation session.

15. Sarat and Felstiner have described the way attorneys in divorce cases also serve to reshape emotional issues (Sarat and Felstiner 1988).

16. See Sudnow's analysis of normal crimes (1965).

17. See Felstiner et al. (1980–81) on the importance of this process of naming and labeling disputes.

18. For further discussion of this process, see Chapter 2. For a detailed analysis of the processes taking place in the clerk's office in Massachusetts, see Yngvesson (1985a, 1988).

19. I am indebted to Barbara Yngvesson for the details of this mediation session.

Chapter Six

A somewhat different version of this chapter was published in *The Yale Journal of Law and Humanities* 2 (1990): 1–35. © 1990 by The University of Chicago. All rights reserved.

1. Although a concern with the power of discourse is found throughout Foucault's extensive corpus of writing, the argument is particularly clear in *Discipline and Punish* (1977) and in *Power/Knowledge* (1980). He describes the power of discourse as follows:

What I mean is this: in a society such as ours, but basically in any society, there are manifold relations of power which permeate, characterize, and constitute the social body, and these relations of power cannot themselves be established, consolidated nor implemented without the production, accumulation, circulation, and functioning of a discourse. There can be no possible exercise of power without a certain economy of discourses of truth which operates through and on the basis of this association. We are subjected to the production of truth through power and we cannot exercise power except through the production of truth (1980: 93).

2. Said's assessment of Foucault's contribution emphasizes the importance of his concept of discourse:

> While it is true that he has been mainly interested in two sides of the same coin—the process of exclusion by which cultures designate and isolate their opposite and its obverse, the process by which cultures designate and valorize their own incorporative—it is now certain that Foucault's greatest intellectual contribution is to an understanding of how the appetite for or will to exercise dominant control in society and history has also discovered a way to clothe, disguise, rarify, and wrap itself systematically in the language of truth, discipline, rationality, utilitarian value, and knowledge. And this language, in its naturalness, authority, professionalism, assertiveness, antitheoretical directness, is what Foucault has called *discourse*. The difference between discourse and such coarser, yet not less significant, fields of social combat as the class struggle is that discourse works its productions, discriminations, censorship, interdictions, and invalidations on the intellectual at the level of base, not of superstructure. The power of discourse is that it is at once the object of struggle and the tool by which the struggle is conducted: in penology, for example, the juridical language identifying the delinquent and the intellectual schema embodied in the prison's physical structure are instruments controlling, identifying, incarcerating felons as well as the powers (withheld from felons obviously) to keep freedom for oneself and deny it to others ([1978] 1980: 120).

3. In her study of the expression of sentiments among the Bedouin, Lila Abu-Lughod suggests that these people employ two discourses, one of poetry and one of everyday talk, each of which is culturally constituted (1985). She suggests that each discourse represents a distinct cultural ideology with associated values and ideals for personhood. The particular life experience of any individual is therefore informed by multiple ideologies (1985: 258). Similarly, the discourses I describe are associated with particular ideologies about human behavior.

4. Weissbourd and Mertz argue that law engages in routine creativity through categorizing particular events, in rendering interpretations (1985: 640). Sarat and Felstiner have explored the power inherent in attributions of motive in interactions between divorce lawyers and their clients (1988). Edelman's analysis points to ways in which one or another form of symbolic language is powerful in determining the social treatment of various kinds of disadvantaged people (1977).

5. In his study of political language, Murray Edelman points to the power of particular languages, such as those of the helping profession, to label people in one way or another, which leads to certain "logical" political consequences (1977). For example, he distinguishes between calling a poor black person jailed for stealing a "criminal" or "political prisoner," labels which have great significance for the way this person is understood and handled. The helping professions exercise a particularly effective form of power through their use of a language which seems value neutral, formal, and professional. He concludes: "The helping professions are the most effective contemporary agents of social conformity and isolation. In playing this political role they undergird the

entire political structure, yet they are largely spared from self-criticism, from political criticism, and even from political observation, through a special symbolic language" (1977: 75).

6. Mather and Yngvesson's analysis of dispute transformation points to the role that the audience to a dispute plays in defining its meaning (1980/81; see also Santos 1977).

7. In the literature, there has been considerable discussion of moral, therapeutic, and legal discourses. See, in particular, Edelman (1977), Lasch (1977), and Bellah et. al. (1985).

8. In contrast, Carol Greenhouse's study of the meanings of conflict for a Baptist community in the American South provides a rich account of a religious discourse of conflict (1986).

9. Stone's distinction between "essential legal relations" and the particular laws derived from these relations is helpful in understanding this legal discourse (1985). Working from Engel's discussion of two distinct but related concepts of legal superstructure, Stone differentiates between the legal conceptions central to the capitalist economic order—legal conceptions such as property, contract, and credit—and specific laws based on these essential legal relations. It is possible to have changes in specific laws with continuity in the general concepts. Essential legal relations are those legal relations which mirror and define the fundamental economic relationships in a society (1985: 50). Particular rules are derivative subrelations. If particular rules are contradictory, the system can survive as long as these essential legal relations are not challenged. Stone suggests that capitalist societies are flexible and adaptive, surviving despite many changes in rules and despite many rules which conflict with the interests of capitalists— and which even restrain or limit property or contract rights—because these rules do not challenge or transform the fundamental legal relations themselves: those of contract, property, and the corporation, which have remained stable over a long period of time and are now embedded in the taken-for-granted social order (1985: 50–64). The legal discourse of working-class Americans in court provides further evidence of the extent to which these concepts are embedded in American culture.

10. This situation is intriguingly similar to the way witnesses are invoked by the Islamic *qadi* judge, who, according to Lawrence Rosen, relies heavily on oral testimony from morally upright individuals to assess both the meaning of the event and the character of the persons involved (1980/81).

11. In their study of litigant talk in small-claims courts, John Conley and William O'Barr observe similar variations in the way people talk about law and morality, although these authors analyze these variations in a somewhat different way. They draw a distinction between rule-oriented and relational modes of talk (1990). Some litigants in small-claims courts organize and present accounts in a relational mode, and some do so in a rule-oriented mode. Conley and O'Barr define these accounts in the following terms: "A *relational* account emphasizes status and relationships, and is organized around the litigant's efforts to introduce these issues into the trial. A *rule-oriented* account emphasizes rules and laws, and is tightly structured around these issues. Relational and rule-oriented accounts are ideal constructs based on our study of almost 100 litigants in the small claims courts of North Carolina and Colorado. Actual accounts usually contain some features of both types, although typically features characteristic of one or the other of these orientational principles will predominate" [emphasis in original] (1990: 2). They suggest that the rule-oriented accounts mesh better with the logic of the law and of the court than do the relational accounts, which are filled with details of background and surrounding social ties which the courts find irrelevant and inappropriate. Although they have neither counted the frequency of the two accounts nor determined who uses which

kind, they suspect that the relational accounts are similar to the style of testifying adopted by relatively "powerless" people (1990: 13). They think that the rule-oriented account may correlate with exposure to the cultures of business and law. In contrast to my approach, however, they see these two forms of account as characteristic of different kinds of people rather than as part of an available repertoire to be used from time to time by all litigants.

12. I am indebted to Donald Brenneis for pointing out this distinction. Julia Tyler, in working with these materials, suggested a similar distinction.

13. Within traditional legal discourse, used by judges and attorneys, the law recognized the concept of sole custodian of the child as a legal category, assuming that the responsibility of the law was to designate the custodial parent and to provide for visitation rights for the noncustodial parent. Within the discourse of the helping professions, however, the symbolic ideal of parental equality led to advocacy of shared parenting arrangements and joint custody. In her analysis of this shift, Fineman highlights the implications that this reframing has for substantive changes in the relations between husbands and wives at divorce: "As this view has become accepted, it has altered the way we articulate and conceive of custody issues. The dominant rhetoric no loner describes divorce as a process that terminates the relationship between spouses, establishing one as the custodial parent with clear responsibilities. Rather, divorce is now described as a process that, through mediation, restructures and reformulates the spouses' relationship, conferring equal or shared parental rights on both parents although one, in practice, usually assumes the primary responsibility for care of the children. This is an important substantive shift" (1988: 732).

14. Here, as in all the other cases, I have changed names and some personal details in order to conceal the identities of the individuals involved.

15. I am indebted to Barbara Yngvesson for the information on the complaint-application form.

16. The process appeared to the clients of the other two mediation programs as somewhat less official. In the independent mediation program, of forty-six people interviewed after mediation sessions, 85 percent of the forty-one who responded said they had a choice about going to mediation. But many were still unsure about whether the agreement was legally binding. Of the thirty-six from the independent mediation program who responded to this question, 17 percent thought it was binding, 25 percent were not sure, and 58 percent said they thought it was not. In the parent/child mediation program, of 114 people interviewed after mediation, 42 percent thought the judge could enforce their mediation agreement, 8 percent were not sure, and 50 percent thought he could not.

17. Rosen also uses Mills's concept of vocabularies of motives to talk about the way social identities are constructed: "motives are the terms with which interpretation of conduct by social actors proceeds" (Mills 1940: 904). He continues by stating that when we attribute motives to others we are trying to define the situation in which we find ourselves. "By tracing the relation between vocabularies of motive and situated actions we may also understand how, by characterizing a situation in a particular way, we may create in the observer a set of expectations and hence an image of the actor's intent" (Rosen 1984: 48).

Chapter Seven

1. Galanter's study of "one-shotters" and "repeat-players" provides valuable insight into the effects of repeated use of the courts and into the benefits in skill and expertise this implies (1974).

2. Sarat and Felstiner describe how divorce lawyers try to put emotional matters aside

and focus on instrumental and financial concerns. In the process, the lawyers create a divided self: a self with a rational, financial side which the law recognizes and an emotional side to which the law is indifferent (1986: 132). The lower courts similarly endeavor to separate the emotional from the rational side of disputes.

3. In order to see how often the same people returned to court with interpersonal problems, I examined all the complaint applications filed in the clerk's office of the Salem District Court in 1981 which had not been issued. Since interpersonal problems are not likely to have complaints issued, nonissued complaints provide a rough indication of how many interpersonal problems arrived in the court altogether. In order to see how many of these people had been in court before, I compared the names and addresses in these 220 cases with those in all the cases referred to the mediation program during 1980 and the first six months of 1981, a total of 336. Most of the cases handled by the mediation program were referred by the court. This is obviously neither a complete set of all interpersonal problems in court nor a study of repeat users over a very long period, but it provides a rough indication of how often the same people returned to court over two years. As is often the case with ethnographic research, I was not thinking about repeat users when I gathered this information but discovered them in the course of examining the information I gathered on case types. These data miss cases with issued complaints, cases in court before 1980, and 1980 cases in the clerk's office which were not referred to mediation. Thus, they underestimate rather than exaggerate the proportion who return to court with interpersonal problems.

4. I determined whether the cases were interpersonal problems by reading the description of the incident on the form and noting the relationship between the parties.

5. Eighteen conflict situations generated forty-two case filings, 19 percent of all filings for interpersonal cases. Twenty-nine of the filings represented two or more filings for the same problem at different times and were generated by eleven problems, and thirteen were multiple filings at the same time and were generated by seven problems. In the most extreme case, one conflict situation generated four filings after a first incident and three after a second, all filings being made by various participants in this large neighborhood conflict.

6. Twenty people appeared as defendants more than once, ten men and ten women, but also accounted for only 8 percent of the defendants.

7. Five were plaintiffs in criminal court and two were criminal court defendants, seven were plaintiffs in small-claims court and three were small-claims defendants, one was a defendant in juvenile court, and most of the rest were observers, witnesses, or involved in divorce or probate matters.

8. Of course, a significant but unknown proportion of cases which arrive in court as "crimes" are actually interpersonal disputes which have escalated into serious violence or retaliatory theft of property (see Merry 1981; Black 1983).

9. In his interviews with twelve working-class people in the early 1980s, Craig Reinerman found that these people generally believe in democracy and support the fundamental aspects of the welfare and regulatory state—government-supported health care, guaranteed employment, public education assistance for the needy, regulatory restrictions on the freedom of capital, and a general support for benefits for the deserving poor—although he also reports that they have a consistent recognition of powerlessness and of collusion between the rich and the politicians (1987: 238). These people acquiesce to their position in a social order which is recognized as stratified and unequal, yet they value their own self-reliance (1987: 67).

10. As I reported earlier, a substantial proportion of the people interviewed after mediation said they had been upset during the mediation session.

11. Complaints are generally less likely to be issued when the accused is represented by a lawyer than when he or she is not.

12. This description is derived from my observation of the mediation session, from detailed interviews with the main parties, from my research assistant Kim Worthington's observations of the court handling of the case, and from Susan Silbey's observation of the final court appearance. In addition, I discussed the case with the mediation program staff and consulted court records.

13. For comparable data on assessments of fairness from people of different social classes, see Tyler's recent study of 652 Chicago citizens' assessments of fairness in their encounters with the police and the courts (1987). His study uncovers widely shared common assumptions, across class and racial lines, about what constitutes fair procedure.

Chapter Eight

1. Although it describes very different kinds of societies from urban American neighborhoods, the anthropological record of life in villages and bands is not all rosy: tied together by strong kinship links and enduring relations of support, such communities are often rife with factionalism, full of gossip, torn by accusations of witchcraft, riven by envy of one another's wealth and good fortune, and consumed with struggles over political power. Some accounts of village life reveal rampant gossip and often harsh consequences—exile, labeling as a witch, and even execution—for the person who comes to be seen as a "bad character" (for a summary, see Merry 1984). Less severe penalties for stepping out of line include the use of mocking nicknames, songs sung out of the dark at night, practical jokes by groups of youths, and a refusal to allow marriage to one's son or daughter. Although senior males may enjoy considerable position and power, the lot of the poor, the young, and women is often one of service and subordination. Many people stay in these communities because they have no place else to go or because the price of leaving is extremely high.

2. Zoning is commonly used to provide order in suburban neighborhoods. The first comprehensive zoning ordinance was passed in New York City in 1916, and zoning gradually became an almost universal feature of the land-use of cities (Friedman 1973: 584). Zoning was popular because it strengthened American patterns of income segregation, dealing with problems at the borders of neighborhoods, and, during the period of black migration to northern cities, providing a way for fearful whites to exclude blacks (Friedman 1973: 584). Within mature urban residential communities, zoning serves to conserve the existing character and shape of neighborhoods (Steele 1986).

3. As Robert Nisbet wrote in 1970, "unhappily, remote power, however omnipotent and encompassing, can oftentimes come to seem preferable to authority at close quarters, a fact that has much to do with the history of centralization and bureaucracy" ([1953] 1970, xiv).

4. As discussed in Chapter 1, this research shows that caseloads have not dramatically increased in recent years, except in the federal courts—and that it has done so there only in a limited range of torts, primarily product liability, medical malpractice, and in response to particular situations, such as the 1980s flood of asbestos litigation (Lieberman 1981; Galanter 1983, 1986; *Justice System Journal* Special Issue 1986).

5. Robert Hayden observes that the complaint of litigiousness focuses on personal injury cases (1989), a type of problem which Americans seem to regard as particularly inappropriate for litigation. In David Engel's analysis of the meaning of court use in a rural Illinois county, for example, he finds that it is primarily personal injury complainants who are condemned as "too litigious" because such people violate a fundamental version of American individualism, that of self-reliance and self-sufficiency (1984). In

his study, Engel finds two distinct types of individualism: one is based on notions of rights, and the other is based on self-sufficiency, so that each individual is responsible for providing for his or her own protection and for absorbing the consequences of injuries without seeking help from others (1984). Personal injury suits violate this second form of individualism.

6. Since the 1920s, sociologists and anthropologists have argued that urbanization weakens the primary bonds of family, neighborhood, and community characteristic of villages and small towns and replaces them with more superficial, transitory, and segmental social ties (Wirth 1938; Short 1971). The resulting social disorganization, anomie, and normlessness of urban life has led to the familiar urban diseases of crime, psychological breakdown, suicide, and mass movements. It seemed clear to the social scientists trying to understand the social life of the vast, sprawling, choked, industrial giant of Chicago in the 1920s and 1930s that the lives they observed—people such as hoboes, dance hall girls, gangs, rooming-house residents—were very different from the lives of people in small-town America at the same time. This contrast served as the fundamental point of comparison for the theory of urbanism (Park 1915; Wirth 1938). The folk society, in contrast to the urban, was consensual, morally homogeneous, integrated, and harmonious. Life was organized around shared rules, a common religious commitment, and a sense of belonging. Normative homogeneity and face-to-face ties created intimate environments in which people were willing to deal with their differences through compromise, to seek conciliation rather than confrontation, and to agree on the rules governing their lives.

7. The history of legal rights activism during the 1960s and 1970s, as chronicled by Handler et al. (1978), shows how the government not only enunciated rights which encouraged working-class people to use the courts but also made available to them experts who could help them find the door. Building on the major advances in civil rights achieved through legal action during the 1950s, the law was viewed as a critical weapon for social change during the 1960s and early 1970s. Legal rights activity shifted from an older, reactive system of legal aid to an activist stance which claimed that the law should serve as a lever to topple unjust power and to create a more just society. Aggressive legal rights organizations uncovered the problems of the poor and minorities and brought them to the attention of the country, persuading courts, agencies, and legislatures that there were legal needs and problems which could be remedied through the legal system. During this period, lawyers assumed a new responsibility for social reform. Law was envisioned as the tool of this change, a powerful weapon which would challenge existing hierarchies of power. By 1979, the Legal Services Corporation, the primary source of civil legal assistance to the indigent, estimated that it was able to provide "minimum access to legal services" for twenty-six million of the nation's twenty-nine million poor (Cavanagh and Sarat 1980: 393). Gradually, this lead to broad cultural shifts in attitudes toward the danger of government infringements on individual liberties.

8. See Neal Milner's discussion of the importance of this rights discourse for the mobilization of reform efforts in the mental health area (1986, 1987, 1988).

9. In this period, there have been substantial changes—in claims, in ways of funding claims, in access, and in rules of standing—which have made law more democratic and more available to the whole citizenry than ever before, according to Jethro Lieberman (1981: 18). There has been an expanding demand for the courts as a result of new rights; federal legal services programs; public-interest law; the use of law in closed institutions such as prisons, schools, and hospitals; and, at least since 1954, increased Supreme Court sensitivity to the legal rights of disadvantaged citizens facing discrimination on the basis of race, gender, or wealth (Auerbach 1983: 122). Auerbach points out that, in

the 1960s and 1970s, "within little more than a decade, legal representation and litigation had been transformed into vital ingredients of social justice in the modern state" (1983: 122). (see, generally, Sarat 1986.)

10. For further discussion of these issues, see Lasch (1977), Bellah et al. (1985), and, on the way patterns of thought become institutionalized, Douglas (1986).

11. As Scheingold points out, the myth of rights is a powerful political resource precisely because there is widespread popular understanding in American society that rights are linked to social justice (1974: 131).

12. Brigham argues that law serves, in this sense, to constitute social practices such as social movements (1987b).

13. Neal Milner describes a similar diminishing of rights, as he terms the process, in a very different context: that of mental health rights. During the 1980s, he argues, the assault on rights discourse, an assault produced both by the erosion of rights advocates on the bench and by a general critique of rights within the legal academy and in other organizations, has reduced the inclination of mental health groups to pursue a rights-oriented strategy for people with mental illness (1986, 1987).

Appendix

1. The breakdown by gender was as follows:

	No. (%)	
	NJC[a] $(N=465)$	Court[b] $(N=533)$
Female complainant/male respondent	191 (41)	429 (81)
Female complainant/female respondent	125 (27)	16 (3)
Male complainant/male respondent	87 (19)	43 (8)
Male complainant/female respondent	62 (13)	45 (8)

[a] Data on the gender of the complainant was missing in twenty-one cases, and data on the gender of the respondent was missing in sixty-eight cases.
[b] Missing data in twelve cases.

(table from Harrington 1985: 134, 167).

2. The complainant's race was missing in 95 of 591 cases referred to mediation, and the respondent's was missing in 169 of 591 cases, 54 of which were organizations (Harrington 1985: 134). The racial breakdown was as follows: of complainants, 226 were whites, 243 were blacks, 21 were Hispanics, 1 was Asian, and 3 were some other race; of respondents 169 were whites, 175 were blacks, 20 were Hispanics, and 1 was some other race. Harrington was able to analyze the race of both complainant and respondent in 359 cases: in 142 both parties were white, in 158 both were black, in 13 both were Hispanic, and in 48 the races were mixed (1985: 135).

3. Harrington reports income data for 410 of the 591 complainants as follows: 228(56%)—0–$6,000; 117(28%)—$6,000–$12,000; 43(10%)—$12,000–$18,000; 17(4%)—$18,000–$24,000; 5(1%)—$24,000–$30,000. Data for respondents are more fragmentary. Of 229 respondents for whom income data are available, the distribution is as follows: 120(52%)—0–$6,000; 65(28%)—$6,000–$12,000; 29(13%)—$12,000–$18,000; 14(6%)—$18,000–$24,000; and 1(4%)—$24,000–$30,000. These income figures were taken from the intake screening form and are self-reported (1985: 135). They refer to the late 1970s.

4. Twenty-three women initiated complaints: 57 percent were about neighbors, 22 percent were about roommates, and 9 percent were about landlord or tenant problems. Eleven men initiated complaints: 27 percent were about neighbors, 9 percent were about roommates, and 27 percent were about landlord and tenant problems (Rothschild 1986: 245–47).

References

Abu-Lughod, Lila. 1985. "Honor and the Sentiments of Loss in a Bedouin Society." *American Ethnologist* 12:245–61.

Amherst Seminar. 1988. "From the Special Issue Editors." *Law and Society Review* 22:629–36.

Arno, Andrew. 1985. "Structural Communication and Control Communication: An Interactionist Perspective on Legal and Customary Procedures for Conflict Management." *American Anthropologist* 87:40–55.

Auerbach, Jerrold. 1983. *Justice Without Law?* New York: Oxford University Press.

Bailey, F. G. 1983. *The Tactical Uses of Passion: An Essay on Power, Reason, and Reality.* Ithaca and London: Cornell University Press.

Baumgartner, M. P. 1985. "Law and the Middle Class: Evidence from a Suburban Town." *Law and Human Behavior* 9:3–24.

———. 1988. *The Moral Order of a Suburb.* New York: Oxford University Press.

Beer, Jennifer E. 1986. *Peacemaking in your Neighborhood: Reflections on an Experiment in Community Mediation.* Philadelphia: New Society.

Bellah, Robert N., Richard Madsen, William M. Sullivan, Ann Swidler, and Steven Tipton. 1985. *Habits of the Heart: Individualism and Commitment in American Life.* New York: Harper & Row.

Bender, Thomas. 1978. *Community and Social Change in America.* Baltimore: Johns Hopkins University Press.

Berger, Bennett. 1968. *Working Class Suburb: A Study of Auto Workers in Suburbia.* Berkeley, Calif.: University of California Press.

Bittner, Egon, 1967. "The Police on Skid-Row: A Study of Peace-Keeping." *American Sociological Review* 32:699–715.

Black, Donald. 1976. *The Behavior of Law.* New York: Academic Press.

———. 1980. *The Manners and Customs of the Police.* New York: Academic Press.

———. 1983. "Crime as Social Control." *American Sociological Review* 48:34–45.

Block, Joyce, and Barbara Kreger. 1982. *Mediation: An Alternative for PINS: A Research Report of the Children's Aid Society's PINS Mediation Project.* New York: Children's Aid Society.

Bluestone, Barry, and Bennett Harrison. 1982. *The Deindustrialization of America: Plant Closings, Community Abandonment, and the Dismantling of Basic Industry.* New York: Basic Books.

Blumberg, Abraham S. 1967. "The Practice of Law as a Confidence Game: Organizational Cooptation of a Profession." *Law and Society Review* 1:15–40.

Bossy, John, ed. 1983. *Disputes and Settlements: Law and Human Relations in the West.* Cambridge: Cambridge University Press.

Bourdieu, Pierre. 1977. *Outline of a Theory of Practice.* Translated by Richard Nice. Cambridge: Cambridge University Press.

Boyum, Keith, and Lynn Mather. 1983. *Empirical Theories About Courts*. New York: Longman.

Brenneis, Donald. 1984. "Straight Talk and Sweet Talk: Political Discourse in an Occasionally Egalitarian Community." In *Dangerous Words: Language and Politics in the Pacific*, edited by D. Brenneis and F. Myers, 69–84. New York: New York University Press.

Brigham, John. 1987a. "The 'Giving Issue': A View of Land, Property Rights and Industrial Development in Maine and Nova Scotia." In *Land Rites and Wrongs: The Management, Regulation, and Use of Land in Canada and the United States*, edited by Elliot J. Feldman and Michael A. Goldberg, 247–68. Cambridge: Lincoln Institute of Land Policy.

———. 1987b. "Right, Rage, and Remedy: Forms of Law in Political Discourse." *Studies in American Political Development* 2:303–16.

———. 1988. "The Bias of Constitutional Property: Toward Compensation for the Elimination of Statutory Entitlements." *Law and Inequality: A Journal of Theory and Inequality* 5:405–29.

Buckle, Leonard, and Suzann Buckle. 1977. *Bargaining for Justice*. New York: Praeger.

Buckle, Leonard, and Suzann R. Thomas-Buckle. 1982. "Doing unto Others: Dispute and Dispute-Processing in an Urban American Neighborhood." In *Neighborhood Justice*, edited by Roman Tomasic and Malcolm Feeley, 78–90. New York: Longman.

Bumiller, Kristin. 1987. "Victims in the Shadow of the Law: A Critique of the Model of Legal Protection." *Signs* 12:421–39.

———. 1988. *The Civil Rights Society*. Baltimore: Johns Hopkins University Press.

Burger, Warren E. 1983. "Conflict Resolution: Isn't There a Better Way?" *National Forum* 63:3–5.

Cain, Maureen and Kalman Kulcsar. 1981/82. "Thinking Disputes: An Essay on the Origins of the Dispute Industry." *Law and Society Review* 16:375–403.

Cannon, Mark W. 1983. "Contentious and Burdensome Litigation: A Need for Alternatives." *National Forum* 63:10–13.

Cavanagh, Ralph, and Austin Sarat. 1980. "Thinking about Courts: Toward and Beyond a Jurisprudence of Judicial Competence." *Law and Society Review* 14:371–420.

Chagnon, Napoleon. 1969. *Yanomamo: The Fierce People*. Holt, Rinehart & Winston.

Chanock, Martin. 1983. "Signposts or Tombstones? Reflections on Recent Works on the Anthropology of Law." *Law in Context* 1:107–25.

Coates, Robert. 1985. "Victim Meets Offender: An Evaluation of Victim-Offender Reconciliation Programs." PACT Institute of Justice Report. Valparaiso, Ind. Mimeograph.

Collier, Jane Fishburne. 1988. *Marriage and Inequality in Classless Societies*. Stanford, Calif.: Stanford University Press.

Comaroff, Jean. 1985. *Body of Power, Spirit of Resistance: Culture and History of a South African People*. Chicago: University of Chicago Press.

Comaroff, Jean, and Comaroff, John. 1986. "Christianity and Colonialism in South Africa." *American Ethnologist* 13:1–22.

Comaroff, John L., and Jean Comaroff. 1987. "The Madman and the Migrant: Work and Labor in the Historical Consciousness of a South African People." *American Ethnologist* 14:191–210.

Comaroff, John, and Simon Roberts. 1981. *Rules and Processes: The Cultural Logic of Dispute in an African Context*. Chicago: University of Chicago Press.

Conley, John, and William M. O'Barr. 1990. "Rules versus Relationships in Small

Claims Disputes." In *Conflict Talk,* edited by Allen D. Grimshaw, Cambridge: Cambridge University Press.

Daniels, Stephen. 1985. "Continuity and Change in Patterns of Case Handling: A Case Study of Two Rural Counties." *Law and Society Review* 19:381–421.

Doeringer, Peter B., and Michael J. Piore. 1971. *Internal Labor Markets and Manpower Analysis.* Lexington, Mass.: D. C. Heath, Lexington.

Donzelot, Jacques. 1980. *The Policing of Families.* Translated by Robert Hurley. New York: Pantheon.

Douglas, Mary. 1966. *Purity and Danger: An Analysis of Concepts of Pollution and Taboo.* Harmondsworth, England: Penguin.

———. 1986. *How Institutions Think.* Syracuse, N.Y.: Syracuse University Press.

Edelman, Murray. 1977. *Political Language: Words That Succeed and Policies That Fail.* New York: Academic Press.

Eisenstein, James, and Herbert Jacob. 1977. *Felony Justice.* Boston: Little, Brown.

Engel, David, and Eric Steele. 1979. "Civil Cases and Society: Process and Order in the Civil Justice System." *American Bar Foundation Research Journal* 1979:295–345.

Engel, David M. 1980. "Legal Pluralism in an American Community: Perspectives on a Civil Trial Court." *American Bar Foundation Research Journal* 3:425–54.

———. 1984. "The Oven Bird's Song: Insiders, Outsiders, and Personal Injuries in an American Community. *"Law and Society Review* 18:551–82.

Farber, Bernard. 1972. *Guardians of Virtue: Salem Families in 1800.* New York: Basic Books.

Feeley, Malcolm. 1979. *The Process Is the Punishment: Handling Cases in a Lower Criminal Court.* New York: Russell Sage.

———. 1983. *Court Reform on Trial.* New York: Basic Books.

Felstiner, William, Richard Abel, and Austin Sarat. 1980/81. "The Emergence and Transformation of Disputes: Naming, Blaming and Claiming . . ." *Law and Society Review* 15:631–55.

Felstiner, William L. F., and Lynne A. Williams. 1980. *Community Mediation in Dorchester, Massachusetts.* Washington, D.C.: U.S. Department of Justice, National Institute of Justice.

Fineman, Martha. 1988. "Dominant Discourse, Professional Language, and Legal Change in Child Custody Decisionmaking." *Harvard Law Review* 101:727–74.

Foucault, Michel. 1977 (1975). *Discipline and Punish: The Birth of the Prison.* Translated by Alan Sheridan. New York: Random House. (Translated 1977.)

———. 1980. *Power/Knowledge: Selected Interviews and Other Writings, 1972–77.* Edited by C. Gordon and translated by C. Gordon, Leo Marshall, John Mepham, and Kate Soper. New York: Pantheon.

Friedman, Lawrence M. 1973. *A History of American Law.* New York: Simon & Schuster.

Galanter, Marc. 1974. "Why the 'Haves' Come out Ahead: Speculations on the Limits of Legal Change." *Law and Society Review* 9:95–160.

———. 1983. "Reading the Landscape of Disputes: What We Know and Don't Know (and Think We Know) about Our Allegedly Contentious and Litigious Society." *UCLA Law Review* 31:4–71.

———. 1986. "The Day After the Litigation Explosion." *Maryland Law Review* 46:3–39.

Geertz, Clifford. 1973. "Thick Description: Toward an Interpretive Theory of Culture." *The Interpretation of Cultures: Selected Essays,* 3–30. New York: Basic Books.

———. 1983. *Local Knowledge.* Basic Books.

Gluckman, Max. 1955. *The Judicial Process among the Barotse of Northern Rhodesia.* Manchester: Manchester University Press.

Goldberg, Stephen B., Eric D. Green, and Frank E. A. Sander. 1985. *Dispute Resolution.* Boston: Little, Brown.

Gordon, Robert. 1984. "Critical Legal Histories." *Stanford Law Review* 36:57–125.

Gramsci, Antonio. 1971. *Selections from the Prison Notebooks.* Edited and translated Quinten Hoare and Geoffrey Nowell Smith. London: Lawrence & Wishart.

Greenhouse, Carol. 1982. "Nature Is to Culture as Praying Is to Suing: Legal Pluralism in an American Suburb." *Journal of Legal Pluralism* 20:17–37.

———. 1986. *Praying for Justice.* Ithaca, N.Y.: Cornell University Press.

———. 1989. "Interpreting American Litigiousness." In *History and Power in the Study of Law,* edited by June Starr and Jane Collier, 252–77. Ithaca, N.Y.: Cornell University Press.

Griffiths, John. 1986. "Recent Anthropology of Law in the Netherlands and its Historical Background." In *Anthropology of Law in the Netherlands: Essays in Legal Pluralism,* edited by Keebet von Benda-Beckman and Fons Strijbosch, 11–66. Dordrecht & Cinnaminson: Foris.

Gulliver, P. H. 1963. *Social Control in an African Society.* London: Routledge & Kegan Paul.

———. 1969. "Introduction to Case Studies of Law in Non-Western Societies." In *Law in Culture and Society,* edited by L. Nader, 11–23. Chicago: Aldine.

Handler, Joel F., Ellen Jane Hollingsworth, and Howard S. Erlanger. 1978. *Lawyers and the Pursuit of Legal Rights.* New York: Academic Press.

Handlin, Oscar. 1941. *Boston's Immigrants.* Cambridge, Mass.: Harvard University Press.

Harrington, Christine. 1985. *Shadow Justice: The Ideology and Institutionalization of Alternatives to Court.* Westport, Conn.: Greenwood.

Harrington, Christine, and Sally Engle Merry. 1988. "Ideological Production: The Making of Community Mediation." *Law and Society Review* 22:709–37.

Hay, Douglas. 1975. "Property, Authority, and the Criminal Law." In *Albion's Fatal Tree: Crime and Society in Eighteenth-Century England,* by Douglas Hay, Peter Linebaugh, John G. Rule, E. P. Thompson, and Cal Winslow, 17–63. New York: Pantheon.

Hayden, Dolores. 1984. *Redesigning the American Dream: The Future of Housing, Work, and Family Life.* New York: W. W. Norton.

Hayden, Robert M. 1987. "Turn-taking, Overlap, and the Task at Hand: Ordering Speaking Turns in Legal Settings." *American Ethnologist* 14:251–70.

———. 1989. "The Cultural Logic of a Political Crisis: Common Sense, Hegemony, ·and the Great America Liability Insurance Famine of 1986." Disputes Processing Research Program working papers, series 9, no. 8. Madison, Wis.: University of Wisconsin Law School, Institute for Legal Studies.

Haydu, Jeffrey, 1987. *Factory Politics in British and American Machine Trades: Changing Agenda for Protest, 1890–1922.* Berkeley, Calif.: University of California Press.

Higham, John. 1955. *Strangers in the Land: Patterns of American Nativism, 1860–1925.* New Brunswick, N.J.: Rutgers University Press.

Hofrichter, Richard. 1982. "Neighborhood Justice and the Social Control Problems of American Capitalism: A Perspective." In *The Politics of Informal Justice,* edited by Richard Abel, vol. 1, 207–48. New York: Academic Press.

———. 1987. *Neighborhood Justice in Capitalist Society: The Expansion of the Informal State.* Westport, Conn.: Westview.

Howell, Joseph T. 1973. *Hard Living on Clay Street: Portrait of Blue-Collar Families.* Garden City, N.Y.: Anchor/Doubleday.

Humphreys, Sally. 1985. "Law as Discourse." *History and Anthropology* 1:241–64.

Hunt, Alan. 1985. "The Ideology of Law: Advances and Problems in Recent Applications of the Concept of Ideology to the Analysis of Law." *Law and Society Review* 19:11–39.

Hunter, Floyd, Ruth Conner Schaffer, and Cecil G. Sheps. 1956. *Community Organization: Action and Inaction.* Chapel Hill, N.C.: University of North Carolina Press.

Ietswaart, Heleen. 1986. "Review of Keebet von Benda-Beckman and Fons Strijbosch (eds.) *Anthropology of Law in the Netherlands: Essay in Legal Pluralism.*" *Journal of Legal Pluralism* 24:161–70.

Justice System Journal: Special Issue: "The Litigation Explosion Debate." 1986. Robert T. Roper, guest ed. *Justice System Journal* 11:259–388.

Kairys, David, ed. 1982. *The Politics of Law: A Progressive Critique.* New York: Pantheon.

Kapferer, Bruce, ed. 1976. *Transaction and Meaning: Directions in the Anthropology of Exchange and Symbolic Behavior.* ASA Essays in Social Anthropology, vol. 1. Philadelphia: Institute for the Study of Human Issues.

Kennedy, Duncan. 1982. "Antonio Gramsci and the Legal System." *ALSA Forum* 6:32–37.

Kett, Joeseph F. 1983. "Review of Franklin E. Zimring, *The Changing Legal World of Adolescence.*" *American Bar Foundation Research Journal* 1983:272–77.

Kidder, Robert. 1980/81. "The End of the Road? Problems in the Analysis of Disputes." *Law and Society Review* 15:717–27.

Koch, K.-F. 1974. *War and Peace in Jalemo.* Cambridge, Mass.: Harvard University Press.

Kolko, Gabriel. 1978. "Working Wives: Their Effects on the Structure of the Working Class." *Science and Society* 42:257–78.

Lan, David. 1985. *Guns and Rain: Guerrillas and Spirit Mediums in Zimbabwe.* Berkeley and Los Angeles: University of California Press.

Larrain, Jorge. 1979. *The Concept of Ideology.* Athens, Ga.: University of Georgia Press.

Lasch, Christopher. 1977. *Haven in a Heartless World: The Family Besieged.* New York: Basic Books.

Law and Society Review: Special Issue: "Law and Ideology." 1988. vol. 22(4).

Law and Society Review: Special Issue: "Plea Bargaining." 1979. Vol. 13(2).

LeMasters, E. E. 1975. *Blue Collar Aristocrats: Life-Styles at a Working Class Tavern.* Madison, Wis.: University of Wisconsin Press.

Lempert, Richard O. 1980/81. "Grievances and Legitimacy: The Beginnings and End of Dispute Settlement." *Law and Society Review* 15:707–17.

Levison, Andrew. 1974. *The Working Class Majority.* New York: Coward, McCann, & Geoghegan.

Lieberman, Jethro K. 1981. *The Litigious Society.* New York: Basic Books.

Linebaugh, Peter. 1975. "The Tyburn Riot against the Surgeons." In *Albion's Fatal Tree: Crime and Society in Eighteenth-Century England,* by Douglas Hay, Peter Linebaugh, John G. Rule, E. P. Thompson, and Cal Winslow, 65–119. New York: Pantheon.

Lipetz, Marcia. 1984. *Routine Justice.* New Brunswick, N.J.: Transaction.

Llewellyn, Karl, and E. A. Hoebel. 1941. *The Cheyenne Way.* Norman, Okla. Oklahoma University Press.

Macaulay, Stewart. 1987. "Images of Law in Everyday Life: The Lessons of School, Entertainment and Spectator Sports." *Law and Society Review* 21:185–218.

Mackenzie, Gavin. 1973. *The Aristocracy of Labor: The Position of Skilled Craftsmen in the American Class Structure*. London: Cambridge University Press.

Malinowski, Bronislaw. 1926. *Crime and Custom in Savage Society*. London: Routledge & Kegan Paul.

Mather, Lynn. 1979. *Plea Bargaining or Trial*. Lexington, Mass.: Lexington.

Mather, Lynn, and Barbara Yngvesson. 1980/81. "Language, Audience, and the Transformation of Disputes." *Law and Society Review* 15:775–822.

Mayhew, Leon, and Albert J. Reiss. 1969. "The Social Organization of Legal Contacts." *American Sociological Review* 34:309–18.

Meggitt, Mervyn. 1977. *Blood Is Their Argument: Warfare among the Mae Enga Tribesmen of the New Guinea Highlands*. Palo Alto, Calif.: Mayfield.

Merry, Sally Engle. 1979. "Going to Court: Strategies of Dispute Management in an American Urban Neighborhood." *Law and Society Review* 13:891–925.

———. 1981. *Urban Danger: Life in a Neighborhood of Strangers*. Philadelphia, Pa.: Temple University Press.

———. 1984. "Rethinking Gossip and Scandal." In *Toward a General Theory of Social Control*, vol. 2, edited by Donald Black, 271–302. New York: Academic Press.

———. 1986. "Everyday Understandings of Law in Working-Class America." *American Ethnologist* 13:253–70.

———. 1987. "Crowding, Conflict, and Neighborhood Regulation." In *Neighborhood and Community Environments*, edited by Irwin Altman and Abraham Wandersman, 35–68. New York: Plenum.

Merry, Sally Engle, and Ann Marie Rocheleau. 1985. *Mediation in Families: A Study of the Children's Hearings Project*. Cambridge: Mass.: Cambridge Children's and Family Services.

Merry, Sally Engle, and Susan S. Silbey. 1984. "What do Plaintiffs Want? Reexamining the Concept of Dispute." *Justice System Journal* 9:151–79.

Miller, Richard E., and Austin Sarat. 1980/81. "Grievances, Claims, and Disputes: Assessing the Adversary Culture." *Law and Society Review* 15:525–67.

Mills, C. Wright. 1940. "Situated actions and Vocabularies of Motive" *American Sociological Review* 5:904–13.

Milner, Neal. 1986. "The Dilemmas of Legal Mobilization: Ideologies and Strategies of Mental Patient Liberation Groups." *Law and Policy* 8:105–29.

———. 1987. "The Right to Refuse Treatment: Four Case Studies in Legal Mobilization." *Law and Society Review* 21:447–86.

———. 1988. "The Denigration and Diminishing of Rights." Paper presented at the Law and Society Association annual meetings, Vail, Colo.

Minow, Martha. 1990. *Making all the Difference*. Ithaca, N.Y.: Cornell University Press.

Morris, Marlene. 1983. *Parent-Child Mediation: An Alternative That Works: The Second Research Report of the Children's Aid Society's PINS Mediation Project*. New York: Children's Aid Society.

Nader, Laura. 1965. The Ethnography of Law. (Special Issue) *American Anthropologist* 67(6), part 2.

———. 1969. "Introduction." In *Law in Culture and Society*, edited by Laura Nader, 1–10. Chicago: Aldine.

———. ed. 1980. *No Access to Law*. New York: Academic Press.

———. 1984. "A User Theory of Law." *Southwestern Law Journal* 38:951–63.

Nader, Laura, and Harry J. Todd, Jr., eds. 1978. *The Disputing Process: Law in Ten Societies*. New York: Columbia University Press.

Nash, June. 1989. "A Redistributive Model for Analyzing Government Mediation and Law in Family, Community, and Industry in a New England Industrial City." In *History and Power in the Study of Law,* edited by June Starr and Jane Collier, 81–113. Ithaca, N.Y.: Cornell University Press.

Nelken, David. 1986. "Review Essay: Beyond the Study of 'Law and Society'? Henry's *Private Justice* and O'Hagen's *The End of Law?*" *American Bar Foundation Research Journal* 1986:323–38.

Newman, Katherine. 1988. *Falling from Grace: The Experience of Downward Mobility in the American Middle Class.* New York: Free Press.

Nisbet, Robert A. (1953) 1970. *The Quest for Community.* Preface to 1970 edition, vii–xix. London and New York: Oxford University Press.

O'Barr, William M., and John M. Conley. 1985. "Litigant Satisfaction versus Legal Adequacy in Small Claims Court Narratives." *Law and Society Review* 19:661–701.

———. 1988. "Lay Expectations of the Civil Justice System." *Law and Society Review* 22:137–61.

Pappas, Gregory. 1989. *The Magic City: Unemployment in a Working-Class Community.* Ithaca, N.Y.: Cornell University Press.

Park, Robert. 1915. "The City: Suggestions for the Investigation of Human Behavior in the Urban Environment." *American Journal of Sociology* 20:577–612. Reprinted in Sennet, Richard, ed. 1969. *Classic Essays on the Culture of Cities,* 91–130. New York: Appleton-Century-Crofts.

Parkin, Frank. 1971. *Class Inequality and Political Order.* New York: Praeger.

Perin, Constance. 1977. *Everything in Its Place: Social Order and Land Use in America.* Princeton, N.J.: Princeton University Press.

———. 1988. *Belonging in America: Reading between the Lines.* Madison, Wis.: University of Wisconsin Press.

Platt, Anthony M. 1969. *The Child Savers: The Invention of Delinquency.* Chicago: University of Chicago Press.

Reinerman, Craig. 1987. *American States of Mind.* New Haven, Conn.: Yale University Press.

Rosen, Lawrence. 1980/81. "Equity and Discretion in a Modern Islamic Legal System." *Law and Society Review* 15:217–46.

———. 1984. *Bargaining for Reality: The Construction of Social Relations in a Muslim Community.* Chicago: University of Chicago Press.

Rosenblatt, Rand E. 1982. "Legal Entitlement and Welfare Benefits." In *The Politics of Law,* edited by David Kairys, 262–78. New York: Pantheon.

Rothman, David. 1980. *Conscience and Convenience: The Asylum and Its Alternatives in Progressive America.* Boston: Little, Brown.

Rothschild, Judith. 1986. "Mediation as Social Control." Unpublished Ph.D. diss., Department of Sociology, University of California, Berkeley.

Rubin, Lillian. 1976. *Worlds of Pain: Life in the Working Class Family.* New York: Basic Books.

Ryan, Dennis J. 1975. "Salem: A Study of Its People's Leadership, Behavioral Patterns, and Political Feelings and Their Relationship to Social Class." Tufts University. Mimeograph.

Said, Edward W. 1978. "The Problem of Textuality: Two Exemplary Positions." *Critical Inquiry* 4:673–714. Reprinted in Philipson, Morris, and Paul J. Gudel, eds. 1980. *Aesthetics Today,* rev. ed., 87–135. New York: New American Library.

Santos, Boaventura. 1977. "The Law of the Oppressed: The Construction and Reconstruction of Legality in Pasagarda." *Law and Society Review* 12:5–126.

————. 1982. "Law and Revolution in Portugal: The Experience of Popular Justice after the 25th of April, 1974." In *The Politics of Informal Justice,* edited by R. L. Abel, vol. 2, 251–80. New York: Academic Press.

Sarat, Austin, 1976. "Alternatives in Dispute Processing: Litigation in a Small Claims Court." *Law and Society Review* 10:339–75.

————. 1977. "Studying American Legal Culture: An Assessment of Survey Evidence," *Law and Society Review* 11:427–98.

————. 1985. "The Litigation Explosion, Access to Justice, and Court Reform: Examining the Critical Assumptions." *Rutgers Law Review* 37:319–36.

————. 1986. "Access to Justice: Citizen Participation and the American Legal Order." In *Law and the Social Sciences,* edited by Leon Lipson and Stanton Wheeler, 519–80. New York: Russell Sage Foundation.

Sarat, Austin, and William Felstiner. 1986. "Law and Strategy in the Divorce Lawyer's Office." *Law and Society Review* 20:93–134.

————. 1988. "Law and Social Relations: Vocabularies of Motive in Lawyer/Client Interaction." *Law and Society Review* 22:737–71.

Scheingold, Stuart A. 1974. *The Politics of Rights, Lawyers, Public Policy, and Political Change.* New Haven, Conn.: Yale University Press.

Schwartz, Richard. 1954. "Social Factors in the Development of Legal Control: A Case Study of Two Israeli Settlements." *Yale Law Journal* 63:471–91.

Scott, James C. 1985. *Weapons of the Weak: Everyday forms of Peasant Resistance.* New Haven, Conn.: Yale University Press.

Sennett, Richard, and Jonathan Cobb. 1972. *The Hidden Injuries of Class.* New York: Vintage.

Sheehan, Brian. 1984. *The Boston School Integration Dispute.* New York: Columbia University Press.

Sheppard, David I., Janice A. Roehl, and Royer F. Cook. 1979. *Neighborhood Justice Centers Field Test: Interim Evaluation Report.* U.S. Department of Justice, Law Enforcement Assistance Administration. Washington, D.C.: U.S. Government Printing Office.

Sherzer, Joel. 1987. "A Discourse-centered Approach to Language and Culture." *American Anthropologist* 89:295–310.

Short, James. 1971. *The Social Fabric of the Metropolis.* Chicago: University of Chicago Press.

Silberman, Matthew. 1985. *The Civil Justice Process.* Orlando, Fla.: Academic Press.

Silbey, Susan S. 1979. *What The Lower Courts Do: The Jurisdiction and Work of Courts of Limited Jurisdiction.* Washington, D.C.: U.S. Department of Justice, OIAJ, Council on the Role of Courts.

————. 1981. "Making Sense of the Lower Courts." *Justice System Journal* 6:13–27.

Silbey, Susan S., and Sally E. Merry. 1986. "Mediator Settlement Strategies." *Law and Policy* 8:7–32.

————. 1987. "Interpretive Processes in Mediation and Court." Paper on file with authors.

Silbey, Susan, and Austin Sarat. 1987. "Critical Traditions in Law and Society Research." *Law and Society Review* 21:165–74.

————. 1988. "Dispute Processing in Law and Legal Scholarship: From Institutional Critique to the Reconstitution of the Juridical Subject." Disputes Processing Research Program working papers, series 8, no. 9. Madison, Wis.: University of Wisconsin Law School, Institute for Legal Studies.

Slater, Philip. 1968. "Social Change and the Democratic Family." In *The Temporary*

Society, edited by Warren G. Bennis and Philip E. Slater, 20–52. New York: Harper & Row.

Smith, Barbara E. 1983. *Non-Stranger Violence: The Criminal Court's Response.* Washington, D.C.: U.S. Department of Justice, National Institute of Justice.

Snyder, F. G. 1981. "Anthropology, Dispute Processes, and Law: A Critical Introduction." *British Journal of Law and Society* 8:141–80.

Starr, June. 1978. *Dispute and Settlement in Rural Turkey: An Ethnography of Law.* Leiden: E. J. Brill.

Steele, Eric. 1986. "Participation and Rules-The Functions of Zoning." *American Bar Foundation Research Journal* 1986:709–55.

Steinitz, Victoria Anne, and Ellen Rachel Solomon. 1986. *Starting Out: Class and Community in the Lives of Working-Class Youth.* Philadelphia: Temple University Press.

Stone, Alan. 1985. "The Place of Law in the Marxian Structure-Superstructure Archetype." *Law and Society Review* 19:39–67.

Sudnow, D. 1965. "Normal Crimes: Sociological Features of the Penal Code in a Public Defender Office." *Social Problems* 12:255–76.

Suffolk County Community Mediation Center. Evaluation Report. 1980. mimeograph.

Susser, Ida. 1982. *Norman Street: Poverty and Politics in an Urban Neighborhood.* New York: Oxford University Press.

———. 1986. "Political Activity among Working-Class Women in a U.S. City." *American Ethnologist* 13:108–17.

Swidler, Ann. 1986. "Culture in Action: Symbols and Strategies." *American Sociological Review* 51:273–86.

Teitelbaum, Lee E. n.d. "Family History and Family Law." Legal History Working Papers, series 1, no. 1. Madison, Wis.: University of Wisconsin Law School, Institute for Legal Studies.

Todd, Harry F. Jr. 1978. "Litigious Marginals: Character and Disputing in a Bavarian Village" In *The Disputing Process in Ten Societies,* edited by Laura Nader and Harry F. Todd, Jr., 86–112. New York: Columbia University Press.

Tomasic, Roman, and Malcolm Feeley. 1982. *Neighborhood Justice, Assessment of an Emerging Idea.* New York: Longman.

Trubek, David M. 1977. *Law and Society Review:* "Complexity and Contradiction in the Legal Order: Balbus and the Challenge of Critical Social Thought about Law." *Law and Society Review* 11:529–70.

———. ed. 1980/81. Dispute Processing and Civil Litigation. (Special Issue) *Law and Society Review* 14(3–4).

———. 1984. "Where the Action Is: Critical Legal Studies and Empiricism." *Stanford Law Review* 36:575–622.

Trubek, David M., and John Esser. 1989. "Critical Empiricism in American Legal Studies: Paradox, Program, or Pandora's Box?" *Law and Social Inquiry* 14:3–53.

Trubek, David M., Joel B. Grossman, William L. F. Felstiner, Herbert M. Kritzer, and Austin Sarat. 1983. *Civil Litigation Research Project Final Report.* Madison, Wis.: Dispute Processing Research Program.

Turner, Victor. 1957. *Schism and continuity in an African Society.* Manchester: Manchester University Press.

Tyler, Tom R. 1987. "What Is Procedural Justice? Criteria Used by Citizens to Assess the Fairness of Legal Procedures." *Law and Society Review* 22:103–37.

Umbreit, Mark. 1985. *Crime and Reconciliation.* Nashville: Abington.

Vera Institute of Justice. 1977. *Felony Arrests: Their Prosecution and Disposition in*

New York City's Courts. Vera Institute of Justice Monograph. New York: Vera Institute of Justice.

Warner, W. Lloyd, J. O. Low, Paul S. Lunt, and Leo Srole. 1963. *Yankee City*. New Haven, Conn.: Yale University Press.

Warner, W. Lloyd, and Leo Srole. 1949. *The Social System of American Ethnic Groups*. New Haven, Conn.: Yale University Press.

Weissbourd, Bernard, and Elizabeth Mertz. 1985. "Rule-Centrism versus Legal Creativity: The Skewing of Legal Ideology through Language." *Law and Society Review* 19:623–61.

Wiebe, Robert H. 1975. *The Segmented Society: An Introduction to the Meaning of America*. New York: Oxford University Press.

Williams, Raymond. 1977. *Marxism and Literature*. London: Oxford University Press.

Wilson, James Q. 1968. *Varieties of Police Behavior: The Management of Law and Order in Eight Communities*. Cambridge, Mass.: Harvard University Press.

Wirth, Louis. 1938. "Urbanism as a Way of Life." *American Journal of Sociology* 44:1–24.

Yngvesson, Barbara. 1976. "Responses to Grievance Behavior: Extended Cases in a Fishing Community." *American Ethnologist* 3:353–73.

———. 1985a. "Legal Ideology and Community Justice in the Clerk's Office." *Legal Studies Forum*. 9:71–89.

———. 1985b. "Reexamining Continuing Relations and the Law." *Wisconsin Law Review* 1985:623–46.

———. 1988. "Making Law at the Doorway: The Clerk, the Court, and the Construction of Community in a New England Town." *Law and Society Review* 22:410–48.

Yngvesson, Barbara, and Pat Hennessey. 1975. "Small Claims, Complex Disputes." *Law and Society Review* 9:219–74.

Index